Sandford Fleming

Lorne Edmond Green

Fitzhenry & Whiteside

Contents

The Canadians A continuing series
General Editor: Robert Read
Consulting Editor: Roderick Stewart
Designer: Susan Budd
Editor: Rosalind Sharpe

Green, Lorne.
 Sandford Fleming

(The Canadians)

Bibliography: p.64
ISBN 0-88902-671-8 pa.

1. Fleming, Sandford, Sir, 1827-1915. 2. Railroad engineers —
Canada — Biography. I. Series.

TF140.F4G74   625.1'00924   C79-094438-3

The Author
*Lorne Edmond Green has served for twelve years with the Canadian
diplomatic service, and is the author of* The Beauty of Canada.

© 1980 Fitzhenry & Whiteside Limited
        150 Lesmill Road
        Don Mills, Ontario M3B 2T5

Printed and bound in Canada by
T. H. Best Printing Company Limited, Don Mills, Ontario

What do Canada's first adhesive postage stamp, the telegraph cable across the floor of the Pacific and a railway line stretching from ocean to ocean have in common? If you said that they all have something to do with communications you would be right, but only partly so. The fact is that all three are due in large measure to the vision, talent and energy of one man: Sandford Fleming.

Prologue

The Canadian Pacific Railway which cemented Canadian unity; the telegraph wires that facilitated communication across Canada and around the world; and four Canadian settlers, who partly owe their way of life, though they may not know it, to the energy and vision of Sir Sandford Fleming.

As if railways, postage stamps and telegraph lines were not sufficient accomplishment, consider this: Fleming conceived and promoted universal standard time, the twenty-four-hour system of time reckoning by which clocks are still set all round the world. He also compiled Canada's first inter-denominational prayer book, undertook some of the earliest detailed surveys of Canadian towns, was chancellor of Queen's University for thirty years and received a knighthood from Queen Victoria. Sandford Fleming was a living example of the pioneer spirit that was necessary to make this country great. He combined a sense of purpose, great courage and creative genius — three important ingredients when transforming a wilderness into a modern nation.

When Fleming first arrived in British America it was a loose collection of isolated colonies. Seventy years later, when he died, Canada was a cohesive, self-governing dominion stretching from the Atlantic to the Pacific, a mature participant in world affairs. Fleming's biography is not only the story of his achievements; it is a chronicle of the birth and early development of a nation. The stories of Fleming and of Canada are inseparable.

The CPR was a challenge and a triumph for the young Canadian nation.

Kirkcaldy Chapter 1

Sandford Fleming was born to Elizabeth and Andrew
Fleming on January 7, 1827, at the family home in
Kirkcaldy, Scotland. The seaport town of Kirkcaldy hugs
the cliffs and shore along the north side of the Firth of
Forth, almost directly across from Edinburgh. With its
long sea front promenade, Kirkcaldy has been known for
years as the "Lang Toun" or Long Town. Kirkcaldy's
best known son was the world-famous philosopher and
author of *The Wealth of Nations*, Adam Smith. The
Fleming family had its own more modest claims to fame:
Sandford's grandfather served in General Wolfe's army
at the Battle of Quebec, and a great-grandfather
accompanied Scotland's Bonnie Prince Charlie into exile
in France.

Sandford's father, Andrew, was well known in and
around Kirkcaldy. He ran a sawmill and construction
company, and he built Kirkcaldy's church a few years
after Sandford was born. These were days of great
activity in Kirkcaldy. The town was enjoying an
unprecedented business boom brought about by the
Industrial Revolution. With the introduction of cotton
spinning, weaving looms appeared everywhere.
Kirkcaldy, however, was essentially a seaport. As a boy,
Sandford would often run down to the docks with his
brothers to watch the tall-masted, wooden-hulled whal-
ing ships unfurl their sails and slip down the firth to the
sea.

The Fleming family lived comfortably by local
standards. Their house stood in gardens with a row of
trees leading to the front door. There was a rabbit shed in
the garden and a stable adjacent to the house. Of his five
brothers and two sisters, Sandford was closest to his
brother David. On Saturday afternoons, Sandford and
David ran along the golden sands of Kirkcaldy's
beautiful stretch of beach, scrambled over the hills at
Burntistand and played in the wooded grounds of Raith
Park, fishing in its lake, riding the donkeys or sometimes
picnicking by the waterfall. In winter they went skating
on the lake, or shot hares for supper.

The children often visited their grandmother at nearby Kennoway, and it was here that Sandford began his schooling. Later, his parents moved him to the Kirkcaldy Burgh School, where the well-known writer Thomas Carlyle had taught twenty years before. Sandford was a good student, with a strong head for figures. He showed a special talent for drawing, and wherever he went, he carried a sketchbook and pencil. He sketched the ruins of ancient Ravenscraig Castle on Kirkcaldy's shore, and the castle in the middle of Loch Leven where he went fishing each summer with his brothers. He loved to sketch the Fifeshire countryside as he travelled about with his father to deliver lumber and collect unpaid accounts.

Sandford's skills in mathematics and drawing suggested that the boy might have an aptitude for engineering, so at the age of fourteen he was apprenticed to the prominent local engineer and surveyor, John Sang. For the next four years he laboured in Sang's workshop from eight each morning till six at night, studying land measurements and calculations, astronomy and the principles of mechanics. In the evenings he practised what he had learned. He drew a plan of his father's stable, made a set of compasses and devised a portrait machine for tracing silhouettes from life models. Sandford's parents dutifully sat for their son while his portrait contraption traced the bumps and hollows of their faces onto a piece of paper mounted on the wall.

Sandford's own drawings were so well executed that they attracted attention in the local community. Several people expressed interest in buying his sketches. The energy and perseverance that were to hallmark his career were already becoming apparent. On New Year's Day, 1845, he recorded in his diary,

I finished a sketch of Ravenscraig Castle in the morning. . . . Mr. Crawford was to make arrangements with Mr. Lizers about the engraving of it. At Mr. Sang's through the day and dined at home with a few friends. Began in the evening to draw on stone Kirkcaldy harbour to be lithographed by Mr. Bryson.

Sandford was up until three a.m. to finish the stone plate. The next day Mr. Bryson accidentally dropped it and the plate shattered into pieces on the floor. Sandford went straight home and drew another harbour scene.

At the workshop, he was mastering the basic skills of engineering and surveying. Sang taught him harbour- and waterworks, and more important for the future course of his life, engaged the boy on railway surveys — especially from Edinburgh to Perth, and from Perth to Dundee.

Sandford Fleming was fortunate to have been associated, if only in a small way, with the early days of steam railway development in Britain, for it was here that the age of steam railway locomotion began. Railway development in Britain and elsewhere gave a great thrust to the surging Industrial Revolution. For the first time the speedy transportation of large numbers of passengers and bulk cargo over land was made possible.

The psychological impact of steam railway transportation was enormous, especially in North America, where vast distances made the prospect of easy transcontinental travel a breathtaking one. When the first through train reached Vancouver in 1886, cheering crowds turned out to greet it. In 1889, when this picture was taken, a steam engine could still generate a lot of excitement among the residents of Medicine Hat, Alberta.

Although steamships had been plying Canadian waters ever since John Molson of Montreal built the forty ton Accomodation in 1809, steam had not been applied to land transportation at this stage. The first use of steam on Canadian soil came in 1830 at Cape Diamond, Quebec, during the construction of the Quebec Citadel. The Royal Engineers used cable cars running along tracks to haul building materials, armaments and general supplies up the steep slope from the river's edge. In 1830 a stationary engine was put into use to replace the horses which previously had done the haulage.

While there had been earlier trials, the first public service steam locomotion railway in the world began with George Stephenson's Stockton and Darlington line in 1825. It is important to emphasize *steam* railway locomotion for there had been earlier lines on which coaches were towed along rails, or tracks, by horses.

Although the Stockton and Darlington line marked a tremendous advance in transportation, there were many problems still to be ironed out. The heavy locomotives often were more than the weak track could bear, and traction was a problem. In the early days the steam railway companies, plagued by such difficulties, sometimes were obliged to uncouple the locomotive from the coaches and revert to horse power of the four-legged kind.

Progress was made, however, and the Liverpool and Manchester Railway became the first public railway on which all traffic was hauled exclusively by steam locomotives when it opened in 1830. The enormous commerical potential of steam railway transportation dawned like a new day, and railway development rushed ahead in Britain, Europe and America. It was in this climate of furious railway construction in the 1830s and 1840s that the teen-age Sandford got his start in railway survey work.

Engraving of a sextant

Fresh Fields Chapter 2

For some time now there had been much talk in the
Fleming household about the attractions of life in the
New World. Kirkcaldy neighbours and friends had sold
their belongings and gone out to Canada: their letters
home told of cheap land and good opportunities. By the
beginning of 1845 Andrew and Elizabeth Fleming had
agreed to allow their two eldest sons, David and
Sandford, to try their luck in Canada. The rest of the
family would follow them if the boys' reports were
favourable. Andrew Fleming called on Mr. Ellice,
Member of Parliament, to make the necessary arrangements for his sons.

Sandford Fleming in 1845

The following months were taken up with anticipation, packing and good-byes. Mr. Sang gave his pupil a pocket sextant as a parting gift; Andrew Fleming presented his son Sandford with a silver watch. By mid-April, 1845, the day of departure was at hand. Sandford and David went to Kennoway to say a final good-bye to their grandmother.

The following morning the boys were up at six to finish packing their iron-bound leather sea trunks. With farewells to their mother, brothers and sisters, Sandford and David set off with their father for Glasgow. Two days later, on April 24, a little after one on a fine spring afternoon the boys cast off on the sailing vessel *Brilliant*.

As a steamer towed the *Brilliant* out into deep water, Mr. Fleming followed the ship to the end of the wharf and gave her three cheers. With a mixture of sadness and excitement, the boys watched the Scottish coast slip from view.

The *Brilliant* was not long out of sight of land when she ran into stormy weather and rough seas. Baggage and cargo broke loose and slid about the decks from one side to another.

One week out of Glasgow the worst of the sea's fury struck. The Flemings struggled not to be pitched from their beds; even the pillows had to be tied down. Sandford recorded the ordeal in his travel journal:

As the evening advanced the storm grew worse. The sea sometimes washed across the deck. I never expected to see daylight again when a great wave swept above our heads. It had a sound as if the sea was closing over us. We slept none all night, the timbers were cracking terribly, the bottles and tins rattling from one side of the floor to the other — pity the poor sailors on deck all night.

Despairing of their fate, Sandford sealed a farewell letter to his father in a bottle and tossed it into the sea. Amazingly, seven months later the bottle with the letter intact washed ashore on the Devon coast and was picked up by a fisherman, who notified Andrew Fleming in Kirkcaldy.

In the meantime, by the end of the second week the weather had cleared and the ocean was calm. Sandford made friends among the sailors, and sketched their likenesses in his journal. He also sketched sailing ships as they passed by the *Brilliant* and, when they neared Canada, recorded the first sighting of land. In the evenings the boys gathered with the passengers and crew in the steerage to sing sea shanties and play chess. When the weather was fine Sandford read on deck and watched for the porpoises, whales and sea birds that passed the ship. The weeks flew by for the Flemings, and the journey neared its end. There was great excitement and a feeling of relief among the travel-weary passengers when land was sighted.

At sunrise on June 5, six weeks after setting out from Glasgow, the boys saw Quebec City with the sun glinting on the tin roofs of the town. The St. Lawrence River was crowded with sailing ships, nearly all loading timber for England, and pilot boats were darting about in every direction. Sandford and David were anxious to go ashore for the first time in the New World. Happy to set foot on dry land again after their long voyage, they set off to see the ruins of a great fire which had swept through the city a week before their arrival, leaving 100 dead and 16 000 homeless. Since the houses and sidewalks were chiefly made of wood, the fire spread rapidly, reducing more than eight hectares of the town to charred rubble.

This painting by Joseph Legaré shows the ruins left by the fire that swept through Quebec City in 1845.

Downcast at the sight of this disaster, the two young men walked pensively out over the Plains of Abraham, where their grandfather had fought with General Wolfe in 1759, then returned to board a river steamer for the next stage of their journey.

The late spring weather was fine, the boys admired the passing scenery and activity of the river, and at night they slept under oil cloths on deck. Fleming observed that the vessel "was pretty well filled with Canadian queer-looking fellows."

The river highway along the St. Lawrence carried them to Montreal, at that time capital of the Province of Canada. Montreal in 1845 was a bustling commercial centre as well as the seat of government. Its population had grown to 60 000 on the strength of its port, the fur trade, and a growing number of business enterprises. While in Montreal, Fleming came across his old school master from Kennoway who had emigrated to Canada and was now the master of the Montreal High School.

Changing steamers once more, Sandford and David carried on up the Ottawa River to the small community of Bytown. Within a few years the little town would be renamed Ottawa and become the new capital of Canada. Further on their way, the brothers passed Kingston and the fledgling Queen's College. Little did Sandford Fleming realize, when he saw the "large plain college," that one day he would return to Queen's University as its chancellor.

Eleven days after leaving Quebec and eight weeks away from Scotland, Sandford and David arrived at their final destination, the town of Peterborough. The boys were not very impressed by their first sight of the new community of 2 000 inhabitants:

It looked rather a poor place when we entered — the stumps of trees still in the middle of the streets, a wood home here and there, with a few good villas with verandahs around.

But a warm welcome awaited them at the two-story stone house of their Kirkcaldy kinsman, Dr. Hutchison, and his wife. The doctor had been one of the first settlers in Peterborough, and was practically the only familiar face in the New World for the boys. Within a few days, however, Sandford met a number of young people in Peterborough. One of the very first was Jeanie Hall, who, ten years later, would become his wife.

The LASER Fund

How to Diversify and Create the Foundation
for a Tax-Free Retirement

Section I
[The Left-Brain Approach]

Douglas Andrew

Emron Andrew

Aaron Andrew

UPDATED EDITION
3DimensionalWealth.com

Also by Douglas Andrew, Emron Andrew, Aaron Andrew

Millionaire by Thirty

Also by Douglas Andrew

Best-Sellers

Missed Fortune
Missed Fortune 101
The Last Chance Millionaire

Entitlement Abolition
Learning Curves
Secrets to a Tax-Free Retirement
Baby Boomer Blunders
Create Your Own Economic Stimulus
How to Have LASER Focus

Original edition published 2018
Updated edition published 2022
By 3 Dimensional Wealth
Salt Lake City, UT U.S.A.
Printed in U.S.A.

ISBN: 978-0-9740087-4-5

The LASER Fund and The IUL LASER Fund are proprietary terms used by the authors of this book as a way to describe a properly structured, maximum-funded Indexed Universal Life (IUL) policy. With any mention of LASER Funds, IUL LASER Funds, properly structured, maximum-funded IUL policies, or related financial vehicle terms throughout this book, let it be noted that any life insurance policy is not an investment and, accordingly, should not be purchased as an investment.

Where appropriate, authentic examples of clients' policies have been incorporated, with names changed to safeguard privacy.

The materials in this book represent the opinions of the authors and may not be applicable to all situations. Due to the frequency of changing laws and regulations, some aspects of this work may be out of date, even upon first publication. Accordingly, the authors and publisher assume no responsibility for actions taken by readers based upon the advice offered in this book. You should use caution in applying the material contained in this book to your specific situation and should seek competent advice from a qualified professional or IUL specialist. Please provide your comments directly to the authors.

Acknowledgments

We wish to express sincere gratitude for the wonderful people who have helped and inspired *The LASER Fund.*

We offer gratitude to Sharee, Doug's wife and mother to Emron and Aaron. She has been by our sides rendering assistance and encouragement with every project we've undertaken. We also express thanks to Emron's wife, Harmony, and Aaron's wife, Heather, and our children, for their never-ending support—and for always teaching us how to lead better lives.

To our family and friends, we offer gratitude for the blessings of life and wonderful support you give us.

We are grateful to Heather Beers at Momentum Communications, our longtime friend and editor. We sincerely appreciate your special talents and your encouragement. We extend special thanks to Toni Lock at ᵗᵐdesigns for her expertise in the layout of this work.

We appreciate the support and contributions of the team at LASER Financial, including Owner Brandon Johnsen and IUL specialists Scott Reynolds, Greg Duckwitz, Karl Nelson, Terry Seeley, Clarence McBride, Sean Nelson, Marcus Maxfield, Tracy Belliston, Tyler Lyman, and Doug Jones.

Special thanks go to our team at 3 Dimensional Wealth, including Bud Heaton, who are dedicated not only to the development and growth of our company, but also to increasing the abundance of others' lives through the 3 Dimensions of Authentic Wealth. Thank you for working with us in our professional and philanthropic endeavors.

Suggestions for reading this book...

IF YOU LIKE A SOLID FOUNDATION
[Chapters 1-3]

Start with this deep-dive education that includes:
- Fundamentals of taxes and insurance
- What makes a prudent financial vehicle
- Why you want liquidity, safety, rate of return, and tax advantages in your financial vehicles

IF YOU LIKE TO FOCUS ON THE "MEAT"
[Chapters 4-10]

Delve into this section that provides:
- How The LASER Fund works
- How it plays out in illustrated scenarios
- How it compares to other financial vehicles
- How 2020 tax laws changed to make max-funded IULs 1/3 less expensive on average

IF YOU LIKE TO KNOW MORE
[Chapters 11-14]

Read this section that explains:
- Why these proven strategies may be new to you or those you know
- How to safeguard your approach
- Why The LASER Fund isn't the only strategy you want ... and how to optimize your portfolio

Table of Contents

[For the Right-Brain Approach – Flip to Section II]

Introduction
WARNING: Are You Sure You Want to Read This Book?

Let's just start by asking, "Are you sure you want to read this book?"

We know most authors would never want to dissuade readers from picking up their book, but we offer this caution from the sincerest of places.

This is NOT your average, run-of-the-mill financial book. It will not contain conventional advice about traditional retirement vehicles. You won't likely feel reassured if you're like millions of Americans who have followed the crowd, adhering to widely accepted strategies when it comes to accumulating wealth and preparing for retirement.

While the principles contained have been helping the affluent achieve greater financial stability for decades—even during some of the nation's worst economic storms—they are not well-known. Mainstream financial professionals are often not familiar with these strategies, and sometimes look upon them with suspicion or doubt. These folks have even been known to dismiss the principles, saying things like, "I've never seen it before, so it can't be real." But that's where one must beg the question, "Have you ever seen gravity, or the wind, or your brain before? Then how can any of those be real?"

The LASER Fund principles we will discuss in this book are very real.

- They've provided people tax-free liquidity—access to their cash—for everything from supplemental retirement income and business capital to children's educations and emergency funds.
- They've provided safety from market volatility when using this financial vehicle.
- They've provided rates of return that can consistently outperform other traditional vehicles.
- Plus, they've provided valuable tax advantages, and upon death, the opportunity for money to blossom and transfer to heirs income-tax-free.
- When we share the advantages of this approach, people invariably call it "a miracle."

That said, this isn't a one-size-fits-all approach. This isn't even the *only* financial vehicle we would recommend.

And this isn't for the faint of financial heart. It's definitely not for financial jellyfish.

These principles are only for the abundance-minded, teachable, responsible, accountable, and self-disciplined. In fact, before we work with anyone, we have them consider whether they have the 8 Mindsets required to pursue this path. Figure I.1 is a condensed version of the 8 Mindsets Scorecard we share with prospective clients. You might want to take a peek to decide if this book is for ... you.

NOTE: The official scorecard includes a range of responses for each mindset and the opportunity to score yourself. For brevity, we've included only the extreme ends of the scorecard here, so you can get a feel for where you are on the scarcity-to-abundance spectrum. Score yourself on a scale from 1 to 10, with 10 being superior.

---

8 MINDSETS – FROM SCARCITY TO ABUNDANCE FIGURE I.1

MINDSET	STOP READING NOW	EMBRACE THE COMING PAGES	MY SCORE (1-10)
It's about "We" Not "Me" / Abundance-Minded	You believe that resources are scarce, your future is bleak, and nothing can change that. You envy the success of others and often think life is unfair to you.	You believe your greater future will be best achieved by collaborating with a team of experts and know that abundance breeds more abundance.	
Motivated to Learn & Change	You are comfortable with the status quo and like things the way they are. You feel that what you've learned is satisfactory to survive.	You are willing to seek for what you don't know, because you understand the progress that will come. You yearn to learn new things to constantly improve.	
Teachable	You are skeptical, doubtful, and usually don't trust others. You often "dig in your heels" and feel that people are trying to manipulate you to do what they want.	You make the time to learn and want to be influenced for a better path to a brighter future. You are willing to get out of your comfort zone to grow more.	
Independent Thinker	You don't know your own opinions. You're not sure what you stand for. You have a tendency to do what the mainstream does.	You think for yourself and don't follow the crowd. When you learn a true principle, you want to implement it immediately to improve and thrive more.	
Decisive	You are unwilling to make decisions, and you consistently second-guess the decisions being made, which causes you to worry and fret about all kinds of things.	You have the ability to weigh options and feel confident in the decision you make. You move forward with determination to make your decisions work for the best.	
Accountable & Responsible	You blame others when things don't go according to plan. You often justify why you can't accomplish things. You feel that nothing ever turns out right for you.	You take ownership for the decisions you make and the actions you take. You respond with all your ability, and you account to others who depend on you.	
Financially Disciplined	You often have too much month left at the end of the money. Things have just never worked out for you financially because you have more challenges than others.	You have a track record of saving and accumulating your financial assets. You recognize new opportunities and want to keep optimizing your assets.	
Courteous & Respectful	You are usually late; you have a hard time following through; and you rarely finish things that you start. You are quick to judge others.	You are always on time; you do what you say you're going to do; you finish what you start; and you are naturally polite and happy and seek to understand others.	

How'd you do? If you're scoring on the high end, congratulations and read on. If your score is low, you might want to put the book down now (or hand it to someone else who's ready).

Pursuing ... More

Status quo. It's a term for "the existing state of affairs," or the way things have always been. As a general rule, mankind tends to stick to the status quo. We follow along known paths. We stay tucked inside our comfort zones. Even if our "existing state of affairs" isn't the best, we often go with the flow because change requires action, ingenuity, and sometimes outright courage.

But if there's a better way, why not challenge the conventional thinking? Thankfully, that's what abundance-minded people have dared to do throughout history.

PIONEERS IN LIFE

Looking back in time, for millennia there was no reliable way for mankind to fight even the simplest of infections. A small scratch could turn to infection, which could abscess, and ultimately lead to death. The same held true for pneumonia, rheumatic fever, and countless other infectious illnesses. Doctors could only stand by and hope for the best—that is until penicillin came along, thanks to an accidental discovery by Alexander Fleming, a British professor of bacteriology.

But it took more than Fleming's moldy petri dish in 1928 to start saving lives. Over the next two decades, it required the work of experts in Great Britain and the US conducting extensive research to develop, produce, and distribute penicillin as treatment.

The advent of penicillin ushered in the era of antibiotics, which changed the course of modern medicine in many ways. But it wouldn't have happened without people who were dissatisfied with the status quo, people who saw patients dying and thought, "We can and we must do better."

The same has held true for most major advancements in medicine, transportation, agriculture, technology, and even commerce. Take the automobile, for instance. During the late 1800s, the Germans and French honed the blueprint for the modern automobile, but it wasn't until Henry Ford wondered if there were a better way to mass-produce cars that the world really started moving.

Steve Jobs was another example of challenging the status quo. He didn't invent the cell phone. He just made a better one. He created one of the most popular cell phones and platforms used worldwide—advancements that have spawned millions of apps. Likewise, Jobs didn't invent the MP3 player. But when he saw the technology, he dared to wonder what would happen if Apple could put thousands of songs in everybody's pocket. At the time, the music industry viewed him as a threat. They resisted his idea that people could download individual songs on iTunes for a nominal fee. While the doubters were busy being scarcity-minded, Jobs started a revolution in the industry—one that continues today with streaming services like Spotify.

And just look at today's game changers in the entertainment industry. Blockbuster built an empire of video rental stores, dwarfing mom-and-pop shops and larger competitors. But then others dared to question the rental store model, and along came competition with things like Netflix's DVD shipping model and that pervasive little kiosk, Redbox. For nearly three decades, Blockbuster had been a video rental titan with as many as 9,000 stores worldwide, but it drifted into history, replaced by ever-advancing entertainment technology. Now streaming services like Netflix, Amazon, and Hulu are dominating. They are not only disrupting the way people get their entertainment, but entertainment itself, launching their own series and movies that rival the best programs on traditional networks, cable channels, and movie screens.

This same principle has also played out in the travel and lodging sector. When it comes to booking lodging, people used to visit with their travel agent, who made the hotel arrangements on behalf of their clients. The internet paved the way for hotels and travel sites like Expedia and Trivago to empower travelers in booking their own hotel stays. With further innovation, sites like VRBO and Airbnb have given travelers even more options, bypassing the hotel chains and empowering people to stay in private condos, homes, or timeshares.

The examples go on and on—including things like long-established taxi companies competing with Uber and Lyft as the "sharing economy" transforms our world. Suffice it to say that the status quo is not always necessarily the best. When pioneers in any area of life dare to explore new routes, it opens the way for others to thrive along better paths. These pioneers are engaging in something called "creative destruction," a term credited to Austrian American Economist Joseph Schumpeter.

CREATIVE DESTRUCTION

In 1942, Schumpeter published a work, *Capitalism, Socialism and Democracy,* in which he pointed out that creative destruction, was a "process of industrial mutation that incessantly revolutionizes the economic structure from within, incessantly destroying the old one, incessantly creating a new one." Essentially, he was pointing out this cycle of something newer killing off and replacing something older.

The financial services sector has benefited from its share of creative destruction. At one time, the only options to preserve your wealth were to bury it in the ground, lock it up, or put it in the bank where it could earn nominal interest. Over time, other financial vehicles emerged—CDs, money market accounts, and qualified investments like IRAs and 401(k)s.

Each of these vehicles has offered Americans a new path to accumulating wealth and saving for retirement, but they have their limitations. In 1980, E.F. Hutton caused another wave of creative destruction when the stock brokerage firm introduced a special kind of insurance policy that could provide a death benefit along with other benefits: cash accumulation, liquidity, safety, predictable rates of return, and tax advantages.

Despite its existence for more than three decades, this revolutionary policy is something relatively few financial experts know about—let alone understand how to properly structure and fund. And even though it has become one of the most valuable financial vehicles for thousands of successful people across the country—helping our clients get through the Great Recession of 2008 and the pandemic of 2020 without losing principal due to market volatility (and many of them even saw significant gains)—it's a strategy that is often misunderstood and even maligned.

But we ask, "Just because all the dogs may be barking up other trees, does that make those the right trees?" We'd rather catch the prize—a brighter financial future—in whichever way is best. In fact, that's what led us to where we are today, one of the nation's pioneers in suggesting a balanced approach to financial strategies that includes incorporating what we call The LASER Fund, which is a properly structured, maximum-funded Indexed Universal Life policy (you'll see we also refer to this as an IUL LASER Fund throughout the book).

We've been called creative disruptors for leading this charge. It's a role we'll gladly accept, because our path to developing these strategies has been hard-earned. These principles were borne out of the crucible of real-life experiences that proved to be turning points, defining moments that have benefited our clients, and even ourselves. We started this movement in the 80s, with Doug Andrew paving the way. These concepts garnered major national attention with the advent of Doug's first book in the early 2000s, *Missed Fortune.* From there, our team taught thousands of financial services professionals these powerful strategies we're about to share with you in this book. Today, our strategies have gone on to help transform entire segments of the financial services and insurance industries—as well as countless lives.

TAKE OWNERSHIP OF YOUR FUTURE

Even when something good comes along in any aspect of life, you often see people clinging to the same old premises. They hold on to concepts or practices they're familiar with, simply because they tend to equate familiarity with comfortability. And we humans like to stay within our comfort zones.

The same holds true in financial planning. There are many principles that people adhere to, even though in actuality they're just myths, such as:

Common Myths

- Choose only tax-deferred financial vehicles because you'll be in a lower tax bracket when you retire.
- Keep all your money in the market. If you're losing significant amounts, just stay in there, and you'll come out ahead.
- The best way to get out of debt and get ahead is to send extra principal payments to the mortgage company to pay off your mortgage as soon as possible.
- During retirement, the best way to save on taxes is to stretch out your IRA or 401(k) as long as possible by taking Required Minimum Distributions (as required by the IRS).

Doug's comprehensive best-selling books explain why these and other myths simply aren't true. All three of us shared these principles in our book, *Millionaire By Thirty*, illustrating how other financial vehicles can provide more critical advantages than the traditional ones. Doug explores these strategies on his 3 Dimensional Wealth YouTube channel and national radio show. And our team delivers these principles at our regular seminars and full-day events.

Why all this effort to help people learn, and let go of old ways of thinking? Because we don't believe in just selling financial products—we believe in empowering people to understand these concepts for themselves so they can make informed decisions. In fact, we often won't meet with potential clients until they've first attended one of our educational events. This is to help them determine for themselves if this is a path they're interested in—and if they're self-disciplined enough to take it.

Our clients actually get involved in their financial strategies. While we see our role as being their guides, we invite our clients to see themselves as competent partners in the process, taking personal accountability and responsibility for their finances, as well. Because there is at least some element of risk in virtually all financial vehicles, our clients are encouraged to do the homework necessary to gain at least a fundamental understanding of financial principles and strategies so they can make decisions for their individual situations.

Our IUL specialists lead them through an 8-Step True Wealth Transformation process. The first step is the Enlightenment Experience, where clients learn the ins and outs of how to incorporate a blend of

strategies. Throughout the 8-Step process, most of our clients invest hours in studying these principles. This way they gain essential knowledge to move forward and have the opportunity to reap the rewards these strategies provide.

Taking this kind of personal ownership for one's financial path corresponds with Marshall Thurber's principle of "dealing above the line." Marshall Thurber, the revolutionary attorney, businessman, author, and educator (and personal friend of Doug's), explains that we must avoid living "below the line," dwelling in blame, shame, and justification. Instead we should live above that line, taking accountability and responsibility for our lives. When it comes to finances, this essentially means it's wise to partner with your financial professionals, essentially becoming "fiduciaries" together so you can take responsibility for your future.

Now the term "fiduciary" has become a hot button topic in ongoing legislative debates related to the future of the financial services industry. According to "The Free Dictionary," as an adjective, fiduciary means, "of or relating to a duty of acting in good faith with regard to the interests of another." As a noun, it means "a person bound to act for another's benefit."

Far too many Americans would rather turn the entire responsibility for their financial future over to their financial professional, essentially making the professional the sole fiduciary. They would rather assume their financial professional knows everything there is to know and is selecting optimal strategies for them—and all they have to do is sign on the dotted line and hope for the best. If anything goes south (which with market volatility, economic storms, rising taxes, and inflation, things often do), they want to be able to blame and penalize their fiduciary financial professional.

How much greater is it to take ownership of your own finances, gain an understanding for yourself, and then partner with like-minded financial professionals to pursue best-possible strategies that incorporate the three marvels of wealth accumulation we'll talk about in Section I, Chapter 3?

Stop and think: who has the biggest stake in your abundant future? You! Who has the most to gain or lose when it comes to the strategies you select? You!

So why wouldn't you want to know more, understand more, and have more control?

We'd like to empower as many Americans as possible to stand up and take ownership for their own brighter days ahead. That's what our company's mission is about. That's what this book is about.

This book is also about getting in motion, now. Not five years from now. Not ten years from now. Wherever you are in your journey toward retirement, you can never start too early—or too late—to adopt better strategies. We've helped thousands of clients break away from the herd and achieve better outcomes using The IUL LASER Fund, which we'll be talking about in this book.

TRAILBLAZING A PATH FOR YOU

For decades, we've been blazing this trail, but industry trailblazers often have arrows in their backs. As one of the first to introduce these strategies, we've taken criticism and skepticism for years, but it's interesting to note that now others realize the path we've helped illuminate is better. We're seeing a migration in America's financial sector. More financial professionals are turning to the strategies we've been helping clients with for decades. What was once a chorus of naysayers has become a group of like-minded professionals.

In his popular series on creative destruction, nationally renowned Strategic Coach Dan Sullivan (a personal friend of Doug's) has cited the impact Doug and our team have had in the industry by saying:

> *Many of our previous industry transformers have continually focused on specific clientele within a specific market. Over a period of time, they are able to continually deepen their value of creation. Doug Andrew started off on his path, with his unique process, the True Wealth Transformer, focusing on helping his own clientele maximize their wealth creation opportunities. It wasn't long, however, before many other advisors began asking Doug to teach them how to transform their practices in the same dramatic fashion as he had his own. It was not too long after he began helping thousands of financial advisors to transform their practices that representatives from other financial subservices sectors made the same request.*

The ripple effect of our work is also seen in the growth of a sector of the insurance industry that provides one of the primary financial vehicles we recommend—the very vehicle you'll be learning about in this book. After Doug started teaching other financial professionals and agents/producers across the nation to utilize this vehicle, some of the country's largest brokerages saw a significant increase in the volume of these policies. And according to industry leaders over the past ten years, the industry has seen an average growth rate of nearly 20% year-over-year on these policies.

As the leading company in the US to recommend these strategies, many of the nation's top insurance institutions now consult with our team when updating their offerings—even flying their executive teams out to our Salt Lake City offices to meet with us in person. These are multi-billion-dollar companies in a multitrillion-dollar global industry, with stellar track records we're proud to recommend.

WOULD YOU LIKE MORE OR LESS?

Often by the time people come to us, they've lost money in the market. They realize during retirement that they're in a tax bracket that is as high or higher than during their working years. Their finances are essentially in Stage IV cancer. While we can often offer the right "treatments" to help them secure a healthier financial future, how great would it have been if they'd taken advantage of prevention rather than seeking a cure? How much better is it to change out the oil regularly than replace the entire engine?

Many people don't realize how the reality of retirement can play out. Let's look at a quick illustration. Let's say you're thinking that in retirement, in addition to other sources of income (pension, Social Security, rental income), you want to pull $3,000 a month out of your 401(k) to cover the extras (travel, medical, charitable giving). That's $36,000 a year.

Now, do you know how much would you have to pull out of an IRA or 401(k) every year to net $36,000?

It's not $36,000. Those dollars inside your 401(k) are pre-tax dollars, so once you withdraw them, it's time to pay taxes. And because you're in a 27% tax bracket, you would need to withdraw almost $50,000 to cover the $13,500 in taxes to finally end up with that $36,000 you wanted

(except where noted, throughout this book we'll be using 27% as an average tax bracket, which is comprised of a 22% to 24% federal tax bracket for incomes over $75,000, and a 3% to 5% state tax bracket).

Let's look more closely at that: $50,000 is 4% of what? It's 4% of a $1,250,000 nest egg. If you're anything like us, we'd be frustrated having accumulated a nice big $1.25 million nest egg, only to be enjoying a measly $3,000 a month from the account during retirement.

But that 4% is consistent with what traditional financial professionals recommend you take every year. In the industry, it's called the 4% rule, something promoted by many "crowd-following" financial professionals who encourage clients to withdraw only 4% a year from their accounts. (The thinking is this will help clients avoid outliving their money during retirement. However, it's important to note that even the 4% rule has come into question within the last few years. Recent analyses and articles show that it may fail in preventing a good portion of retirees from outliving their money, due to market volatility and longer life expectancies.)

In this book, we'll show how it's possible to enjoy a 7% payout a year, on average—tax-free. This would mean with a $1,250,000 nest egg, you could be pulling out more than $87,000 a year to live on—again, tax-free. That's over $7,000 a month, which is more than two times what you would be getting from your IRA or 401(k) in this example.

So we beg the question: would you like access to more or less money when you need it most?

We're guessing your answer is *more.*

AS YOU TURN THE PAGES

This book is designed to help you learn how to achieve more. We want to help you prevent any further pain from less-than-optimal financial strategies. Throughout Section I, we'll discuss several financial vehicles—the most significant of which is The IUL LASER Fund. We'll take an in-depth look at how it works, how it complies with IRS rules and guidelines, and how it can dramatically impact your financial future. We'll also discuss why you can't call The IUL LASER Fund an investment (let us repeat, this is NOT an investment—but we'll get to that later).

In Section II on the book's flip side, we'll explore the numerous ways The IUL LASER Fund can be utilized to empower you, your family, and even your business to thrive, including:

- Death Benefit
- Retirement Planning
- Working Capital
- School, Family, and Life
- Lump Sums
- Business Planning
- Life's Emergencies
- Estate Planning
- Real Estate
- Strategic Rollouts
- Tax Reduction

The principles, strategies, and knowledge in this book can help you diversify your retirement approach. This book can help you lay out a plan to revolutionize the Financial Dimension of your life. It can empower you to maximize your Legacy Dimensions (Foundational and Intellectual). It can bring you closer to the life you'd like to have now ... and down the road. Essentially, it can help you pursue ... more. Welcome to your opportunity for a more abundant future.

DISCLAIMER: With any mention of The LASER Fund, The IUL LASER Fund, maximum-funded tax-advantaged insurance policies/contracts, or related financial vehicles throughout this book, let it be noted that life insurance policies are not investments and, accordingly, should not be purchased as an investment.

TOP 5 TAKEAWAYS

1. To achieve a meaningful transformation in any aspect of life, you must dare to step outside your comfort zone, shake up the status quo, and be willing to re-think your thinking.

2. Creative destruction has led to significant advances in everything from medicine to media to financial services.

3. As you take ownership of your own life and invest in exploring powerful knowledge, wisdom, and strategies, you are empowered to create a present—and future—with more abundance.

4. Many Americans do not realize that they are at risk of outliving their money when following conventional retirement planning.

5. As you turn the pages of this book, you will discover financial (and abundant living) strategies that can be life-changing, not just for you, but for your posterity.

Escape the Tax Trap

One of our favorite places to go is Alaska—it's an outdoor paradise. As avid fishermen, the chance to catch Pacific salmon as they surge up Alaska's pristine rivers is unparalleled. From herds of caribou to black wolves (one of which Doug came face-to-face with—a story he shares in his book, *Learning Curves*), breathtaking wildlife is everywhere. And so are brown bears.

There was a time when trappers made their living snaring bears like these in leg-hold traps. Steel-jawed, with razor sharp teeth and a vice grip—these traps were strong enough to keep an unsuspecting 1,500-pound beast tethered once caught. For humane reasons, these toothed traps have been outlawed throughout much of North America.

But there's another kind of trap, equally menacing, that's perfectly legal and snares millions of Americans ... the tax trap.

Too many Americans fail to comprehend that at retirement they will likely find themselves in a tax bracket that's as high or higher than during their working years. Why? We call it the Deduction Reduction.

Many will have paid down or paid off their mortgage by the time they retire. This means they're no longer enjoying those tax deduction benefits

if they itemize. Their children are usually grown and have moved away, along with their dependent deductions. For many, their former business write-offs have also retired. And many stop contributing to their IRAs or 401(k)s, losing that annual deduction (which could be as high as $26,000 for maximum contributions to a 401[k]). It's often not until retirees start accessing money from their tax-deferred accounts that they realize they're being taxed in a higher tax bracket than they anticipated—and those taxes are taking a sizable chunk of the very retirement income they were counting on.

PROCRASTINATING & PARTNERSHIPS

You may still be thinking, "I should be good. I've got tax-advantaged retirement plans in place, like my IRAs and 401(k)s." Sure, these are technically tax-advantaged. But notice *when* those advantages take place: when you're putting your pre-tax dollars into these accounts. Everyone tells you this is great, because you can put in more now, and worry about paying taxes down the road, when you access your money during retirement. That's why these accounts are also called "tax-deferred."

Still hoping it sounds good, right?

Not so much. Postponing taxes is essentially *procrastinating taxes.* In some cases, traditional "tax-deferred" strategies should be called "tax-procrastinated" strategies.

Think back to your school days. When did procrastinating a big report or project ever make things better? Or at work, is it ever beneficial to procrastinate resolving an issue with employees or clients? Procrastinating only tends to compound problems, rather than alleviate them. And when it comes to your money, the only compounding you want is positive interest.

Think about it: who designed tax-deferred accounts like IRAs and 401(k)s? The same guy who set that trap, Uncle Sam. And why would that uncle of yours want you to procrastinate your taxes? Could it be that there's something in it for him? By putting your money into traditional accounts like IRAs and 401(k)s, you're essentially making Uncle Sam your partner in your wealth accumulation endeavors.

Is he really the kind of partner you want?

We often offer the following proposition to our audiences, saying, "Let's say you and I go into business together. You're going to do all the work, but I'm your partner. If the business struggles along the way, you're on your own; I won't offer any financial protection. And from the word go, whatever you build this business to be worth, when you sell it or liquidate it, I get one-third. Okay? I get a third guaranteed, but if I'm hard up at the time, I reserve the right to increase my percentage. And if you want to sell early, I'll charge a 10% penalty in addition to my third. And if you want to sell it later than I want you to, I can force you to sell and pay me my portion sooner than later. How many of you would go into business with somebody like that?"

The crowd always laughs—until we say, "I just described an IRA or 401(k) to you." Consider this: when it comes to your IRA or 401(k), who earns the money that goes into your account? You do—along with matching 401(k) funds from your employer, in many instances. If the economy tanks, your account tanks, too. When you begin to take distributions during retirement, who takes about one-third of your withdrawals in taxes? Uncle Sam. Could that tax rate increase? You bet it can, and many experts think it will. (Uncle Sam DOES have a huge pile of debt with more than 20 trillion reasons to hike the tax rates in the future.) If you withdraw money before age 59½, you get a 10% penalty in addition to your taxes. And after age 72, you MUST take Required Minimum Distributions—or face a 50% penalty—so Uncle Sam can start taxing your withdrawals.

Now we're not entirely disparaging IRAs and 401(k)s. They can have a valuable place in comprehensive wealth accumulation strategies, particularly with company matching benefits. As a side note, we would not recommend putting in anything above your company's match. If you have extra money to set aside beyond that, consider putting it into financial vehicles like The IUL LASER Fund. This will diversify your retirement tax base, as well as further diversify your retirement strategies. That said, IRAs and 401(k)s should be handled with caution. Let us explain why with an illustration.

Let's assume that you have $1 million saved in your 401(k) for retirement. To be generous, we'll say that your million bucks is earning an average return of 10% a year. With $100,000 a year in interest, most people could live fairly comfortably. You'll be able to pay for the necessities of

life, as well as travel a bit, donate to your favorite charities, and create a strong family legacy.

But you must consider inflation—it can take a toll on your retirement planning. That's because inflation increases your cost of living. Thus, ten, fifteen, and twenty years down the road, that $100,000 income will buy you less and less. But even worse, the real danger is the amount of taxes you could be paying.

Many Americans are in 25% to 30% tax brackets between what they pay in federal and state taxes. For the sake of this illustration, we'll use a 27% marginal tax bracket. At that tax rate, how much would you need to withdraw from your 401(k) in order to net $100,000? The answer is $137,000, because roughly a third of your money will be going to pay taxes. If you live in California or New York, your marginal rate will be more like 33% between federal and state. If that is the case, you would need to withdraw $150,000 in order to net $100,000.

Going back to our million-dollar example, as you can see in Figure 2.1, if you take $137,000 to $150,000 a year, but your money is only earning $100,000 a year, it would take you just twelve to thirteen years to deplete your hard-earned nest egg. And even if you withdrew less in order to make your nest egg last, the government will continue to collect taxes on whatever you withdraw from your IRA or 401(k)—and those taxes will likely be going up.

FIGURE 2.1

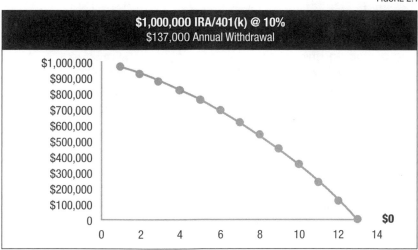

Does this reality leave you worried that your future might not look as bright? Are you feeling a bit stuck? Snared in a vice grip? Well, guess who left that trap lying around? Yep, Uncle Sam.

And why would he want to trap you, ensuring he can continue to tax you handsomely, even during your retirement years?

Because he's spending himself silly, and he needs your money to support his out-of-control habits. No matter which side of the political aisle you find yourself on, it's pretty much a consensus that even if taxes temporarily go down, they will eventually go up again—often without the deductions that were previously allowed.

WHAT GOES UP ... AIN'T COMIN' DOWN

Because of the runaway national debt, experts agree that despite temporary tax cuts (often politically motivated for the short-term), we will be entering an overall era of rising taxes. In 2007, the national debt reached $9.2 trillion. With approximately 100 million taxpayers in America then—if every American were to have paid his or her equal share of the national debt—every single American taxpayer would have had to write a check for $92,000 to eliminate the national debt.

Since then, the debt has escalated to more than $30 trillion (at the time of the printing of this edition), with US unfunded liabilities escalating in the hundreds of trillions, as well. US unfunded liabilities include what the government owes those of us who have faithfully paid into the system for programs such as Social Security and Medicare. The government has withheld the money for these programs from our paychecks throughout our working careers, and it now owes all that in future Social Security and Medicare benefits to us. The reason that this is referred to as unfunded liabilities is because the government technically does not have that money in its coffers to provide future Social Security and Medicare benefits to retirees. And the only place the government can get money to fund these programs in the future? Taxes. Unlike the national debt, the government cannot print money to cover the cost of Social Security and Medicare. It must come from taxes.

And then there's defense spending. With unrest throughout the world and the US's involvement in several foreign conflicts, national defense

is a hefty budget item—one that's not likely to decrease soon. If an all-out war were to break out, taxes could surge. If history is any indication, around the time of World War I and World War II, according to Tax Foundation, federal income taxes were over 90% for the nation's top earners.

It's not out of the realm of possibility for taxes to skyrocket in the coming years. In its "Solutions 2016" report, The Heritage Foundation announced that our national debt is three-quarters the size of the US economic product, adding, "The Congressional Budget Office estimates that without fiscal restraint, public debt could exceed 100 percent of GDP by 2030, within less than one generation." The report also cautioned, "Projected deficits are large and growing, and raising taxes to pay for this spending would require doubling tax rates even for the lowest income brackets. Such a policy would deal a devastating blow to the economy." Our nation is effectively in a scarcity spiral, which could cause another big crash.

Indeed, with an escalating national debt; ongoing military action; unfunded liabilities; costly healthcare programs; and anticipated low returns to a recession (or worse!), it's a pretty good bet that your taxes won't be going anywhere but up in the long run.

Think of that example, the $1 million nest egg tucked into your IRA or 401(k). You'd like to have $100,000 a year to pay for all your living, travel, medical, and other costs during retirement (which as we pointed out, you'll need that much because of inflation). And let's say you're in a 33% combined tax bracket. To cover the cost of taxes and net $100,000, you would have to pull out an additional 50% from your IRA or 401(k), or $150,000 a year.

Because you're pulling out that extra 50%, your nest egg will be cracked, empty, and dried up in just twelve years. Twelve years. Most people think $1 million will be enough to last throughout retirement.

Sadly, many Americans will outlive their money, especially considering increasing life expectancies. You may be thinking, "What about Social Security—that should help, right?" The reality is folks are living longer than when Social Security was first introduced. Back then, they were expecting men to only live seven years beyond age 65. Now, at least one individual in a baby boomer couple is likely to live until age 96.

This makes it clear why financial strategies that use post-tax dollars for contribution on the front end—and provide distributions that are income-tax-free on the back end—are critical for maximizing your financial future.

TAXES ON THE SEED VS. THE HARVEST

Let's explore this principle a little more. Imagine you're a farmer. Winter is about to give way to spring's warmer days, and you're getting ready to prepare your fields for the growing season. As you look out across your acres, you can picture the seedlings that will take root. You can see summer's sun radiating life into your emerging crops. You can even look ahead to the fall, when you'll be harvesting your bounty.

Here's a question for you: when would you rather be taxed? Would you rather pay taxes on the front end, when you purchase your seed? Or would you like to wait until the harvest, when you're selling your crops?

Now apply this same question to the issue of financial planning. Would you rather pay taxes on your earnings before you "plant" them in a financial vehicle to give them a chance to grow? Or would you prefer to pay taxes on your "harvest," when you go to withdraw money for retirement or other ventures?

Most Americans choose the harvest. They listen to traditional advice and follow the crowd—often without realizing there's any other way to do it. They put their pre-tax dollars into their IRA, thinking it's better to put as much as they can into the account during the contribution phase. Then when they get to the distribution phase and access their money after age 59½, they pay taxes on those withdrawals. As we've discussed, that's when most Americans find an ugly surprise: they're often in a tax bracket that's as high or higher than during their earning years. Now they're taking the full brunt of those taxes on their distributions at a time in life when they need the income the most. They're enjoying less of a harvest than they anticipated. And they're often worried the pantry will run dry before it's time.

This is why we recommend paying taxes on the seed rather than the harvest on a portion of your retirement portfolio, in order to be tax diversified.

This goes along with the idea of prevention rather than a cure, a point that is well-illustrated in one of our favorite poems, *A Fence or an Ambulance*.

A Fence or an Ambulance
by Joseph Malins (1895)

'Twas a dangerous cliff, as they freely confessed,
though to walk near its crest was so pleasant;
but over its terrible edge there had slipped
a duke and full many a peasant.

So the people said something would have to be done,
but their projects did not at all tally;
some said, 'Put a fence 'round the edge of the cliff, '
some, 'An ambulance down in the valley.'

But the cry for the ambulance carried the day,
for it spread through the neighboring city;
a fence may be useful or not, it is true,
but each heart became full of pity
for those who slipped over the dangerous cliff;

And the dwellers in highway and alley
gave pounds and gave pence, not to put up a fence,
but an ambulance down in the valley.

'For the cliff is all right, if your careful, ' they said,
'and if folks even slip and are dropping,
it isn't the slipping that hurts them so much
as the shock down below when they're stopping.'

So day after day, as these mishaps occurred,
quick forth would those rescuers sally
to pick up the victims who fell off the cliff,
with their ambulance down in the valley.

Then an old sage remarked: 'It's a marvel to me
that people give far more attention
to repairing results than to stopping the cause,
when they'd much better aim at prevention.

Let us stop at its source all this mischief, ' cried he,
'come, neighbors and friends, let us rally;
if the cliff we will fence, we might almost dispense
with the ambulance down in the valley.'

"Oh he's a fanatic," the others rejoined,
"Dispense with the ambulance? Never!
He'd dispense with all charities, too, if he could;
No! No! We'll support them forever.

Aren't we picking up folks just as fast as they fall?
And shall this man dictate to us? Shall he?
Why should people of sense stop to put up a fence,
While the ambulance works in the valley?"

But a sensible few, who are practical too
Will not bear with such nonsense much longer;
They believe that prevention is better than cure,
And their party will soon be the stronger.

Encourage them then, with your purse, voice, and pen.
And while other philanthropists dally,
They will scorn all pretense, and put up a stout fence
On the cliff that hangs over the valley.

Better guide well the young than reclaim them when old,
For the voice of true wisdom is calling,
"To rescue the fallen is good, but 'tis best
To prevent other people from falling."

Better close up the source of temptation and crime
Than deliver from dungeon or galley;
Better put a strong fence 'round the top of the cliff
Than an ambulance down in the valley.

"AT-RETIREMENT" TAX BILL

Since the amount of taxes you pay during retirement can have a significant impact on the quality of your Financial Dimension during your golden years, it is helpful to consider your "at-retirement" tax bill. We're talking about how much you'll pay in taxes throughout your retirement years, based on your financial portfolio strategies.

Once you have a projection of your at-retirement tax bill based on your current strategies, you can look at diversifying your at-retirement tax bill. You can make adjustments to ensure your financial portfolio is not top-heavy with financial vehicles that are taxable as you take out money for retirement income. Instead you may want to aim for a balanced approach during the distribution phase, using a blended financial portfolio featuring up to four different types of income:

- Investment income
- Real estate income
- Guaranteed income
- Tax-free income

This can help you increase your net spendable retirement income during perhaps one of the most critical times of your life. We'll touch more on this in Section I, Chapter 14.

FAIR TAXES, YES – UNNECESSARY TAXES, NO

You deserve to have a consumer advocate to help protect you from the tax trap. And while we'll always encourage you to avoid financial pain and protect yourself, let us clarify that we're not vilifying taxes altogether. We see taxes as an asset. Every time we as fortunate Americans drive down a highway; take off from an airport; take our children to the library; watch our young ones graduate from public high school; send them off to fine state universities; call on police and firefighters; and benefit from the service and protection of our men and women in the armed services—all of these are made possible by the taxes we pay. It is a privilege to enjoy these advantages in a blessed country like America, and for that, we believe we, as Americans, should pay our fair share of taxes.

At 3 Dimensional Wealth, we're strong believers in the necessity and power of a tax-paying nation. However, we also believe there are positive, productive ways to contribute to society other than paying unnecessary taxes. By escaping the tax trap and saving on taxes where legally prudent and possible, it frees that money to be put to use for charitable efforts to benefit those in need. It empowers Americans to put their resources in business and capital investments that can go on to create jobs, and to create self-sufficiency in healthcare and retirement living.

In the next chapter, we'll examine the marvels of wealth accumulation and delve into the impact of taxes, lending critical knowledge to help you avoid the drain of unnecessary or untimely taxes, empowering you to maximize your financial future.

TOP 5 TAKEAWAYS

1. Postponing taxes is more like procrastinating taxes. Arriving at retirement with only tax-deferred accounts can play a role in putting you in a tax bracket that is as high or higher than your earning years.

2. Uncle Sam can prove to be a selfish "partner" when it comes to your retirement strategies, taking more in taxes than you anticipate at a time when you need money the most.

3. With a rising national debt, unfunded liabilities, and out-of-control government spending, it is likely taxes will increase over the long-term.

4. Americans would do well to consider that it is advantageous to pay taxes on the seed, rather than the harvest.

5. To avoid outliving your money during retirement, it is important to plan for your "at-retirement" tax bill to understand your net spendable retirement income.

What Successful Folks Know

Here's a little exercise we often do with our audiences. Ready? Pick a number, any number, between one and ten. Now take that number (the one you chose between one and ten), and double that number. Next, add eight to that number. Now divide that total in half. What number do you have? Next, subtract the original number you started with from your latest number.

You should have a final number in your head now. Take that final number you arrived at, and pick the corresponding letter of the alphabet that number represents. For example, if your last number was one, that would be the letter A. Two would be B; three would be C; four would be D; and so on. So what is your letter of the alphabet?

Now take that letter of the alphabet and pick a country in Europe or the Baltics (using the American name for countries) that starts with that letter. It's going to be near the beginning of the alphabet, so you can choose from countries like England, Germany, Ireland, France, Belgium, Czechoslovakia, Austria, and Italy. Up in the Baltics, you've got Finland, Denmark, and Estonia.

Now think of the country that starts with the letter of the alphabet you ended up with. Take that country, then think of the last letter of that

country's name. Now pick a zoo animal—an animal that is not indigenous to the United States but one you'd probably find in a zoo in the United States—that starts with that letter (the last letter of your country you chose).

Do you have a zoo animal in your head? Now take the last letter of that zoo animal and pick a common fruit that starts with that letter, okay? So, you should have a country, a zoo animal, and a common fruit.

Now when we do this with our audiences, we know what 80% of people are thinking: Denmark, kangaroo, orange. Is that what you thought? (Maybe you thought Denmark, koala, apple.) Either way, you're like 80% of people who perform this exercise.

Why is this? It's called predictability. Most of the time, 80% of people will get to these three items when they arrive at the number four. (If you did not get to four as the final answer on your number, well, maybe consider brushing up on your math.)

Predictability is critical in many aspects of life. In business, delivering predictable results with your company's service, products, and marketing is integral for retaining and growing a customer base. In relationships, predictably providing kindness, compassion, honesty, and trustworthiness is paramount to maintaining those bonds that matter most. And when it comes to planning for your financial future, paying attention to factors that are predictable is likewise critical.

While economists do their best, unfortunately there's no crystal ball that can accurately forecast exactly how the economy and market will perform in five, fifteen, or thirty years. But in planning for your financial future, there are some things that are predictable, like taxes. We can bet: 1) they'll always be there; 2) they're likely going up over time; and 3) during retirement, you're likely going to be in a tax bracket that is as high or higher than during your earning years. When you plan for that likely inevitability, you'll be prepared to escape the unnecessary tax trap.

Conversely, you can also apply predictability to employ sound financial strategies—like utilizing the three marvels of wealth accumulation—to give yourself the opportunity to enjoy abundance rather than scarcity.

These three marvels are what affluent and successful folks have implemented for generations. They are:

- Compound interest
- Tax-favored accumulation
- Safe, positive leverage

THE MARVEL OF COMPOUND INTEREST

The first marvel of wealth accumulation is compound interest. Many people think they understand interest. They know it's the amount that a bank or credit union pays you for the privilege of "holding" your money (which the bank then invests, or puts to work). Conversely, it's the amount of money you pay the bank for using its funds, with tools like business loans or mortgages.

But what many don't understand is there are two methods of computing interest—simple and compound. When you borrow money for your house, it is usually calculated as simple interest as you make payments on the debt. When you deposit money in a bank, you earn compound interest.

The difference between simple and compound interest can be the difference between paying hundreds of dollars on a simple interest, declining balance that may be tax-deductible (as in your mortgage), versus thousands of dollars climbing exponentially, in a financial vehicle that provides compounding interest, which we will explain later.

Here's why: simple interest is calculated on the original balance or principal. But when you earn compound interest, you make money not only on your original deposit, but also on your accumulated gains.

As an illustration, let's say you're putting away $500 a month, earning 7.2%. With simple interest, after ten years, you have set aside $60,000 and earned $1,980 dollars in interest, for a total of $61,980. With compound interest, however, you have earned $28,026.51 in interest, for a total of $88,026.51.

That difference of roughly $26,000 between simple and compound interest may not seem too significant after ten years, but watch what happens over a longer period of time, say forty years. Over forty years, you

will have set aside $240,000 of principal. With simple interest, you will earn $29,520 in interest, and your principal-plus-interest total would be $269,520. With compound interest, you will earn $1,127,280 in interest, and your principal-plus-interest would be $1,367,280 (see Figure 3.1 for the difference in interest earned).

FIGURE 3.1

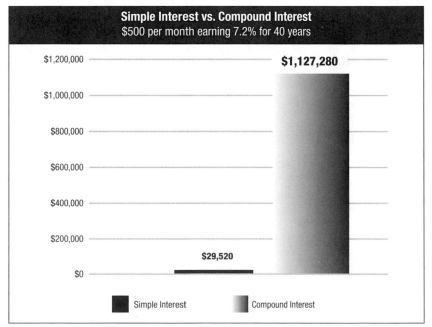

If this comes as a surprise to you, you're not alone. We've found that many CPAs, tax attorneys, and financial professionals—people who are astute in so many areas—think they understand the power of compound interest. But a quick test proves they are not as well-versed as you would think. In training classes, we've asked them to imagine taking an 8.5" x 11" sheet of paper and folding it in half once, then in half again.

We then ask them to picture folding that sheet of paper in half a total of forty-eight more times. We invite them to estimate how thick that piece of paper would be, folded a total of fifty times. Many of these sophisticated CPAs and tax attorneys who work with numbers on a daily basis give us typical answers such as: one-quarter of an inch, half an inch, or three inches. Once in a while someone who understands compound interest will reply, "Well, it's probably a mile or two high."

FIGURE 3.2

Folding a 26 lb (97.83 g/sq meter) Sheet of Paper 50 Times				
# of Folds	Equivalent # of pages	Thickness		
		Inches	Feet	Miles
0	1	0.005	0.00	0.00
1	2	0.01	0.00	0.00
2	4	0.02	0.00	0.00
3	8	0.04	0.00	0.00
4	16	0.08	0.01	0.00
5	32	0.17	0.01	0.00
6	64	0.34	0.03	0.00
7	128	0.67	0.06	0.00
8	256	1.35	0.11	0.00
9	512	2.7	0.22	0.00
10	1,024	5.4	0.45	0.00
11	2,048	10.79	0.90	0.00
12	4,096	22	1.80	0.00
13	8,192	43	3.60	0.00
14	16,384	86	7.20	0.00
15	32,768	173	14	0.00
16	65,536	345	29	0.00
17	131,072	691	58	0.00
18	262,144	1,381	115	0.02
19	524,288	2,763	230	0.04
20	1,048,576	5,526	460	0.09
21	2,097,152	11,052	921	0.17
22	4,194,304	22,104	1,842	0.35
23	8,388,608	44,208	3,684	0.70
24	16,777,216	88,416	7,368	1.40
25	33,554,432	176,832	14,736	2.79
26	67,108,864	353,664	29,472	5.58
27	134,217,728	707,327	58,944	11.16
28	268,435,456	1,414,655	117,888	22
29	536,870,912	2,829,310	235,776	45
30	1,073,741,824	5,658,619	471,552	89
31	2,147,483,648	11,317,239	943,103	179
32	4,294,967,296	22,634,478	1,886,206	357
33	8,589,934,592	45,268,955	3,772,413	714
34	17,179,869,184	90,537,911	7,544,826	1,429
35	34,359,738,368	181,075,821	15,089,652	2,858
36	68,719,476,736	362,151,642	30,179,304	5,716
37	137,438,953,472	724,303,285	60,358,607	11,432
38	274,877,906,944	1,448,606,570	120,717,214	22,863
39	549,755,813,888	2,897,213,139	241,434,428	45,726
40	1,099,511,627,776	5,794,426,278	482,868,857	91,452
41	2,199,023,255,552	11,588,852,557	965,737,713	182,905
42	4,398,046,511,104	23,177,705,114	1,931,475,426	365,810
43	8,796,093,022,208	46,355,410,227	3,862,950,852	731,619
44	17,592,186,044,416	92,710,820,454	7,725,901,705	1,463,239
45	35,184,372,088,832	185,421,640,908	15,451,803,409	2,926,478
46	70,368,744,177,664	370,843,281,816	30,903,606,818	5,852,956
47	140,737,488,355,328	741,686,563,633	61,807,213,636	11,705,912
48	281,474,976,710,656	1,483,373,127,265	123,614,427,272	23,411,823
49	562,949,953,421,312	2,966,746,254,530	247,228,854,544	46,823,647
50	1,125,899,906,842,620	5,933,492,509,061	494,457,709,088	**93,647,293**

In actuality, if a sheet of copy paper, which is five-one-thousandths of an inch thick, were to be folded in half fifty times, the thickness of the sheet of paper would double fifty times. The ensuing pile of paper would be equivalent to more than ninety-three million miles high—in other words, from here to the sun. If you could fold over the piece of paper one additional time (to a total of fifty-one times), it would be from here to the sun and back (see Figure 3.2).

Here's another analogy: imagine a pond, and in the middle of the pond a single lily pad appears. The next day there are two. The following day, four. Every day the lily pad patch doubles in size. Forty-eight days later, the entire pond is covered in lily pads. So if it took forty-eight days to take over the surface of the pond, how many days did it take to cover just half the pond? Most people burst out with: twenty-four. But not so. The answer is: forty-seven. The day before, the pond was half-covered, and then it doubled the next day, covering the entire pond.

Here's one you might want to use the next time you're on the golf course. Ask your pals when you're starting a round, "Hey, what if we bet twenty-five cents on the first hole, then doubled it every hole?" They're likely to say yes ... until you let them know that would mean they'd owe $32,000 if they lost the eighteenth hole alone.

People who understand the dynamics of money—those who realize how money socked away and left to earn compound interest can burgeon into wealth—are more likely to be making headway toward a livable retirement.

THE MARVEL OF TAX-FAVORED ACCUMULATION

Once you grasp the power of compound interest, you're ready to see how it relates to the next marvel, tax-favored accumulation. Let's do that by comparing money compounding in a tax-favored versus taxed-as-earned environment.

Imagine you start with one dollar; yes, just one little dollar, that will double every period for twenty periods in a tax-favored environment. It becomes $2, then $4, then $8, and so on for a total of twenty periods. Believe it or not, that $1 will grow to $1,048,576. That's the power of compound interest in a tax-favored environment.

FIGURE 3.3

$1 Doubling 20 Times			
Tax-Favored	Taxed-As-Earned at 25%	Taxed-As-Earned at 33.3%	Tax-Deferred
$2.00	$1.75	$1.67	$2.00
$4.00	$3.06	$2.78	$4.00
$8.00	$5.36	$4.63	$8.00
$16.00	$9.38	$7.72	$16.00
$32.00	$16.41	$12.86	$32.00
$64.00	$28.72	$21.44	$64.00
$126.00	$50.27	$35.73	$126.00
$256.00	$87.96	$59.55	$256.00
$512.00	$153.94	$99.25	$512.00
$1,024.00	$269.39	$165.41	$1,024.00
$2,048.00	$471.43	$275.70	$2,048.00
$4,096.00	$825.01	$459.50	$4,096.00
$8,192.00	$1,443.76	$765.86	$8,192.00
$16,354.00	$2,526.58	$1,276.45	$16,354.00
$32,768.00	$4,421.51	$2,127.46	$32,768.00
$65,536.00	$7,737.64	$3,545.84	$65,536.00
$131,072.00	$13,540.88	$5,909.85	$131,072.00
$262,144.00	$23,696.54	$9,849.95	$262,144.00
$524,288.00	$41,468.94	$16,416.90	$524,288.00
$1,048,576.00	$72,570.64	$27,362.05	$1,048,576.00

Figure 3.3 shows what happens when that same dollar doubles every period for twenty periods—but this time it's in a taxed-as-earned environment (meaning you pay taxes on any gains as your money earns a positive rate of return).

Let's start at the beginning again. One dollar doubles to two dollars— but you have to pay a 25% tax on that gain, so you only have a $1.75 after taxes. During the next period, your new balance of $1.75 doubles to $3.50, at which point you have to turn around and pay 25% tax on that gain; you only result in $3.06.

If we look at the twenty-period results, a dollar doubling for twenty periods, taxed-as-earned in a 25% tax bracket, only grows to $72,571 (only 7.2% of its potential value). What if the taxes are higher, as in 33.3%? If that dollar doubles every period for twenty periods but is taxed-as-earned in a 33.3% tax bracket, the ending value equals just $27,362. It only grows to 2.7% of its potential value.

When people hear us teach this, they say, "My money in my IRAs and 401(k)s grows tax-deferred. Isn't that better than taxed-as-earned?" Well, it is better during the accumulation phase. But it still doesn't help

you during the distribution phase (we'll discuss the 4 Phases of Retirement Planning—contribution, accumulation, distribution, transfer—a little later in this chapter).

Let's look at what that dollar does in a tax-deferred vehicle (in these vehicles, you don't pay taxes on your money before you put it in the account, or while it grows in the account; you only pay taxes when you withdraw money out of your account). So in a tax-deferred vehicle, that one dollar doubles twenty times to $1,048,576. Now let's say you're in retirement, and you'd like to withdraw your interest earnings to live on. Let's assume it's earning an 8% annual average rate of return. You could pull out about $80,000 a year, right? But is all of that $80,000 yours to use as you please? No. Keep in mind you now have to pay tax on that $80,000—especially if your money is in an IRA or 401(k)—because those funds were only tax-deferred.

To explore this concept further, let's change our illustration. Let's say you have a million-dollar nest egg averaging a rate of return of 7.2%. You want to withdraw just your interest earnings (so you don't deplete your principal of $1 million), which would be $72,000 per year, or $6,000 per month. What if that $72,000 is on top of other income, such as Social Security or a defined benefit pension? You would have to pay tax of probably about 27% to 29% on that $72,000. Doing the math, after paying tax in a 29% tax bracket, your $72,000 would only net $51,120. Therefore, a taxable distribution of $72,000 would create a tax liability of $20,880, just under one-third of the $72,000.

Now you can see how that $6,000 per month is not all of your money. The government has had a permanent tax lien on your IRAs and 401(k)s the entire time that you were accumulating and saving that money. In other words, $6,000 a month of income would require a tax of $1,740, only netting you about $4,260 a month to buy gas, groceries, prescriptions, and golf green fees during your retirement years.

But what if you need to have a net of $6,000 a month after paying tax? In a 29% tax bracket, you would need to withdraw $101,408 and pay $29,408 in income tax to Uncle Sam to enjoy your net $72,000 a year. You might be thinking that sounds doable. But not for long. Because now you're withdrawing more than your interest earned, which means you're beginning to deplete your $1 million nest egg. Which means it won't last as long. Which means you're at risk of outliving your money during your retirement years.

In a survey conducted by Allianz Life Insurance Company of North America, 61% of boomers surveyed said they feared outliving their retirement money more than they feared death ("Reclaiming the Future: Challenging Retirement Income Perceptions," May 2010). Why is this such a big fear? Because it will be a reality for far too many Americans.

FIGURE 3.4

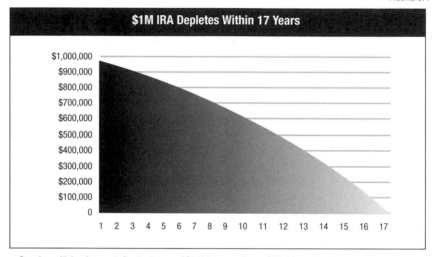

Based on withdrawing a net after-tax income of $6,000 per month on a $1M IRA earning 7.2%, in a 29% tax bracket.

As you can see in Figure 3.4 where the million-dollar nest egg is depleted within 17 years, taxes can have a profoundly negative impact on retirement income. If your retirement planning vehicle is tax-free during the harvest (as explained in Section I, Chapter 2), that million-dollar nest egg earning 7.2% would allow you to withdraw $72,000 per year tax-free and never deplete your million-dollar principal. This is why it's important to optimize when and minimize how much you're taxed—but more on that during our discussion of the 4 Phases of Retirement Planning, later in this chapter.

THE MARVEL OF SAFE LEVERAGE

Think of the last time you had to change a flat tire. Unless you called AAA to replace the tire, you could have either: 1) called six of your strongest buddies and asked them to lift the car for you, or 2) gone to the trunk,

pulled out your jack, and raised that two-ton-plus vehicle far enough off the ground.

There's a reason everyone chooses Option #2: safe leverage. Safe leverage is something the nation's wealthiest banks, companies, and individuals use every day. It's the idea of taking something relatively small to gain something greater.

There's a saying, "There are two kinds of people in the world—those who pay interest, and those who earn it." Actually, there is a third kind of person in the world, one who understands leverage and is willing to pay some interest to earn even more interest.

Even though leverage is one of the three marvels, many people cringe when they hear "pay interest." Why? Because their parents and teachers warned them against debt, urging them to avoid paying interest wherever possible. We, too, are strong opponents of borrowing to consume—paying useless interest on credit cards or loans to acquire luxuries like TVs, laptops, or vacations. However, we are proponents of borrowing to conserve—using prudent leverage to get ahead.

This very principle is taught in The Bible, in the Parable of the Talents. In Matthew 25:14-30, the verses tell the story of a man who gives one servant five talents, another two, and a third servant just one talent. The first servant grows his five talents to ten; the second grows his to four; the third buries his in the ground until his master's return. The master praises the first two for "being faithful" over what he has given them and promotes them to be a "ruler over many things." The third he chastises for being "slothful" and gives the one talent away to the first.

Clearly, this principle of leverage has been around for millennia, and it's something you're likely implementing without even realizing it—with your mortgage.

Most people don't usually buy a home outright with cash—even if they have hundreds of thousands or more to cover the listing price. Why? They understand that if they hand all the money over at once, it would be tied up in the house, leaving zero liquid cash for emergencies or other ventures.

Instead, most people put a down payment on a house and finance the re-mainder of the purchase price with a mortgage. This is leverage in action. They're using a small amount of cash to own or control a greater asset.

Just like with your down payment and mortgage, banks and credit unions use leverage every day. They essentially "borrow" the money you've deposited with them, paying you nominal interest for your savings ac-count. They then turn around and put that money to work to earn greater interest—and the difference is their profit. Banks are actually glad to pay you that interest, because it accelerates their accumulation of money.

To illustrate, say you deposit $1 million in the bank. They pay you 1% interest on your money, or $10,000. Someone else goes to the bank to get a million-dollar loan. The bank lends her that $1 million and charges her 5% interest. The bank will earn $50,000 in interest on that loan. How much more is five than one? Don't be tempted to say four; it's five times, or 500%.

Would you hire an employee for $10,000 if the employee made you $50,000? Would you buy a widget machine for $10,000 if the widget machine made you $50,000? The answer is: YES.

The nation's top banks put at least 30% to 40% of their Tier 1 assets to work in financial vehicles that earn rates of return that are six times or more what they are paying for those assets. Can you do the same thing? Can you bypass the middleman on your serious cash and earn 6% or more—and get safety and liquidity to come along for the ride? The an-swer is: YES.

Keep in mind: leverage is good—in fact, it's what makes the world go around. But leverage without matching liquidity is stupidity. We'll explain later why liquidity is the No. 1 feature to look for in prudent strategies.

LIFT, THRUST & DRAG

To summarize the power of the three marvels of wealth accumulation, we can compare them to the principles of aerodynamics. In order to overcome the weight of an airplane, the plane has to overcome gravity (which we compare to taxes and inflation) by using three other forces:

- **Lift** – The Bernoulli Principle explains how air flowing over and under the wings of an airplane creates lift. Because of the wing's shape, the faster moving air on top creates less air pressure; the slower moving air on bottom has more air pressure. This difference in air pressure causes the plane to lift upward. This is just like the effect of compound interest, raising your balance higher and higher.

- **Thrust** – As air flows through an airplane's jet engine or propeller, it creates thrust, moving the plane forward at high speeds. Tax-favored accumulation is like thrust. Tax-deferred accounts (like IRAs) would be like flying in a propeller engine aircraft, whereas tax-free would be more like soaring in a jet engine plane.

- **Drag** – Drag is caused by the friction of the air surrounding the plane. Most people don't understand why it's necessary to have drag, but without that friction or resistance, your airplane would never get off the ground. We compare drag to paying interest. When you use drag—safe, positive leverage—by borrowing OPM (other people's money), you can earn more interest.

Ideally, you want to maximize all three forces, or marvels of wealth accumulation, to arrive at your destination—a future filled with abundance.

4 PHASES OF RETIREMENT PLANNING

When it comes to accumulating wealth, we summarize the process in four key phases:

1. **Contribution** – When you put your money into a long-term financial vehicle (where you won't access it for five years or longer)
2. **Accumulation** – When your money grows inside that vehicle (usually in the form of interest or dividends)
3. **Distribution** – When you access your money (also called the withdrawal phase)
4. **Transfer** – When you pass away and leave your money behind to heirs (*and* Uncle Sam, if you're not careful)

As you look at these four phases, which one do you think is the most important to protect from taxes? If you're like most people in the audience at our events, you might be guessing: contribution. Why? Because conventional financial advice encourages individuals to put pre-tax dollars into financial vehicles like 401(k)s to get as much money as they can into the account before the accumulation phase.

In our audiences, you can also hear soon-to-be-heirs pipe up with, "The transfer phase!" which makes us all chuckle (of course, they want to inherit as much as they can—they really want that phase to be tax-free). But the rest of the crowd typically hollers, "Distribution!" They're thinking about the time in life when they're accessing their money, and how they'd like to do that without Uncle Sam taking a big bite out of each withdrawal.

While the distribution phase matters, it falls behind the most important phase to protect from taxes: the accumulation phase. Why the accumulation phase? Because as we demonstrated earlier with the marvel of compound interest, when your money is compounding tax-advantaged, that's when you'll see the most growth. Now if you can protect your money from taxes in more than one phase, that's all the better.

Let's say you want to have at least $1 million set aside to live on during retirement—to pay for living expenses, groceries, gas, prescriptions, travel, and/or hobbies. Different financial strategies can set the pace for your race to an abundant future. The question to ask yourself is, how fast do you want to complete the Million-Dollar Dash—do you want to crawl, walk, jog, or sprint?

- **Crawling** – Taxed-as-earned investments would be like "crawling" toward the finish line to achieve financial independence. Money set aside in taxed-as-earned investments is contributed with after-tax dollars, and any interest or dividends are taxed each year as they are earned. But the taxes don't stop there. Any capital gains are also taxed during distribution, and upon death your money is subject to income tax and possibly estate tax. Unfortunately this is one of the most common ways Americans save for retirement, in traditional vehicles like mutual funds and savings accounts at banks or credit unions, and typical taxable investments. Here's why it is so slow-going. If you recall in Figure 3.3, when you

have $1 doubling in a tax-favored environment in each period for twenty periods, you will end up with over $1 million. But if your dollar is doubling in a taxed-as-earned environment, where you are taxed at 33.3% on your earnings, you only have a 67-cent gain. After twenty periods, you'd only have just over $27,000 (see Figure 3.5). That's a lot less than $1 million. That's like getting 2.7% of the way around the race track.

FIGURE 3.5

Taxed-As-Earned at 33.3%
$1.67
$2.78
$4.63
$7.72
$12.86
$21.44
$35.73
$59.55
$99.25
$165.41
$275.70
$459.50
$765.86
$1,276.45
$2,127.46
$3,545.84
$5,909.85
$9,849.95
$16,416.90
$27,362.05

- **Walking** – When you set aside money with after-tax dollars into tax-deferred investments (such as tax-deferred annuities), these kinds of vehicles are only tax-favored during the accumulation phase. Upon distribution from a tax-deferred annuity, the IRS taxes all withdrawals or distributions on a LIFO basis (which means last-in, first-out). This is like "walking" toward the finish line—you're only going to get about one-third of the way around the track.

- **Jogging** – How about a nice jog toward that finish line of financial independence? Join the millions of Americans who set aside pre-tax dollars in traditional IRAs and 401(k)s. With these kinds of vehicles, you're able to save with 100% tax-advantaged dollars on the front end. But don't forget that you

must pay taxes when you access your money. You're essentially electing to have a tax break on the front in exchange for paying tax on the back end.

- **Sprinting** – Why crawl, walk, or jog when you could sprint? This happens when you contribute after-tax dollars in a tax-favored environment, when you can access it tax-free, and when it transfers income-tax-free to your heirs upon your passing. This is where unique vehicles, like the one we'll be talking about in-depth in this book, can help you win life's race.

As you can see, not all financial vehicles provide the same momentum, especially with the winds of taxes blowing your way. This is why it behooves you to learn as much as you can about your options, weighing the pros and cons of each vehicle for your needs and goals. As we've demonstrated throughout this chapter, the more tax-advantaged your approach can become, the more opportunity you'll have to take greater ownership of your life. And congratulations—by reading this book, you're on your way.

TOP 5 TAKEAWAYS

1. Just like the Denmark, kangaroo, orange exercise demonstrates, predictability is key, especially when it comes to financial strategies.

2. The three marvels of wealth accumulation can predictably provide opportunities for financial growth: 1) the marvel of compound interest, 2) the marvel of tax-favored accumulation, 3) the marvel of safe leverage.

3. The 4 Phases of Retirement Planning are: 1) contribution, 2) accumulation, 3) distribution, and 4) transfer.

4. The most important phase to protect from taxes? Accumulation.

5. To sprint toward retirement, you want to be able to contribute after-tax dollars in a tax-favored environment, access your money tax-free, and transfer it income-tax-free to your heirs upon your passing.

What Does LASER Stand For?

Our family likes to work hard, very hard, and when it comes time to play, we play equally as hard. Every couple of years, we all get together for a Family Retreat with a Purpose at one of our favorite destinations, Hawaii. (We'll touch on Family Retreats with a Purpose, in Section II, Chapter 1, which are part of our overall Authentic Wealth strategy for maintaining family Values and Vision.) Between those big, bonding trips to Hawaii (where each family saves up for two years and pays their own way to stay in affordable timeshare lodging), we often take off for a week here and there to places like Wind Rivers, Wyoming. With Doug and Sharee leading the pack, we caravan with all six Andrew kids, spouses, and sixteen grandchildren. Once we arrive, we trek back into the picturesque mountain range, with towering peaks, rushing rivers, and deep blue lakes.

Before we head out on the six-hour drive to Wind Rivers, we always make sure to load up our SUVs with the fundamentals: equipment, food, and clothing. And of course towing along extras like the ATVS adds to the experience.

Now, here are some interesting questions. Could we still go on the trip if we didn't have 100% of those fundamentals? Reasonably, we could make do without most of our camping equipment. But it wouldn't be quite the

same trip without the Coleman stove and the tents. As for food, we could probably survive off the fish we caught and the berries we gathered, but it's so much tastier to fry up the trout in lemon pepper and butter and unveil a sweet Dutch oven peach cobbler for dessert. As for the clothing, yes, we could keep the same outfit on that we arrived in, but after five days, none of us would be able to stand downwind of each other. And could we do without the ATVs? Of course, but some of our favorite memories have come from heading out on a beautiful trail ride to explore a new valley.

Like that trip, there are a few fundamentals you need to make the most of your financial journey. Whenever you're positioning serious cash—money you're setting aside for future goals, such as retirement or your children's college education—you want to make sure your financial vehicle is loaded with the essentials:

- **Liquidity**
- **Safety**
- **Rates of return** that are predictable
- **Tax-advantages**

Now, can you still move forward on your journey if you don't have an optimal level of all factors for a prudent financial vehicle? Sure, millions of Americans do. But that's where we ask: why not put yourself in a position to have the best possible outcome? Like St. Jerome said, "Good, better, best. Never let it rest. 'Til your good is better and your better is best." To help you weigh your options and make informed decisions, let's take a closer look at these fundamentals.

LIQUIDITY

As an illustration, let's say we have a family, the Thompsons. The Thompsons are conscientious about their money. They don't have a lot of extra assets, but what they do have, they safeguard well. They live in a beautiful $300,000 home with their three children (for which they made a $50,000 down payment and started with a $250,000 mortgage). They've been diligently sending extra payments to the lender for years. Like many Americans, they're following traditional advice, which says the best way to get out of debt and get ahead is to pay off your mortgage as soon as possible.

Over the past several years they've paid down the $150,000 principal (comprised of the $50,000 they would have normally paid off through minimum payments, and an extra $100,000 through extra payments). They're thrilled to only owe $100,000 on the mortgage. But then Jason Thompson's company downsizes, and he finds himself out of work. Kendra Thompson still has her job in human resources, but it's just enough to cover the basics: groceries, insurance, car payments, etc. After a few months, they get behind on their mortgage, and they really wish they could get access to some of those extra payments they sent the mortgage company. But they can't. It's been applied toward their balance, and it is absolutely, positively, NOT liquid. A few months later, they fall so far behind on their mortgage that the bank forecloses on their home.

What if, instead, that extra $100,000 were set aside in a financial vehicle that provided liquidity—with no income taxes? When Jason loses his job, they could access the money to continue making mortgage payments, which could carry them through until Jason finds new employment.

Now let's say Jason never loses his job. The Thompsons could still set that money aside in a prudent financial vehicle, letting it accrue interest. They would have peace of mind knowing that if they wanted to pay off their mortgage sooner, they could. In fact, by accumulating that money in a tax-favored, liquid side fund compounding, they would likely have enough to pay off the mortgage about 2.5 years sooner than sending that money against their mortgage. But they don't have to physically pay it off. And should they need that money for anything else, they would have access to it, as well.

This is just one example of why liquidity is the No. 1 element you should look for in prudent financial strategies. Without it, not just individuals, but businesses can also go bankrupt. When there are insufficient funds to cover costs—the building lease, payroll, vendor accounts—otherwise viable businesses can go under.

This is why entrepreneurs need as much liquid capital as possible to seize opportunities and withstand cash-flow crunches. The IUL LASER Fund is an excellent solution for working capital, as you don't have to pay government penalties if you choose to use cash from your policy for reasons other than retirement. (See Section II, Chapter 4 for real-life examples of using The IUL LASER Fund for working capital.)

Liquidity is especially imperative when you're in the beginning stages of setting aside money for the future. If something goes wrong, caring for your immediate financial needs will be much more important than saving for your retirement down the road. In short, it's a lot better to have and not need, than to need and not have. Liquidity is like being safe in a submarine as the storms rage overhead—providing absolute calm despite the torrent.

The moral is: life is full of surprises. Some are unpleasant ones, like losing a job or suffering the loss of a loved one. Others are more pleasant, like an opportunity to invest in a business or additional real estate. And one more note on liquidity: we believe it is wise to prioritize liquidity with your entire financial portfolio, not just one vehicle. More on this in Section I, Chapter 14.

SAFETY

Now let's look at the real-life story of an older couple, whom we'll call the Wells, who were in their mid-70s in early 2008. They had done well financially throughout most of their lives. However, a few years earlier they had suffered some financial setbacks (from about age 65 to 75) that required them to exhaust most of their retirement savings to pay off former business debts.

By the time they were in their mid-70s, they weren't able to retire yet. They still had to work full-time jobs to make ends meet. Jim Wells had his mortgage license, and Sarah Wells was working as an office manager. A little later in 2008, Sarah's mother passed away, leaving behind a substantial amount of money in accounts with Lehman Brothers. They were sad to bid farewell to her mother, but grateful for the financial relief that was coming their way from that inheritance.

But notice this was 2008. The Wells had no idea what economic hurricane was headed their way (and everyone else's) later that year. In the fall of 2008, the economy took such a bad turn that it ushered in the Great Recession. As it happened, Lehman Brothers was the first to fold, largely due to its bad bets on real estate holdings. The Wells' inheritance disappeared almost overnight, right alongside Lehman Brothers.

The Wells were faced with no option but to sell their home of over thirty years, downsize to a smaller home, sell their second car, and continue working for another few years. Today they get by on Social Security and a small monthly withdrawal from the 401(k) Sarah had accrued while working at her office job. They're grateful to have enough—but it's just barely enough. No vacations. No helping the grandkids with their education. Nothing more than mortgage, groceries, doctor's bills and medicine.

That inheritance money could have made a big difference in their lives, but it lacked one of the most critical elements of a financial vehicle: safety. It wasn't safe. It had always been at risk of disappearing, and it did, because it was with an institution—and in financial vehicles—that were vulnerable to the economic storms that hit in 2008.

The Wells weren't the only ones. As we've mentioned, millions of Americans lost as much as 40% of their money in their IRAs and 401(k)s that were invested in the market—twice—between 2000 and 2010. Exposure to this kind of loss demonstrates the importance of safety.

Safety has two components:

- Safety of the institution in which the money is entrusted
- Safety of principal

When it comes to your serious cash, look for financial institutions that have a long-term track record of safety. Consider what happened with Lehman Brothers. It had been a Wall Street icon for decades. But like many big financial institutions at the time, it had been dealing in financial strategies that did not protect the consumer. When the Wall Street house of cards began to crumble, so did millions of Americans' financial futures.

Now when we talk about safety of principal, ideally what you want is to be able to protect your principal from loss. Even more, you want any gains you've experienced to become newly protected principal. In other words, say you have $100,000 in a financial vehicle that earns a net rate of return of 7% this year. At the end of the year, you want to have $107,000 as your newly protected principal—which means even if the market drops and the rate of return is less than 0% the next year, your principal of $107,000 would be intact. You wouldn't lose a dime due to market volatility.

When it comes to your financial future, safety is also a priority.

RATE OF RETURN

Marshall Thurber once shared a story about Dr. Edwards Deming. Deming, the American statistician, professor and Total Quality Management engineer, emphasized the importance of predictability in designing manufacturing systems. In the 1970s, he consulted with America's "big three" auto companies, GM, Ford, and Chrysler. His recommendation: ensure more predictable quality. (There's that predictability factor again.)

Well, they ignored him.

Not long after, a consumer report came out suggesting that consumers should buy American cars that were built on a Wednesday. The reason? Workers would typically show up on Monday at the plant hungover from the weekend, unfocused, and sloppy. They made a lot of mistakes. Tuesday's cars were a little better, and by Wednesday, the workers were in the flow. Thursday they'd be looking forward to the weekend, and by Friday they had completely lost focus again.

After the report went nationwide, American car dealers found that cars built on Mondays, Tuesdays, Thursdays, and Fridays were just sitting on the lot. No one wanted them. They had to discount them deeply or send them back to the factory to be double-checked. Clearly, American auto manufacturers had lost the trust of their consumers. And Deming had tried to warn them.

Even though the American companies had disregarded Deming's advice, Japanese manufacturers were eager to listen. Prior to Deming's influence, Japanese products—from automobiles to electronics—did not have a reputation for quality; they were considered junk.

But Deming changed that.

He provided his strategies for Total Quality Management, and Japanese companies implemented them. Within a decade, Japanese cars and electronics began to dominate the market. From Sony and Samsung to Toyota, Honda, and Nissan, Japanese makers became household names. For decades since, American auto manufacturers have been doing their darnedest to come up to speed (no pun intended), with the quality of Japanese cars.

Predictable quality matters. Today, the Deming Prize is a coveted award, recognizing individuals and organizations for their contribution to and achievements in Total Quality Management.

Just as in manufacturing, when it comes to your finances, you want predictability, particularly with your rate of return. To explain:

- When it comes to **rate of return**, the goal is to earn a competitive rate of return that historically has beaten inflation.

- If you can have that rate of return under **tax-favorable circumstances**, it will dramatically increase not only the end result, but also the net spendable income available during your "harvest" years (as explained in Section I, Chapter 2).

LASER RATING

Now that you see how important liquidity, safety, and rate of return are to your financial future, what do you want in your financial vehicles? Just one or two of them? Or all three? And in what order of importance? Many investors rank rate of return above liquidity. But in actuality, liquidity is No. 1. Safety is No. 2. Rate of Return comes in third.

Going back to our analogy of packing for the Wind Rivers trip, ideally you want to take all of the essentials on your journey. Since the same holds true with financial vehicles, optimally, you want vehicles that can provide the essentials of good **liquidity**, **safety**, **rate of return**. And of course, you want the difference-maker—**tax advantages**—along for the ride.

Take a moment now to consider your current financial strategies. How well do they deliver on liquidity, safety, rate of return, and tax advantages? We've developed a proprietary LASER Rating System™ that helps examine specific financial products' uses and risks, as compared to other financial vehicles.

We'll talk about this more in Section I, Chapter 14, but for now, we've developed a LASER Scorecard for you to perform your own analysis on each of your current financial vehicles, to rate how they fare with liquidity, safety, rate of return, and tax advantages. When scoring yourself, assess a score of where you are today, and where you optimally would like to be in the future (see Figure 4.1).

FIGURE 4.1

The LASER Scorecard										
Key Principle	1	2	3	4	5	6	7	8	9	10	Present/
Objective ⇨	Poor ⇨		Fair ⇨		Good ⇨		Better ⇨		Best ⇨		Future
Liquidity Ability to Access Your Money	Your assets are mostly tied up and cannot be converted quickly to cash for emergencies		You can access your money but could incur penalties or suffer a loss due to markets		You can access your money but not without incurring cost (by tax or other penalties)		You have predictable cash flow income but have limited access to lump sums, if needed		You have tremendous liquidity and can access your money electronically within hours or a few days		/
Safety of Principal	You're susceptible to market volatility, and the potential for loss is extremely high		Some of your money is in institutions that do not have strong safety ratings		You diversify by offsetting high-risk vehicles with some low-risk vehicles		Your money is in a safe vehicle, but the tradeoff is very low rates of return		Your vehicle has very low risk. Your money is protected from market volatility		/
Rate of Return	Any returns are usually negated by downturns in the market— very little net growth		0%-2% rates of return (pathetically low), while inflation outpaces gains and erodes principal		2%-4% rates of return, and you're set up on a 4% payout to avoid outliving your money		5%-12% average returns, but returns are taxable when you withdraw your money		5%-10% historic average returns; tax-free during accumulation and distribution phases; hedging against inflation		/
Tax-Advantaged On the Seed or the Harvest?	Savings and investments are taxed-as-earned (on the seed AND harvest)		Traditional IRAs/401(k)s (tax-deferred accounts); seed money not taxed; pay tax on harvest		Roth IRAs and 401(k)s; pay tax on the seed but a tax-free harvest; IRS limitations/rules		Tax-free accumulation; access and transfer of money with greater flexibility and benefits		Tax advantages on contribution, accumulation, distribution, and transfer phases		/

How did you do? We've found when we ask folks how well they think their financial vehicles will score in these four critical areas, they assume it will be high. But when they take the time to really analyze it on this kind of scale, they realize there is room for improvement.

If you find yourself in a similar place, don't worry. The first step to getting anywhere is to acknowledge where you are, right now, and then create a plan for getting where you want to go. We wish you the best as you set your sights on not only improving your score, but also your financial future.

There is give and take with each financial vehicle. As we'll discuss in Section I, Chapter 14, for example, a savings account in a local bank is safe and liquid, but it does not typically offer good rates of return. A Roth IRA fares well with tax advantages, but it can be limited on safety for those who are invested in the market. There is no single perfect financial vehicle, but we will introduce you to what we believe scores the highest across the LASER Rating System™.

TOP 5 TAKEAWAYS

1. The four fundamentals of prudent financial strategies are: 1) liquidity, 2) safety, 3) predictable rates of return, and 4) tax advantages. It can be beneficial to choose financial strategies that fare well on the LASER Scorecard. As a side note, we coined the term LASER to stand for **Liquid Assets Safety Earning Returns**.

2. Liquidity is the ability to access your money when you need or want it.

3. Safety relates to your principal—protecting your money from loss due to volatility in the market, and the safety of your financial institution—working with reliable companies that can weather economic storms.

4. When it comes to rates of return, you want to earn a competitive rate of return that has historically beaten inflation, and ideally, you want that rate of return under tax-favorable circumstances.

5. Tax-advantaged financial strategies can help you avoid paying unnecessary taxes and safeguard you from outliving your money during retirement.

The "Miracle" Solution

In 1974, when Doug was in his early twenties, he started his career in insurance and securities. He built his clientele door to door, relationship to relationship, studying the intricacies of the financial services industry as he went. Within a few years, he was a rising star at his firm. He loved what he was doing. But there was an aspect of his work that troubled him—particularly watching his clients suffer when the economy suffered.

His first real experience with this came in 1980, when the Iranian oil embargo sparked a chain of events that led to a devastating nationwide recession. In the second quarter of that year, the US saw its worst quarterly decline in GDP since the Great Depression (at the time). The economy recovered after six months, but the reprieve didn't last long. By the start of 1982, America's economy crashed yet again. It was painful—unemployment rose as high as 11% and hovered at 10% for ten months.

With every drop in the economy, Doug's heart would drop. He would worry about his clients, who had inevitably lost part of their hard-earned money when their investments tanked. He would visit with his clients, answer their fearful calls, and feel his stomach churn. All he could offer them was the same feeble reassurance every other financial

professional was using, "Hang in there. The market always comes back. Hopefully you'll make up your loss sooner than later."

Doug wasn't immune to these financial crises, either. He shares in this snippet from his book, *Entitlement Abolition,* how his own encounter with major setbacks changed everything.

I had more financial ease than I had all my years growing up. In fact, my wife, Sharee, and I were excited to be building our "dream home" in central Utah. It was 6,400 square feet, with cathedral-beam, wood-decked ceilings, and a master bedroom deck where we could watch the deer and elk bed down in the scrub oak below. We thought we had the world by the tail! Two years later, in 1980, a bad recession hit America, and us.

We experienced unexpected, major setbacks due to a dishonest supervisor in the company I was working for. While the supervisor was being audited, my earnings (and that of two other producers) accumulated and were held in an escrow for nearly a year. As a result, we all found ourselves without an income, which meant Sharee and I got behind on our mortgage payments. Fortunately, we owned a rental duplex which we sold, and used the equity to bring the delinquent mortgage current.

But we got behind again. We owned a timeshare at a ski resort that we sold for triple what we had paid for and were able to bring the mortgage current a second time. When we fell behind a third time, we realized we had no other liquid assets. With no light at the end of the tunnel in the foreseeable future, we decided to sell our house.

We listed our home for sale for $295,000, because it had appraised four years earlier for $305,000. No takers. (When supply is greater than demand, real estate values plummet.) We quickly lowered the price several times to $285,000, $275,000, $265,000; then down to $225,000 and even $195,000; but to no avail. We will never forget the day we went to the county courthouse in Provo, Utah, and on the steps at the sheriff's auction, we watched our beautiful home auctioned off in foreclosure proceedings. The other two producers that had their income put on hold also lost their homes in foreclosure.

Fortunately, Sharee and I were able to buy another home immediately thereafter with no money down—even with a foreclosure on our record—because of a process I developed call The Negative Experience Transformer, a method for turning any negative experience it into a positive learning opportunity that can bring about a better future. Since that negative experience, I have maintained liquidity on my real estate equity by keeping it safely separated from the property, which has enabled me to sail through several more recessions without losing real estate equity, even when the property dropped in value.

The experience of losing a house in foreclosure was a defining moment for me as a financial professional and retirement planning specialist.

After his own personal story of loss, Doug had enough. He wasn't going to continue following the crowd, perpetuating traditional financial advice that left his clients—and his own family—vulnerable to the winds of change in the economy. He knew there had to be a better way.

He found it. Within a few years, he and his were utilizing the primary financial vehicle we discuss in this book, one that fares well in The LASER Rating System.™ And one Monday morning in October of 1987, he couldn't have been more grateful.

Doug awoke from a bad dream—one in which he thought a bear was shaking the cabin. He was on a hunting getaway at the family cabin in Sanpete County. It took him a moment to realize it wasn't a bear, but a mild earthquake rattling Utah. Later that same day, he learned, along with the rest of the country, that something far worse was rattling the entire nation. With a 22% drop, America experienced the worst single-day stock market decline since the Great Depression (again, at the time). What had been 1987's booming bull market turned into a bear market in a matter of hours.

"I remember I was out deer hunting, riding my four-wheeler at the top of the knoll, when I turned on the radio. I heard everyone wailing over the stock market crash," said Doug. "Instead of having to say to myself, 'I've got to rush back to the office to field those desperate phone calls,' I could relax. So could my clients. They knew their principal was protected. And they knew they would still be credited 11% that year. I felt good, because my clients weren't losing."

Doug was able to find this new path thanks to that special type of insurance policy that emerged in 1980. Over the years, he and the rest of our team have honed our strategies for making the most of this vehicle— something that has been called a "miracle solution" because it provides liquidity, safety, rate of return, and income-tax-free advantages. Upon death, it also blossoms as it transfers to heirs income-tax-free.

In this chapter, we'll give you an in-depth look at how The IUL LASER Fund works (so you can understand the "what"). In the next chapter we'll look at how indexing can help your IUL LASER Fund do even more for you. And in Section I, Chapter 7, we'll see how The IUL LASER Fund came about and how it can provide income-tax-free advantages in accordance with legislation and Internal Revenue Code (so you can understand the "how").

CONSTRUCTING YOUR FUTURE

To begin our discussion, let's say you were going to build an IUL LASER Fund policy with the assistance of one of our trained IUL specialists. Since you can create anything from a modest to a mammoth-sized policy, your IUL specialist will help you determine how much cash you'd like to place into your policy.

Through a unique process, your IUL specialist will then identify the minimum amount of insurance you'll need to be in full compliance with the IRS tax code. Did you notice that we said the minimum amount? Why? This ensures that money inside the policy, once it is in force, qualifies for tax-free access, can grow tax-deferred, and provide the most optimal rate of return. (One of the most common mistakes made on these policies is that the death benefit is too high for the premium going into the policy, which dramatically inhibits the policy's ability to grow efficiently. This is why you want to work with an IUL specialist who is well-versed in structuring these kinds of policies.)

The IUL LASER Fund can be compared to owning an apartment building. Now think about it: if you were to own your own five-story apartment building, what would be your goal? To rent out all five floors in order to maximize profit and minimize expenses, right? Because if only the first floor were rented out and the remaining floors were left vacant, costs would remain extremely high and eat away your profits.

The IUL LASER Fund is similar. To maximize your returns and minimize your expenses, you want to fill up your policy with maximum planned premiums (this is like renting out all the available space). To be compliant with TAMRA guidelines, this can be accomplished in four to seven years (this is dependent on your age; typically it's five years for most policyholders—see Section I, Chapter 7 for more on TAMRA).

There are four distinct, yet equally important phases when creating and funding your insurance policy, which we'll take a closer look at:

1. Design & Approval
2. Acquisition
3. Maximum Funding
4. Profits & Distribution

PHASE I – DESIGN & APPROVAL

Based on your financial and retirement goals, your IUL specialist helps determine the size of The IUL LASER Fund policy. These policies can be structured to hold thousands or even millions of dollars. Depending on the size of the policy, they can be filled using only monthly or periodic deposits (such as $1,000 a month, or $10,000 a quarter), or they can accommodate large lump sum deposits (such as $100,000 to $500,000 or more per year). They can also be funded using a combination of both.

Based on your financial objectives and assets available, the IUL specialist designs the policy to comply with IRS guidelines to allow for tax-deferred growth and tax-free access. It is important to remember that Phase I is the planning and approval phase, and the realization of tax-deferred growth and tax-free access is achieved through Phases II, III, and IV.

The plan then gets submitted to pre-selected insurance companies for approval and underwriting. While in underwriting, the insurance company will look at the size of the insurance policy, the need for insurance, insurability, and a variety of other factors. (It may surprise you to know that people with previous medical conditions or people who may be older can often get excellent rates with some insurance companies.)

We can't stress enough the importance of working with IUL specialists who are experienced in designing and coordinating The IUL LASER Fund. A lack of experience can have dire consequences. Think of how difficult it is to make changes regarding structure and floor plans once an apartment is built. Just the same, an insurance policy may be difficult to change down the road without incurring significant expense, especially if it was structured incorrectly from the beginning. The process of proper and effective IUL LASER Fund design is significant and necessary in order to maximize long-term profits, minimize risks, and keep it flexible.

And be aware that not all insurance companies have the products that perform well when structured this way. To be specific, out of the massive insurance industry in the United States, only a select few companies have the ratings and the products that have passed our high standard of scrutiny—fewer than a dozen, in fact. This is not a short-term home for cash.

PHASE II - ACQUISITION

Once Phase I is complete and your insurance policy has been designed and approved, the next stage begins when you put it in force. This simply means that you make the first premium payment, which officially puts the policy in force.

When the money is received by the insurance company, the death benefit is in place, in order to better protect your estate and assets. If an unforeseen death were to occur, the premiums you would have paid into the policy would blossom into a death benefit for your family or the estate.

Consider the entire first year the policy is owned to be Phase II. During this year, it's best to fill up the policy with all the planned premium payments. Near the end of the first year, also called the anniversary date, you receive an annual statement from the insurance company that details the amount of premium paid, cash value (also known as accumulation value—we'll use both terms interchangeably throughout this book) that has accumulated, and costs that have been charged during this year. An annual review is also held with the IUL specialist.

Every insurance policy is different, but generally the minimum amount of time it takes to maximum fund an insurance policy is five years,

according to IRS guidelines (TAMRA). In other words, the IRS doesn't let anyone put the entire amount of planned cash into the policy in one year—they make you spread it over a period of years, often five. (Note that if you were to fund your account faster than TAMRA allows, you would not be in compliance with the tax citation. When you went to access the money, it would not be totally tax-free.)

At the end of Phase II, The IUL LASER Fund is usually about one-fifth maximum-funded. Designing and funding The IUL LASER Fund the first year is similar to renting out just the first floor of the apartment building. It isn't profitable ... yet. It needs to be maximum-funded over the next four years or more.

PHASE III – MAXIMUM FUNDING

The IUL LASER Fund's next phase focuses on filling the policy with all the planned premiums. This phase generally takes place during Years 2 – 5, but can take longer, depending on the way you structure and fund the plan. We recommend that clients meet with IUL specialists annually to set goals and make adjustments as necessary.

During Years 2 - 5, optimally the individual will continue to fill up the policy with all the planned premiums. It's a lot like when renting out more floors of the apartment building—you have more rent payments coming in, offsetting the costs of running the apartment building. Similarly, when you're filling up your policy, your cash value is growing, giving you the opportunity to earn more interest—which can offset your fees. What's more, your cash value will not lose principal due to market volatility—even if the economy and stock market take a serious dive.

As the years progress, the cost of the insurance can go down as you get older. This is because the amount of insurance at risk to the insurance company is reduced as it is replaced with your money and the interest earnings on that money. The goal is to have a small portion of interest earned paying for the insurance, which is required by the IRS for it to qualify as a tax-free policy—thus eventually earning a net tax-free rate of return that is very attractive.

One of the best parts of The IUL LASER Fund? As the accumulation value begins to accumulate in your policy, these funds may be accessed at

any time by requesting a transfer from insurance company. They will promptly put a check in the mail or perform an electronic transfer. The best time to access money from the policy is after it is funded to the maximum amount allowed. But if you absolutely need to, you can choose to access from the policy in the first five years (just keep in mind that policies perform best when they are maximum-funded first).

Filling the policy up to maximum levels is like finally renting out the entire apartment building. With your building completely leased out, it is now optimized for profits.

PHASE IV – PROFITS & DISTRIBUTION

Phase IV is like having the building fully rented, and with The IUL LASER Fund maximum-funded, you can work with your IUL specialist to decide when to take distributions, how often, and how much to access from the accumulation value on a tax-favored basis. The policy can continue to grow through the marvel of compound interest. Based on the index it is linked to, the policy can be credited with interest earned.

When it comes to your money, you want cost-effective financial vehicles. And one of the many benefits of these policies is when they're maximum-funded, they can become very inexpensive in Phase IV, due to the large amounts of accumulation in the policy. Let's say someone has had her policy in force for ten years; the policy has a death benefit of $1,000,000; and it has accumulation value of $800,000. She's only going to pay costs to cover the remaining $200,000 of insurance that is at risk to the insurance company—the remainder is now her own money. If the insured were to pass away, the beneficiary would receive a total death benefit of $1,000,000.

This is by far the superior way to accomplish what the "buy term and invest the difference" proponents say, because individuals are actually becoming self-insured, but this way it's totally tax-free, and it's faster and performs much better. (More on this in Section I, Chapter 13.)

The best way to access money from the policy is through tax-free loans, as we'll explain later in this book. As long as the policy remains in force, no tax will be owed on these loans. (If, however, an individual were to surrender the policy and cancel it, that may create a taxable event. That

would not be smartest exit strategy, but nonetheless, any cash put directly into the policy, or the basis, would remain tax-free, as it has already been taxed.) Furthermore, as we will explain later, while you can choose to repay loans on your policy, it is not mandatory. You simply need to keep the policy in force to avoid a taxable event (which should you decide not to repay your loan, any loan balances will be automatically paid off with the cash value/death benefit upon your passing).

TOP 5 TAKEAWAYS

1. Hard-won lessons and national economic upheaval led to our focus on The IUL LASER Fund as a powerful financial vehicle, with its unrivaled liquidity, safety, predictable rates of return, and tax advantages.

2. Constructing an abundant financial future with The IUL LASER Fund could be compared to building and leasing a five-story apartment building.

3. Just as you would create blueprints and plans for your apartment building, during Phase I, your IUL specialist works closely with you to design a policy that fits your circumstances and goals while maintaining flexibility—and that complies with TEFRA/DEFRA tax citations.

4. Phase II and III could be compared to building and leasing all five floors of your building. Here, you typically fund your policy over five or more years, in accordance with the TAMRA tax citation and your policy design.

5. Phase IV is like reaping the profits from your fully leased building. You can work closely with your IUL specialist to optimize your indexing strategies, decide when to take out income in the form of tax-free loans, etc.

The Power of Indexing

Another valuable advantage of The IUL LASER Fund is the opportunity to "index" your policy. (If you recall, throughout this book we are using the terms IUL LASER Fund and LASER Fund interchangeably to represent a properly structured, maximum-funded Indexed Universal Life policy.) Indexing allows the money in your policy to gain interest when the stock market goes up, and to be completely protected from losses due to market volatility when the market goes down.

How is this possible? Because your money isn't directly IN the stock market, it's simply LINKED TO the market.

One of the many advantages of indexing is you can also choose a single indexed account, or you can link your policy to a combination of them. And you can change your indexing strategies over time.

Let's start by exploring some of the most common types of indexed accounts.

ONE-YEAR POINT-TO-POINT INDEXED ACCOUNT

Let's say you have $1 million in an IUL LASER Fund, and you opt to link your policy entirely to a one-year point-to-point S&P 500 indexed account.

Let's pause for a moment to explain what we mean by annual point-to-point. It's a crediting method wherein most companies typically use the 15th of the month in which you add money to your policy as the "beginning" point, and the 15th of the month one year later as the "end" point.

It does not matter what happens to the index each day of the coming year—it only matters where it started, and where it ended.

So say you add your premium to your policy on December 5. It will earn the current fixed rate until the 15th. On the 15th, your beginning point starts. One year later, on December 15, your return is calculated based on where the index ends. If the index went up from point-to-point, your policy will gain, typically up to a cap.

Let's say in this scenario, that cap is 10.5% with a minor fee of 0.8% (for those who want to avoid fees with this indexed account, the no-fee cap would be around 8%). If the index went down over the previous year, you have the peace of mind of a guaranteed floor of zero (which means you won't lose any principal due to market volatility—which is why we often say, "Zero's the hero.").

Now let's look at a specific scenario to understand it even better. Let's say on December 15 of last year, the S&P was at 1,000. On December 15 of this year, the S&P increases to 1,100 (a 10% increase). The insurance company is contractually obligated to pay you the yield, which is 10%. On $1 million, that means they will put $100,000 into your policy. That $100,000 is locked in as new principal.

Now, the following year, there's a financial disaster, and the economy tanks. While most Americans invested directly IN the S&P could lose a significant amount (which millions of Americans did, losing as much as 40% between 2000 and 2003 and again in 2008) ... here's the great part ... you don't.

With indexing, your principal is completely safeguarded from losses due to market volatility. What's more, when you come to the end of your one-year point-to-point period, your indexed account resets for the coming year.

To summarize, by using indexed accounts, your returns are: 1) calculated annually point-to-point, 2) those gains are locked in, and 3) your index resets on that date for the coming year.

To illustrate this further, let's use historical numbers for a moment, using an example where you're starting with $500,000 in your financial

vehicle (see Figure 6.1). Let's say to calculate your annual return from December 15, 2006, to December 15, 2007, the S&P 500 gained 2.98%. You would have received a 2.98% addition to your principal. With The IUL LASER Fund, that additional $14,900 would have been locked in and protected as new principal. (With a market-based financial vehicle, that $14,900 would still be at risk in the market.)

On December 15, 2008, the S&P 500 index dropped 40.83% from the previous year—this would have been a devastating loss if you were IN the market, but since your IUL LASER Fund has an index floor of 0%, you would have lost nothing due to market volatility, and your return of 2.98% the previous year was locked in.

The index would have reset for the coming year, and by December 15, 2009, it gained 28.27%—your IUL LASER Fund would have gained up to your cap of 10.5%. Again in 2010, you would have hit the cap of 10.5%.

As you look at Figure 6.1, as you move forward to 2012, you can see how much better off you would be with an indexed policy versus having your money actually in the market.

If money were actually IN the stock market, you would still be trying to recover from the losses of the 2008 crash. With your IUL LASER Fund, your gains would be locked in every year, so you wouldn't lose any of those gains every time your policy reset. And in the down years, you would have been protected with a 0% floor, which is why "zero's the hero."

FIGURE 6.1

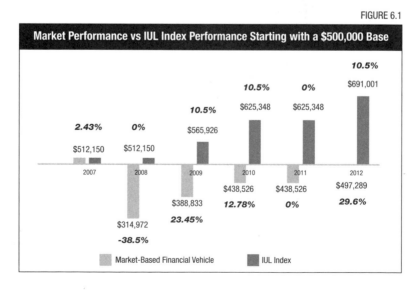

Market Performance vs IUL Index Performance Starting with a $500,000 Base

So in up years, your policy gains, and in down years, your policy's value is protected from losses due to market volatility. With most indexed accounts, the floors are 0%, and the gains are capped (caps vary by indexed account, and insurance companies can change them from year-to-year). To illustrate, currently the S&P 500 is capped at 10.5%. If the S&P saw a 15% increase this year, your earnings would be capped at 10.50%. But if the S&P 500 lost 2% this year, you would see a 0% gain, and your principal would be protected from losses due to market volatility.

ONE-YEAR POINT-TO-POINT INDEXED ACCOUNT WITH NO CAP

If your insurance company offers it, you could also choose a one-year point-to-point indexing strategy with no cap, with a threshold/spread. (To explain the threshold/spread, this is a rate the insurance company subtracts from indexed account growth. It can change depending on the market, and is typically between 5% and 10%.)

There are distinct advantages to this type of indexed account. For example, from March 2019 to March 2020, the S&P 500 dropped 15.04% (largely due to the onset of the pandemic and sudden market volatility). With the guaranteed 0% floor, our clients with this indexing strategy didn't lose anything due to market volatility (again, zero's the hero here).

With the annual reset, our clients were in a position to benefit from what happened during the next period. As we look at the point-to-point change a year later (March 2020 to March 2021), the S&P 500 gained 66.33%. The threshold/spread on this indexed account was 5% at the time, so our clients with this indexed account received a 61.33% return over that one-year period (which is the 66.33% return minus the 5% threshold). Note, even if the threshold/spread had been 10%, the return would have been 56.33%, which can still make a difference in the account's bottom line.

A little later in this chapter, you'll also learn about multipliers, which can boost your policy's earning power. Let's say you had this multiplier turned on with this exact account March 2020 to March 2021. For a multiplier fee of 7.5% that year, your return would have had the benefit of a 2.7 multiplier. This means you would have seen approximately a 165.5% gross return (which is 61.33% multiplied by 2.7). We need to also factor in the fee of 7.5%, which means you would see a net gain of approximately

158% (which is 165.5% minus 7.5%). Stay tuned; we'll explain the multiplier in more depth soon.

PARTICIPATION RATES & VOLATILITY CONTROL INDEXED ACCOUNTS

Let's explore volatility control indexed accounts for a moment. To begin, let's look at another factor in calculating your index return: the participation rate. Most index strategies have a participation rate of 100%. So if the index return is 10%, you will participate in 100% of that return, gaining the full 10%.

Other indexed accounts have a higher participation rate and are uncapped, often with different components than the S&P 500.

With these indexed accounts, the insurance companies can offer a higher participation rate than 100% with no cap, because they have low volatility. There is a trade-off with these accounts—some years these accounts will not gain as much as the S&P 500. Other years, they will gain more than the S&P 500 (because there is no cap).

For example, many of the volatility control indexed accounts our clients use have participation rates that range between 115% to 220%, with no cap. Insurance companies can offer no cap and higher participation rates than 100% because these indexed accounts have lower volatility than the S&P 500. Some accounts require a nominal charge—often 1%—to activate the optional higher participation rate.

Some of these low volatility strategies are one-year point-to-point account, others are two-year point-to-point accounts (we'll explain two-year point-to-point accounts in more detail in the next section).

So let's say you have a one-year point-to-point volatility control indexed account with a 130% participation rate, and the index does 10% this year. You would get 130% of 10%, which is a 13% return. Let's say the index goes up next year to 15%; you would get a return of 19.5% (which is 130% of 15%). And note that even if the index were to go down, you would still have the protection of your 0% floor.

These indexed accounts can be impactful. For example, one of these one-year point-to-point indexed accounts achieved a 26% return in 2017, largely due to the participation rates (and having no cap).

These volatility control indexed accounts are innovative and relatively new, appearing on the scene around 2016 and later. To understand their potential impact, it helps to project what would have happened had they been in play historically. For example, looking back over a recent twenty-year period (2001 to 2021), historical returns for some of these indexed accounts would have been 6% to 10.5%. And some newer volatility control indexed accounts have historical returns that would have been as high as 13.97% and 15.31% over the past seventeen and fifteen years.

It's important to note that even during volatile seasons, some volatility control indexed accounts can still see a positive return. To explain, some of the volatility control indexed accounts we're talking about would have seen positive returns from mid-2000 through the beginning of 2003 (due to the dot-com crash and 9/11), and again in 2008 (the start of the Great Recession).

Keep in mind, the caps and participation rates with each of these indexed accounts can change year-to-year. This is a good thing, because the insurance company needs to be able to afford the cap and participation rate with the current market conditions (e.g., current interest rates and cost of options).

We have seen times when the caps and participation rates go down, and times when they go up. (It is actually beneficial that you're not locked in, because if interest rates rise, your caps and participation rates can rise as well). Note that changes don't happen immediately; there is usually a lag of a few years between market condition changes and changes to caps and participation rates.

TWO-YEAR POINT-TO-POINT INDEXED ACCOUNT

Up to now we have talked about one-year point-to-point crediting strategies. There are also powerful multi-year indexed accounts (such as two-year and five-year accounts) you may want to consider.

With a multi-year indexed account, because it's longer term, the insurance company can afford to offer higher caps and/or higher participation rates than on the one-year point-to-point accounts.

As we will mention in the next section, the insurance company uses options to achieve these index returns. With a longer term strategy, like two years or five years, the option costs are cheaper, and the insurance

company can offer a higher upside when choosing a two-year or five-year strategy.

For example, with a two-year point-to-point strategy linked to the S&P 500, the insurance company might offer a cap of 19%, with a 100% participation rate and no extra fee (similar to the one-year strategy in the "One-Year Point-to-Point" section at the beginning of this chapter).

To figure your return, you would look at the S&P 500 on the 15th of the month (the month when you put money into the policy). Then fast forward two years to the 15th of that same month, and calculate your return based on the change in the S&P 500. If the growth was above 19%, you would get the cap of 19%. If the growth was 15%, you would get 15%. If the S&P 500 was negative, you would not lose; you would get 0%. (And remember, your indexed account would reset at that point.)

As a side note, if your insurance company offers it, you could also opt for another type of two-year point-to-point indexing strategy, with no cap and a threshold/spread historically around 10% (similar to the one-year point-to-point no cap indexed account we mentioned earlier in this chapter). Let's say the market goes up 30% over a two-year period, you would get a 20% return over that two-year period (which is the 30% gain minus the 10% threshold).

FIVE-YEAR POINT-TO-LAST-YEAR-AVERAGE INDEXED ACCOUNT

Now if you want even more upside potential, you may want to go to a five-year strategy, one that typically has no cap and a participation rate of 110%. This strategy is often called a five-year point-to-last-year-average. That's a mouthful, so we'll help you understand how it works.

To figure your return on this indexed account, you would look at the S&P 500 on the 15th of the month (when you put the money into the policy), then move ahead five years (sixty months). Instead of the rate being based on a point-to-point method like the other strategies we've mentioned, it's point-to-last-year-average, so the company averages the S&P 500 the last twelve months of the sixty-month period.

For example, let's say you put money into your policy on March 15, 2015. On March 15, 2020, if you had used the point-to-point method,

the growth would have only been 14.65% because of the crash in March 2020 (a crash that was spurred by the COVID-19 crisis). However, if you had used the point-to-last-year-average, because the company averaged the last twelve months, your return would have been 49.77%. You can see this strategy helps to protect against what exactly happened in March 2020 - a sudden crash toward the end of your five-year period.

This strategy can have tremendous upside potential, because it has no cap. It also locks in your gains every five years, after which it resets, and your gains are tax-free. However, compare this strategy to what happens when your money is directly IN the stock market, where you never lock in gains until you sell and get out, and any gains are usually taxable.

There are some downsides to the five-year strategy to keep in mind. First, you have to wait five years to see a return. (You are still getting the compounding of the market with no cap, but you are not locking in those gains until the five years are up.)

On the other hand, the one-year strategy can be more beneficial to lock in those gains annually. But, the one-year strategies have their cap.

MAKING INDEXED ACCOUNTS WORK FOR YOU

You have a lot of choice and control when choosing your index strategies. As we mentioned earlier, you can diversify between multiple index strategies within the same policy the company offers. For example, you might put 40% in a one-year strategy, 40% in a two-year strategy, and the remaining 20% in a five-year strategy.

Keep in mind not all insurance companies offer all of these choices, so it's important to know which companies you can turn to for these index strategies. And insurance companies often release new index strategies that may be even more advantageous than what is currently available, so stay in touch with a qualified IUL specialist to optimize your approach. Furthermore, we have seen there is no silver bullet—you may not find a single index strategy that checks every box for you, which is why we recommend diversifying your approach to index strategies.

In summary, The IUL LASER Fund has specific safety and rate of return benefits:

- You're linked to an index (or your choice of multiple index strategies)
- Your money is not IN the market, so "zero's the hero" (with your 0% floor)
- Depending on the indexed account, you have the opportunity to earn up to the cap (or no cap with volatility control indexed accounts or the five-year S&P 500 index strategy)
- You also have the opportunity to have participation rates ranging from 115% to 220% (typically the high participation rates are on the volatility control indexed accounts)
- You benefit from locked-in gains at the end of each indexed account's cycle (one year, two year, or five years)

(Reminder: Not all IUL LASER Funds—especially those initiated years ago—offer the same features. Every company and policy is different, so be sure to check with your IUL specialist on the features and benefits of your policy.)

HOW INDEXING WORKS

How can insurance companies give you all the upside benefits of the market while protecting you from the downsides? Let's take a look behind the scenes to see how indexing is possible.

FIGURE 6.2

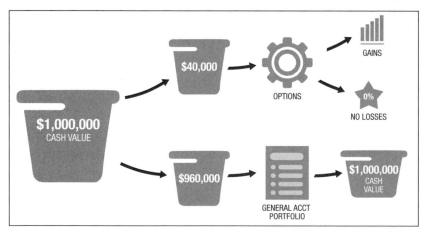

Looking at Figure 6.2, let's say your "policy value bucket" is $1 million (in other words, you have a cash value of $1 million). Your insurance company puts your money into its General Account Portfolio (GAP), with the lion's share of that money in safe, conservative investments like AAA and AA bonds with typically stable rates of return. Let's say in this example, out of your $1 million, the insurance company puts $960,000 into the GAP.

This money is going to grow back up to $1 million during the year, which essentially guarantees your principal of $1 million. This growth is due to the GAP earning a fixed rate of return (currently 4% to 4.5%), regardless of market performance. How is this possible? Because as we just mentioned, the $960,000 is invested in safe, conservative investments that offer fixed annual rates.

The only portion of your money that is "at risk" is the remaining $40,000. The insurance company takes that $40,000 of your $1 million to buy options based on the index strategy you have chosen. Options may be risky, but remember your policy's cash value has guarantees and your cash value is not at risk. Insurance companies can do this, because they are only putting the $40,000 into options, not the other $960,000.

Options are complex, so we'll offer a simplified explanation here, examining what could happen to that $40,000 in different scenarios.

Let's say you have chosen a one-year volatility control indexed account with no cap and a 125% participation rate. If this index goes up 10% over the next year, you would get 12.5% (which is 125% of 10%). With the option strategy, after one year, your $40,000 grows to $125,000, which is a 12.5% return on your $1 million.

Now let's say the index goes down 10%. With the way the options work, the $40,000 is lost, but your $1 million doesn't go down 10%. Even if the index were to drop precipitously, say 40%, the options are still worthless—the $40,000 is gone—but you don't lose any of your $1 million principal in cash value. Your $1 million principal is guaranteed a 0% floor because of the GAP.

Now you may be wondering, why can caps and participation rates vary from year to year? The insurance company sets the cap/participation rate based on variables like their options costs and the rate they're

earning on the GAP. If interest rates in America are going up and the GAP is set to earn more this year, they will likely put less (like $950,000) of your cash value into the GAP, put more (like $50,000) to work in options, and raise the cap/participation rate slightly for the year—because they are likely to get stable returns in the GAP.

As a reminder, caps and participation rates can go down, and they can go up. As market conditions (like interest rates and the cost of options) change, you'll often see related changes to caps and participation rates. And remember, it's advantageous that you're not locked in, because if interest rates rise, your caps and participation rates can eventually rise as well (that change can take a few years).

UNDERSTANDING MULTIPLIERS

We gave you a taste of the multiplier concept earlier in this chapter. Now let's dive in for the full meal and examine the strategy in greater depth.

Multipliers are like putting a supercharger on a car. If you're a gearhead, you know a supercharger enhances the performance of the engine and adds significant horsepower, giving the vehicle more speed and power.

Similarly, multipliers can empower your policy to earn even higher returns. For example, one of the high-end multipliers our clients use allows you to multiply your returns by 2.7 times, for an additional cost of 7.5% per year.

To explain the cost, that 7.5% fee essentially takes 7.5% of your policy's cash value and adds that dollar amount to the options budget (see the How Indexing Works section above for clarification on the options budget). For most companies, this cost is contractually obligated to be used for options strategies only (e.g., the insurance company cannot use the money for operating expenses, commissions, etc.).

Let's look at an example. Let's say the indexing strategy you've chosen is the two-year point-to-point strategy with a 19% cap. With the multiplier strategy, your policy would incur the 7.5% fee for two years, for a total cost of 15%. So let's say you received the 19% return after the two-year period. Now multiply that return by 2.7 times, which equals 51.3%. When you subtract the 15% cost, you would net a gain of approximately 36%.

You can see this is well worth the 7.5% cost to get approximately 36% net return versus 19%.

You might be thinking, "That sounds great, but what if the market tanks during those two years?" You would still be protected by a 0% floor, so your policy value would not drop due to market volatility. However, you would have incurred the 15% fee. So there is some risk to consider with multipliers. On the other hand, there are also the upsides to weigh. As mentioned earlier in this chapter, our clients with the no cap strategy received a 61.33% return in March 2021. With the multiplier, they saw a net gain of approximately 158% tax-free (in just one year!).

To explore the multiplier concept a different way, let's look at a historical comparison of returns without a multiplier, and with a multiplier. Let's say you have a policy with 50% of your cash value allocated to the one-year point-to-point high cap strategy (with a 10.5% cap); 25% to the two-year point-to-point strategy (with a 19% cap); and 25% to the five-year point-to-last-year-average strategy (with no cap and 110% participation rate).

Now let's apply these allocations to see what would have happened to your policy from 1981 to 2021 (for a forty-year period). As you can see in Figure 6.3, without a multiplier, your average annual return would have been approximately 7%. But what if you had a multiplier on this same policy to supercharge your returns? Your average annual return over the same forty year-period would have been approximately 10.83% (that's net, after applying the multiplier and subtracting the multiplier costs).

FIGURE 6.3

40-YEAR HISTORICAL AVERAGE ANNUAL RETURNS	
Without multiplier 7%	With multiplier 10.83%*

*Net of the multiplier fee. Returns are approximate.

Now just for fun, let's see what would have happened if you had 100% of your money in the five-year point-to-last-year-average index strategy

during that same forty-year time period. Looking at Figure 6.4, without the multiplier fee, your average annual return would have been 9.14%. With the multiplier, your average annual return would have been 15.32%, net of the multiplier fee. (This is largely due to the five-year strategy having no cap.)

However, most people do not put all their money in the five-year strategy—most diversify among one-year, two-year, and five-year strategies.

In Figure 6.4, let's explore the two-year strategy for a moment, looking at 100% of your money in the two-year strategy from 1981 to 2021. Without the multiplier, you would have had an average annual return of 7.04%. With the multiplier, you would have seen an average annual return of 11.33%, net of the multiplier fee.

FIGURE 6.4

40-YEAR HISTORICAL AVERAGE ANNUAL RETURNS— 100%		
	5-YEAR INDEX STRATEGY	2-YEAR INDEX STRATEGY
Without multiplier	9.14%	7.04%
With multiplier*	15.32%	11.33%

*Net of the multiplier fee, based on index strategy allocation: 100% - five-year point-to-last-year-average strategy (with no cap and 110% participation rate); 100% - two-year point-to-point strategy (with a 19% cap)

There are a few things to consider with multipliers. Keep in mind like with other features of IUL LASER Funds, returns earned via multipliers are tax-free. Also, they come in different "sizes," meaning the multiplication factors and costs can vary. For example, you might get a multiplier factor of 1.48 times the return, for a fee of 2%.

Sometimes multipliers don't start until the second year or so of the policy, and they may ramp down to lower multipliers after twenty years or so. Additionally, some policies allow you to turn multipliers on or off. And finally, keep in mind, just as with other features we've mentioned, not all policies offer multipliers so if this is something you'd like to utilize, talk with your IUL specialist to find insurance company policies that offer strategies that are best for you.

WHAT ABOUT AN INTEREST BONUS?

A lot of insurance companies will offer extra bonus interest typically, starting from about the eleventh year (some start a little earlier, some start a little later). These interest bonuses can range vastly from company to company, and some can be guaranteed, others are non-guaranteed.

If a bonus is not guaranteed, it helps to look at the insurance company's track record to see how they have handled paying these bonuses in the past. In some cases, insurance companies may choose to not pay non-guaranteed bonuses, due to shortfalls or other reasons. This is why we are selective on which companies we use, understanding the insurance companies' integrity and reputation.

As a side note, it's helpful to understand the difference between a mutual holding insurance company and a publicly traded insurance company. With a mutual holding insurance company, the policy and contract owners are members of the company. Because it is not a publicly traded company, it is not driven by stock performance when making decisions. As a result, it can make decisions that benefit the customers and long-term strength of the company.

On the other hand, a publicly traded company answers first and foremost to its stockholders. While some publicly traded companies have excellent reputations, others can seem to make decisions that adversely affect the policyholders. For example, a publicly traded company may not pay a non-guaranteed interest bonus. Or it might increase the cost of insurance rates. Or it might decrease caps and participation rates on older policies, while offering higher rates to new policies.

Typically, mutual holding companies have stronger track records with keeping caps and participation rates the same for both established and new clients, keeping cost of insurance rates the same (or even lowering them), and in keeping with their promises by paying non-guaranteed bonuses in the policies.

Now back to bonus interest. Let's look at an example of a thirty basis point bonus interest. From the eleventh year on, with our example policy, you would receive an interest bonus of 0.3%. Let's say your policy has a $1 million cash value, so you would receive $3,000 in interest bonus.

Many times, your interest bonus can exceed the cost of insurance at this point in the policy. This difference between your large interest bonuses and the fees can make a big impact on your long-term bottom line.

Other companies have a complex formula for their bonus interest. For example, one company gives large bonus interests from the eleventh year to the thirty-fifth year, at a rate much higher than the bonus mentioned above.

Depending on the insurance company, there are various names for bonus interest, including: additional credit, persistency credit, and conditional credit. Here again, we recommend talking to your IUL specialist to understand the features you're looking for to determine what's best for you.

NOW THAT YOU UNDERSTAND THE BASICS

These are just the basics of indexing to help you get an idea of the choices you have, and how it all impacts the growth of your policy. Savvy IUL specialists can help you navigate the intricacies to make the appropriate selections for you and your situation.

Suffice it to say for now, combining properly structured insurance policies and indexing strategies can help you achieve your financial goals with safety, liquidity, and rates of return that also provide peace of mind.

As you look at your own future, imagine having the confidence and calm that a financial vehicle like this can bring. Just as Doug's clients back in the 80s, who went from feeling vulnerable to the winds of market change, to having a sense of calm amid the storm, you, too, can take a financial path that leads to brighter days.

Plus, with The IUL LASER Fund as part of your overall portfolio, you get the added advantage of insurance benefits that can bless those you care about in times of need. And in the end, that's what it's all about—bringing greater abundance to our lives, our families, loved ones, and communities.

TOP 5 TAKEAWAYS

1. IUL LASER Funds offer a powerful advantage over many other traditional financial vehicles: indexing.

2. Indexing allows the money in your policy to gain interest when the stock market goes up, and to be completely protected from losses due to market volatility when the market goes down.

3. Depending on your insurance company, you can choose from among several different index strategies, including S&P 500 and volatility control indexed accounts.

4. You can choose among strategies like the one-year point-to-point, two-year point-to-point, and five-year point-to-last-year-average. You can also incorporate no cap and multiplier strategies for opportunities to enhance your returns.

5. You have the flexibility to make choices that work for you, such as whether to leave your selected index strategies as your default, or to change it up to accommodate shifts in the market. Your IUL specialist can help you optimize your IUL LASER Fund strategies.

7

The Insurance Revolution

Now that you have a basic understanding of what The IUL LASER Fund, or "miracle solution," is, let's look at how it came to be, how it works in relation to taxes, and how to ensure your insurance can provide so much more than just a death benefit. (As a reminder, we use the terms IUL LASER Fund and LASER Fund interchangeably to represent a properly structured, maximum-funded Indexed Universal Life policy.)

THE EMERGENCE OF UNIVERSAL LIFE

As we mentioned earlier, Universal Life had its start in 1980, when E.F. Hutton (a brokerage firm—not a life insurance company) came up with the idea of how to buy term and invest the difference, protected under the tax-free umbrella of permanent life insurance.

Universal Life was originally designed as an instrument in which people could technically structure a life insurance policy to perform better than the "buy term, invest the difference" approach that called for buying term insurance, and investing the difference in an external account that was subject to income tax. (You can essentially accomplish the same thing by buying term and investing the difference, but doing so

under tax-favorable circumstances by keeping it qualified to be tax-free under the life insurance policy in accordance with section 72[e] of the Internal Revenue Code.)

Recognizing the tax benefits that life insurance had for many decades, E.F. Hutton basically designed Universal Life to take advantage of the tremendous safety and liquidity life insurance can provide, as well as the expertise life insurance companies have demonstrated in money management. (Many insurance companies are some of the best money managers in the world.)

So E.F. Hutton is generally credited for being the mastermind behind structuring life insurance in a way that allows greater safety and a less volatile rate of return on a tax-free basis. The company paved the way for people to pursue a more predictable, tax-favored rate of return.

To illustrate, would you rather try to earn 7% in a volatile stock market and then, after paying tax in a 29% tax bracket, only net 4.97%? Or would you prefer to predictably earn an average of 7% and net 6%, cash-on-cash tax-free return ... while being protected from market loss due to volatility ... and knowing there's an income-tax-free death benefit waiting for your heirs? (That 1% difference over the life of the policy is not tax expense, but rather the cost of the insurance the IRS requires for it to qualify as tax-free under the definition of life insurance.) We think the answer is clear.

In the early 1980s, many people chose to go the more predictable, tax-favored path. They began repositioning their serious cash into maximum-funded Universal Life insurance policies for the primary purpose of accumulating their capital on a tax-free basis for future goals, such as retirement. They were taking out small life insurance death benefits and putting in the most premiums allowed.

For example, they were buying a $50,000 death benefit policy, and paying a premium of $500,000. In this case, they were clearly focused on finding a tax-free, reliable place to grow their money; they were not as focused on the death benefit. In other words, they were trying to take out the least amount of insurance that was required while paying the most premium as fast as they could into those policies.

The IRS came in and challenged what was being done. They went to court, and in the "Hutton Life Rulings," E.F. Hutton won the case

because they were in full compliance with the Internal Revenue Code. To this day, we've been able to benefit from the early work E.F. Hutton did in paving the way for smarter, safer financial strategies.

HISTORICALLY SPEAKING

In the decades since 1980, the tax laws and codes related to Universal Life have evolved. Since taxes have a profound impact on your wealth accumulation, it's wise for you to understand these important codes. And congratulations—you're about to learn about as much if not more than most CPAs know.

First, let's take a little stroll through tax history. There was a time when federal income tax wasn't the norm—it was only implemented for temporary periods to cover the cost of wars. But in 1913, the US added the 16th Amendment to the Constitution, making federal income tax a permanent fixture in American life. Income taxes reached their highest point during the Roosevelt years, topping out at 94% for America's highest earners. This income tax rate eventually receded to between 50% and 80% over the next three decades, during which time Social Security and Medicare taxes were also added to the mix. The message was clear: the more you make, the more they take.

When Reagan became president of the United States in 1980, the financial planning landscape began to see a series of changes. E.F. Hutton had introduced its fresh take on the Universal Life policy, and by 1982, the concept was challenged by Congress and the IRS.

Subsequently, legislators passed the Tax Equity Fiscal Responsibility Act of 1982, known as TEFRA. Two years later, the government passed the Deficit Reduction Act of 1984 (DEFRA). Under TEFRA and DEFRA, what we call the TEFRA/DEFRA corridor was established. The TEFRA/DEFRA corridor dictates the minimum death benefit required (based upon the insured's age, gender, and health) in order to accommodate the aggregate desired premium basis that will be allowed into the life insurance policy. Once these laws were in place, if people didn't comply with TEFRA/DEFRA, their policy would exceed the definition of life insurance. It would no longer be protected under tax-free status under Internal Revenue Code Section 72(e), nor would it allow them to access their money tax-free (which is covered specifically under Internal

Revenue Code Section 7702, along with other guidelines for Universal Life policies).

TEFRA/DEFRA provided parity. TEFRA/DEFRA essentially said that the older the policyholder was, the less death benefit would be required to accommodate the amount of money the policyholder wanted to put into the insurance policy.

For example, after passage of TEFRA/DEFRA, a male age 60 who wanted to put $500,000 into a Universal Life policy would need to have a death benefit of around $1.3 million. By contrast, a male age 35 who wanted to put $500,000 into a Universal Life policy would need to have a death benefit of around $4 million.

It's important to note that the sixty-year-old and thirty-five-year-old would have the same amount of fees, it's just that the thirty-five-year-old would have a lot higher death benefit. Universal Life policies would work at all ages—younger or older folks could still take advantage of all the benefits while paying comparable costs at any age.

As more Americans started to see the value of putting their serious cash into these kinds of policies, banks and credit unions started to complain. In response, the government passed the Technical and Miscellaneous Revenue Act in 1988 (TAMRA) to slow the flow of money into Universal Life policies.

The TAMRA tax citations simply meant that after June 21, 1988, insurance policies could not be funded in one single premium at the maximum TEFRA /DEFRA guideline and still allow the policyholder to enjoy tax-free income streams. The intention was to deter Americans from pulling their money out of other financial vehicles in one lump sum to reposition it in insurance policies.

For example, they didn't want anyone yanking all $500,000 out of their other financial vehicles and immediately being able to put it into a Universal Life policy. Instead, they wanted to slow the flow by requiring the rollout to take place over several years. After TAMRA passed, if you wanted to reposition $500,000 from other financial vehicles into an insurance policy, the most you would usually want to liquidate would be about one-fifth that amount per year (approximately $100,000 annually). This typically would spread the transfer over at least five years.

The Guideline Single Premium is the most that can be paid into the policy during the initial ten to fourteen years, depending on age. Because people wanted to fund the GSP amount in the first year, TAMRA required it to be spread out typically over a five- to seven-year time frame in order to have tax-free access (note that for younger people, TAMRA can allow for as few as four years to fund the policy). Whole Life insurance must not be funded any faster than seven relatively equal installments. It is sometimes referred to as the "7-pay test." The 7-pay test, however, does not apply to Universal Life. Generally, you can maximum fund your Universal Life policy in about five years on average. (Keep in mind, it's different for different ages, ranging from four to seven years).

NEW TAX CODE CHANGES IN 2021

Things shifted for IUL LASER Funds at the beginning of 2021 with the passage of H.R. 133. Tucked into that larger COVID relief bill that passed December 27, 2020, an adjustment was made to Internal Revenue Code Section 7702. The great news is the change improved the premium-to-death-benefit ratio related to the TEFRA/DEFRA corridor.

This is a huge benefit to anyone opening an IUL LASER Fund January 1, 2021, or later. This adjustment allows policyholders to purchase less death benefit than before.

For example, before the bill passed, a male age 60 who wanted to put $500,000 into an IUL LASER Fund would have had to purchase about $1,300,000 of death benefit. After the bill, he would only need to purchase about $1,000,000 of death benefit.

As another example, before the bill passed, a female age 40 who wanted to put in $500,000 would have had to purchase about $3,800,000 of death benefit. As of January 1, 2021, she would only need to purchase about $2,000,000.

As you can see, the revised 7702 reduces some of the policy fees/expenses and cost of insurance by about 20% to 40%. It's true that you may be getting less death benefit (in the first example, the age 60 male's heirs would receive $1,000,000 vs. $1,300,000 income-tax-free upon his passing). However, for most people, the primary objective with their IUL LASER Funds is to get the least death benefit with the lowest

expenses, yielding higher tax-free income. This is even easier now with the passage of H.R. 133.

Why was this adjustment made? The original premium-to-death-benefit ratios were based on interest rates in the 1980s (when Universal Life policies started to take shape). Interest rates are lower in our current world, and the 7702 change adjusts for that.

The change makes this an advantageous time to open a new IUL LASER Fund, as it's more cost-effective to fund and utilize your policy for tax-free income.

INSURANCE AS A FINANCIAL STRATEGY OPTION

Going back to the early 80s, this was the era when Doug stopped recommending that people put their serious cash at risk in the market, and started showing his clients how to find greater safety in Universal Life policies. Many of his more than 3,000 clients ended up moving their money from mutual funds to Universal Life insurance policies. These policies were being credited 9% to 12% fixed interest rates at the time. That interest was, of course, tax-deferred. He was able to design these life insurance policies so that if they were credited 11%, the net internal rate of return, cash-on-cash would be 10%. In other words, the cost of the insurance only "drained out" about 1 of the 11 percentage points, resulting in a net cash-on-cash internal rate of return within 1% of the gross crediting interest rate.

Doug had many clients who paid $500,000 into a Universal Life insurance policy and were therefore able to take out $50,000 a year, or a net of 10% tax-free, each year in income without depleting their $500,000 principal. This was an incredible financial tool for many retirees.

Keep in mind that the early 1980s was a high-interest environment. In the 1990s, interest rates returned to normal, and Universal Life insurance was crediting more like 7%, 8%, and 9%. It was still an attractive vehicle, however, because if you earned 9%, you were still netting 8% cash-on-cash if the insurance policy was structured properly.

We can say that since, people we have worked with have felt much more at peace about preparing for their retirement with what has evolved into

The IUL LASER Fund (as a reminder, these are Indexed Universal Life policies, structured as maximum-funded, tax-advantaged policies). With these IUL LASER Funds, they're able to maintain safety, earn predictable rates of return, and enjoy tax-free income.

Currently, a retirement nest egg of $1 million can predictably (based on historical averages) generate an annual income stream averaging 5% to 10%. That would mean that theoretically a retiree could withdraw about $50,000 to $100,000 per year without depleting a principal of $1 million. Keep in mind this income is totally tax-free; because it is not regarded as earned, passive, or portfolio income, it is not subject to income taxation.

HOW TO PUT THE LEAST IN, GET THE MOST OUT

As always with life insurance policies, you need to demonstrate more than just a desire for a strong financial vehicle, you need to establish a need for the life insurance—indicating that it will be necessary upon death for things like income replacement, estate preservation, or wealth transfer. (Your IUL specialist can help you do this properly.) After you've determined the need for the life insurance policy, let's talk about how The IUL LASER Fund can be used for tax-deferred accumulation and tax-free income.

It doesn't matter whether you open a life insurance policy designed to accommodate $200 per month in premiums, $1,000 a month in premiums, a lump sum of $1 million, or a lump sum of $10 million. For the sake of simplicity let's say that you want to design a life insurance policy to accommodate $500,000. Let's say this year, you turned 60 years old. At age 60, if you're a male in excellent health, you're required under TEFRA/DEFRA to have a death benefit of approximately $1,000,000 to be allowed to deposit up to $500,000 into your new IUL LASER Fund. (Note before January 2021, the minimum death benefit would have been $1,300,000. The new ruling regarding Section 7702 gives you lower costs related to lower death benefit requirements.)

TAMRA dictates that you must spread the payments out typically over a minimum of five to seven years, until you reach your funding maximum of $500,000. Keep in mind that you could purchase considerably more

life insurance than $1,000,000 for a single premium of $500,000. But in this case, that is not your objective.

Rather, your objective is to take out the least amount of life insurance you can under TEFRA/DEFRA guidelines to accommodate the full $500,000, and have it grow with the best internal rate of return. In other words, if the primary objective is to have the best internal rate of return, you can opt to take out the LEAST amount of insurance possible so the net internal rate of return can be the GREATEST.

So at age 60, the minimum amount of life insurance required is approximately $1 million. Note that the amount of life insurance required is contingent on age. If you were only a twenty-two-year-old, the minimum amount of life insurance required to accommodate $500,000 would be about $3,350,000. If you were age 75, the minimum amount of life insurance required to accommodate $500,000 would be $620,000.

On the other hand, the net rate of return could be the same for the sixty-year-old as the twenty-two-year-old. With your policy, you can earn an average rate of return of let's say 7% and have the insurance only cost you about one of those percentage points over the life of the policy, so your net internal rate of return is averaging let's say 6%.

STRATEGIES MOST PROFESSIONALS DON'T KNOW

When designing an insurance policy to perform as a superior capital accumulation tool and produce a tax-free income stream, it is critical to understand several other tactics, such as how to "squeeze down" the life insurance death benefit to accommodate the Guideline Single Premium.

Many financial professionals and insurance agents/producers are not taught these strategies, nor do they understand them. This is why it is imperative to work with someone who knows how to structure the insurance correctly to perform in an optimal way. Otherwise, even though the insurance policy may earn, let's say a 7% average gross rate of return, it may only net you over the life of the policy as low as 1%, 2%, or 3% rate of return (because the cost of the insurance may be higher than it needs to be). Too much life insurance could be assigned to the policy, or it may not be funded properly to have it perform at its best.

When you decide the amount of money you would like to set aside over a certain time-frame, the amount of life insurance required under TE-FRA /DEFRA tax citations can be calculated using sophisticated software. Please keep in mind that even though you may establish an insurance policy designed to accommodate up to say, $500,000 in the example we are using, you are not obligated or required to pay the full $500,000 into the policy.

That said, it would behoove you to fund the full $500,000 into the policy as soon as you can and as fast as the IRS allows. But even if a policy is only 50% to 60% funded (or half-full), it could continue to keep a life insurance policy in force probably the remainder of your lifetime. That's because the interest that is being credited on the premiums that have already been paid into the policy would likely be sufficient to cover the actual cost of the insurance. This is even more powerful with the 2021 change to the Section 7702 tax code, which allows for an even lower death benefit (and thus lower fees), making IUL LASER Funds even more cost-effective.

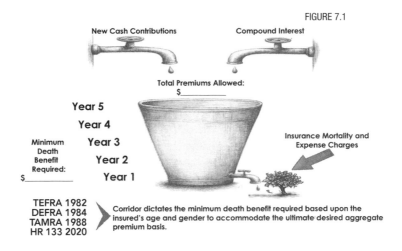

FIGURE 7.1

New Cash Contributions — Compound Interest

Total Premiums Allowed: $_____

Year 5
Year 4
Year 3
Year 2
Year 1

Minimum Death Benefit Required: $_____

Insurance Mortality and Expense Charges

TEFRA 1982
DEFRA 1984
TAMRA 1988
HR 133 2020

Corridor dictates the minimum death benefit required based upon the insured's age and gender to accommodate the ultimate desired aggregate premium basis.

Now let's compare your IUL LASER Fund to a bucket (see Figure 7.1). Throughout this book you'll hear us refer to "buckets" in a couple ways: the "premium bucket" (which is the Guideline Single Premium, or the maximum amount you fund your policy with) and the "policy value bucket" (which is the cash value of the policy—an amount that can grow year-over-year with no limits, according to your index performance).

In this example, you have a premium bucket big enough to accommodate $500,000, which will provide about $1,000,000 in minimum life insurance. Over five years, you fill up your premium bucket in five equal annual payments of $100,000 each.

There are annual costs to your insurance, which include the pure cost of the life insurance, or the term component inside the insurance policy, and any other fees associated with managing the policy. In this illustration, the cost of the insurance is represented by the spigot on the bottom right of the bucket.

Now before you see that "cost flow" as a negative, consider this. The little stream of water is actually going to work for you. It's what's paying for your policy, which in the end will provide a valuable death benefit to your loved ones. It's essentially "watering" a nice little money tree that will blossom and transfer whatever was left in the bucket to your heirs or beneficiaries, income-tax-free, upon your death.

When you open an insurance policy, you want this spigot to drain out the least amount of costs as possible so that your internal rate of return will be the highest possible. As indicated, the average annual return that most people have achieved during the last thirty years is 5% to 10%. This spigot has drained out an average of about 1% over the life of the policy, thus netting an average of about 4% to 9% interest compounded annually on a tax-deferred basis (and being able to access it tax-free for income).

Please keep in mind that there is no limit to what your money can grow to tax-deferred under Section 72(e) inside your insurance policy. The only limit established by TEFRA /DEFRA is the amount of basis that you design the policy to accommodate in aggregate premiums to be paid into the policy.

CREATING A MEC

Just to explore other options (so you can thoroughly understand these principles), what if you didn't want to be in compliance with TAMRA? What if, like some of our clients, you wanted to fund your policy in one fell swoop?

Essentially, you would be creating a Modified Endowment Contract (MEC). With a MEC, the money in your policy can still grow tax-deferred. When you die, the death benefit still passes on to your heirs

income-tax-free. The difference between The IUL LASER Fund and a MEC is the tax treatment on any income you take out. With The IUL LASER Fund, you take money out as a tax-free loan. With a MEC, any money you withdraw will be taxable under last-in, first-out (LIFO) treatment.

Keep in mind that violating TAMRA and creating a MEC can be intentional. There are times when people want the benefits of The IUL LASER Fund, but they do not anticipate needing to take out any income from the policy. They want the policy solely for transferring wealth to their heirs, income-tax-free. Even if they do decide to take out income, they do not mind paying taxes on the money they withdraw.

MECs are a simple, powerful way to see a significant increase on money you intend to transfer to your heirs. One of our clients, for example, had about $500,000 to set aside to pass along to his children. The challenge was, his money was currently in IRAs. He had recently reached the age when he would need to start taking RMDs or face penalties—and any money he withdrew would be taxed at the highest effective tax rate possible (40% between federal and state). He wanted a better strategy for transferring that wealth.

He didn't need the money for retirement income—he had marked it solely for transferring to his heirs. He wanted it to put it in an optimal environment, where it could grow tax-deferred, without the risk of loss due to market volatility. He decided to get his taxes over and done with and create a MEC. He paid $200,000 in taxes and put the remaining $300,000 into his policy. The policy was structured to maximize the death benefit, so that $300,000 purchased $1.5 million in death benefit. This meant his heirs would receive $1.5 million, income-tax-free, upon his passing. That sum was considerably greater than what they would have netted after his passing, if he had left his money in his IRAs.

There are other situations where creating a MEC may be advantageous. Say you have a large sum of money in a traditional bank, where it's earning the current rate of less than 1%. It may be liquid; it may be safe from downturns in the market; but it is growing at a snail's pace—and you're paying taxes on those gains. By putting that money to work in a MEC, you're now benefitting from tax-deferred growth at higher predictable rates of return (let's say it's averaging 7%) and continued safety from market turmoil. Should you need to access it, your money is still liquid; should you never need to touch it, its value just continues to grow. When you pass away, it blossoms and transfers income-tax-free to your heirs.

Or let's say you have money in the market, in a brokerage account, and you're tired of the market volatility (plus you don't want to pay taxes on any gains every year). You want to get all of it in a protected environment, right away, so you choose to move it into a MEC. Now your money is safe—with a guaranteed floor of 0%, you'll never lose money due to market volatility again. It's growing at an average rate of let's say 7%, and you're not paying any taxes on those gains. You will only pay taxes on money you may decide to withdraw. When you die, well, you know the rest: your death benefit transfers income-tax-free to your beneficiaries.

For all these reasons to create a MEC, it is wise to be aware that it is possible to inadvertently create a MEC, by overpaying premiums in those first five to seven years. If this happens, it is possible to "perfect the MEC" by asking the insurance company for a refund of the premiums that were overpaid in violation of TAMRA. This must be done within a sixty-day window following the next policy anniversary from the date that it became a MEC. (A well-trained IUL specialist can help you avoid violating TAMRA and thereby avoid a MEC, or they can help you perfect a MEC in the event that it is accidentally created by violating TAMRA.)

THE IUL LASER FUND'S TAX ADVANTAGES

Remember, we call maximum-funded, tax-advantaged IUL policies The IUL LASER Fund because they pass ... what? The LASER Test. They can provide unrivaled liquidity, safety of principal, rates of return, and another huge benefit: tax advantages.

To be clear, the tax advantages of these policies are no secret or shadow game. They're completely compliant with Internal Revenue Codes and tax laws, which we'll talk more about later in this chapter. When structured correctly and then funded properly, these policies shelter you from the danger of increased taxation. Here's how:

Tax Savings #1

Money put into these insurance policies has already been taxed at today's rates, not tomorrow's. With tax rates predictably going up in the future, getting taxes over and done will likely be important and financially significant. Paying taxes on the seed money rather than the money you harvest is always sound advice.

Tax Savings #2

Money taken out of your policy, when done optimally—in accordance with Internal Revenue Code guidelines—is not regarded as taxable income, as opposed to income from a traditional IRA/401(k). This isn't a new advantage. For more than one hundred years in America, the money that accumulates inside of a life insurance policy does so tax-favored. You can also access your money tax-free using several methods. As we mentioned before, the smartest way to access your money from an IUL LASER Fund is via a loan, rather than a withdrawal. [1]

Here's why: when done correctly, it is a loan made to yourself that is never due in your lifetime. To be in compliance with IRS guidelines, an interest rate is typically charged, but then that interest is offset with interest that is credited on the money you didn't "withdraw" but rather, remained there as collateral for your loan, thus resulting in a zero net cost in many instances.

Rather than just a zero net cost (which is often referred to as a Zero Wash Loan), you can also choose an Alternate Loan (some companies call this an Alternative Loan, Participating Loan, Indexed Loan, Variable Loan, or a Spread Loan). Essentially these types of loans allow the money in the insurance policy (e.g., the cash value that is collateral for the loan) to continue to earn the indexed rate (which typically averages 5% to 10% tax-deferred).

The insurance company is charging interest (as required to keep the cash flow tax-free under the IRS code) at a lower variable rate, say 5%. This strategy often allows you to take out a higher tax-free income because you are borrowing at a lower rate (in this example, at 5%), and your money stays in the policy, earning at a higher rate (in this example, let's say 7%).

---

[1] Policy loans and withdrawals will reduce available cash values and death benefits and may cause the policy to lapse, or affect guarantees against lapse. Additional premium payments may be required to keep the policy in force. In the event of a lapse, outstanding policy loans in excess of unrecovered cost basis will be subject to ordinary income tax. Tax laws are subject to change and you should consult a tax professional. Policy loans are not usually subject to income tax unless the policy is classified as a Modified Endowment Contract (MEC) under IRC Section 7702A. However, withdrawals or partial surrenders from a non-MEC policy are subject to income tax to the extent that the amount distributed exceeds the owner's cost basis in the policy.

So let's recap: In this scenario, you borrowed at 5%, and the money in the policy continued to earn 7%. This creates a 2% positive spread. (We'll explain more about Alternate Loans and Zero Wash Loans in Section I, Chapter 8.)

Remember, loans taken from your policy ARE NOT TAXED. Why? Because ever since the 1986 tax reform, taxpayers pay income tax on only three types of income (see Section 7702 of the Internal Revenue Code):

1. Earned income – This is money that you earn by working, including wages, salaries, and bonuses.
2. Passive income – This would be the type of income you receive from renting or leasing property.
3. Portfolio income – This comes in the form of interest and dividends.

Since loans on IUL LASER Funds are not earned, passive, or portfolio income, the money is yours, tax-free. Although the insurance company does not require you to pay back any loans during your lifetime (because any loan balances are cleared away when the death benefit is ultimately paid), you can pay back some or all of the loan if you choose.

In essence, any loan repayment is actually considered new cash put into policy. This allows tax-free interest on "new money" placed into a policy—even though it may have been once "maxed out." This is a brilliant strategy used by people who want to use the insurance policy as a working capital account, which we'll explain on the flip side of this book, in Section II, Chapter 4.

Tax Savings #3

As a "life insurance policy" increases in value due to competitive interest being earned, no taxes are due on that gain, as long as the policy remains in force. Many financial instruments, such as savings accounts, CDs, mutual funds, and money markets will typically have tax liability on their gain (see Section 72[e] of the Internal Revenue Code).

Tax Savings #4

Upon your death, the money in your insurance policy transfers to your heirs and beneficiaries completely income-tax-free (see Section 101[a] of the Internal Revenue Code).

HOW DOES WHOLE LIFE COMPARE TO THE LASER FUND?

We often get the question: how does Whole Life compare to The IUL LASER Fund? Like The IUL LASER Fund, Whole Life policies provide a safe place for you to set aside your money where it can grow tax-deferred. Also like The IUL LASER Fund, you can access your money through tax-free loans or tax-free withdrawals up to basis (and then pay taxes on any money taken out over and above basis), and your heirs will receive an income-tax-free death benefit upon your passing (the income-tax-free benefit applies to both state and federal income taxes).

As for differences, with Whole Life insurance you can receive dividends (which currently average 4% to 5%), and you can choose to reinvest your dividends into the policy to increase the cash value and death benefit. With The IUL LASER Fund, you don't receive dividends, but your policy can earn interest based upon index strategies (which have historically averaged 5% to 10%). And with multipliers, you can see potential averages of up to approximately 11% to 15%. So there are plenty of opportunities for growth with IUL LASER Funds (see Section I, Figure 6.4).

Whole Life policies also come with guarantees: a guaranteed cash value and a guaranteed death benefit amount. The IUL LASER Fund's cash value can vary, growing in market up-years and remaining static during down-years (based on your index performance, with the protection of a 0% floor during market downturns). The IUL LASER Fund's death benefit can increase due to policy performance and can decrease if there are any outstanding loans or if you make adjustments to your policy to save on costs.

The thing to keep in mind is that whenever a company builds guarantees into a financial vehicle, those guarantees come at a price. Generally, Whole Life policies are more expensive than comparable IUL LASER Funds. And even more challenging, Whole Life expenses and surrender charges are often not clearly disclosed, so you also have less transparency with Whole Life policies than IUL LASER Funds (see Section I, Chapter 9 for a look at the sheer transparency of expenses in IUL LASER Fund illustrations).

Whole Life policies also tend to be less flexible than IUL LASER Funds. Say you have a setback to your income while you are in the midst of funding your policy, and you cannot make your premium payment. You are expected to pay your Whole Life premium each year. If you don't make

that payment, the policy can lapse or go into what's called a non-forfeiture option (such as extended term insurance or a premium loan which allows you to take money out of cash value to pay the premium).

With The IUL LASER Fund, you have enormous flexibility when funding your policy. You can miss a year or two and catch up. Or say you're only able to fund it 50%, you can work with your IUL specialist to make adjustments, still enjoy tax-free access to the money in your policy, and pass along an income-tax-free death benefit to your beneficiaries.

When it comes to accessing money from your policy, the interest rate on Whole Life policy loans tends to be higher than the policy's interest crediting rate. To explain, let's say your Whole Life policy is currently earning 4% interest. You borrow $10,000 from your Whole Life policy. Loan rates are typically 1% to 2% higher than crediting rates, so you end up paying 5% or 6% on that $10,000.

If you do not repay that loan, over time this can create a situation where the policy loan is increasing faster than the cash value. If your policy does not have a Loan Protection Rider (which we will explain in more depth in the next chapter), this can cause the policy to lapse, which can be disastrous from a tax perspective.

We had a client, for example, who came to us after his Whole Life policy had lapsed. He told us that he had received a 1099 that year for $199,000 (which would have been the amount of cash value over and above what he paid in premiums). He did not have the cash on hand to pay the taxes, so not only did he no longer have a Whole Life policy, but he also had to get a home equity loan just to pay Uncle Sam.

Overall, Whole Life policies do have some merits, especially when compared to traditional financial vehicles that are at risk in the market, but they also have some limitations when compared to IUL LASER Funds. For example:

- Whole Life policies are typically more expensive than IUL LASER Funds.
- The loan features are not as favorable with Whole Life policies when compared to IUL LASER Funds. (This is why professionals who specialize in Whole Life policies rarely show policy illustrations with loans, because the tax-free loan income tends to be low.)

- Whole Life policies are not as flexible with delayed premium payments.
- Returns with Whole Life policies tend to be much lower than what IUL LASER Funds can average (refer to Section I, Chapter 6 information about the returns on IUL LASER Funds).

Make sure to explore your options carefully when deciding which financial vehicles you will include in your financial portfolio.

THE IUL LASER FUND – A STRONG FOUNDATION

In summary, during the four-plus collective decades that we have worked in the financial industry, we have not seen any other money accumulation vehicle that accumulates money totally tax-favored; then later allows you to access your money totally tax-free; and when you ultimately pass away, it can increase in value and transfers to your heirs totally income-tax-free.

As we'll explain in Section I, Chapter 14, we don't recommend that every dollar you set aside be in The IUL LASER Fund. Just know that large amounts of taxes can be reduced by including this type of insurance policy in your retirement portfolio—especially by making it your primary retirement planning strategy like thousands of other highly-successful, wealthy people.

We've covered the basics of what an IUL LASER Fund is and how it provides tax savings—in the next chapter we'll demonstrate how The IUL LASER Fund lives up to its name, providing superior liquidity, safety, and rate of return.

TOP 5 TAKEAWAYS

1. The IUL LASER Fund had its genesis in the 80s, when E.F. Hutton introduced Universal Life Insurance.

2. As more Americans turned to Universal Life, the government passed laws regulating the policies: the TEFRA/DEFRA tax citations determine the minimum death benefit based on policy specifics, and the TAMRA tax citation requires the maximum funding of the policy to be spread out typically over no fewer than five to seven years. With changes to the Section 7702 tax code in 2021, IUL LASER Funds have become even more cost-effective, allowing for an even lower death benefit (and thus lower fees).

3. Universal Life has come a long way since the 80s, with sophisticated policies that can offer even more compelling liquidity, safety, rates of return, and tax advantages, along with the income-tax-free death benefit and a variety of indexing strategies. We call this financial vehicle The IUL LASER Fund.

4. There may be situations where you would like many of the advantages of an IUL LASER Fund, but you want to fund the policy with a lump sum. If so, you can create a MEC, which can be a powerful way to transfer wealth to your heirs. Just be aware of the tax differences if you decide to access money from your policy.

5. When structured and funded properly, The IUL LASER Fund provides four key tax advantages: 1) after-tax contributions can help you save on taxes in the long run; 2) you can access money in your policy tax-free for everything from retirement income to working capital and more, 3) your money can grow in your policy on a tax-deferred basis, with no taxes on the gains; and 4) upon your passing, your money transfers to your heirs as an income-tax-free death benefit.

LASER Focus

We hear the term "laser-focused"—but what does it mean? It's often used to describe a person, a campaign, or an organization that has a sharp, specific goal or approach.

The phrase is based on the concept of the literal laser, a highly concentrated light traveling in a powerful beam. Laser light is different from regular light in a few important ways. White light (like that emanating from your desktop lamp) contains all different colors, with all different frequencies, traveling in a jumbled fashion. Visible laser light is strictly one color (often red or green), because it's all one frequency, coherent, with the crests of each wave aligned with each other.

We use lasers for everything from DVD players to bar code readers (those beeping wands at the grocery store), to manufacturing (clothes are often cut with lasers), and surgery (LASIK, anyone?). In this book, we call these policies The LASER Fund for more than just the reference to **Li**-quidity, **S**afety, and **R**ate of Return. (Remember, we use the terms IUL LASER Fund and LASER Fund interchangeably to represent a properly structured, maximum-funded Indexed Universal Life policy.)

We also use the term because it alludes to the laser focus this vehicle can provide in helping you move toward your financial goals, which may be income during retirement, or money to empower your family's

Legacy Bank and loved ones' worthwhile efforts, capital investments, or other objectives. Indeed, it can be a sound financial vehicle—made powerful by its knack for delivering those key elements of a prudent financial strategy. In this chapter, we'll explore how The IUL LASER Fund provides these critical elements, and how these qualities have benefited people in real-life situations.

L: LIQUIDITY

As we discussed in Section I, Chapter 4, liquidity is the ability to access your money when you need it. And while there are plenty of financial vehicles that offer liquidity, most of them have significant strings attached. On the other hand, with The IUL LASER Fund, liquidity is practically string-free. As long as your policy is structured and funded correctly—and you pull your money out correctly—you can access your money income-tax-free.

But that's the important part—pulling out your money *correctly.* We often teach that there are three ways to access your money from an IUL LASER Fund:

1. The Sad Way
2. The Dumb Way
3. The Smart Way

The Sad Way is simply … passing away. While we don't recommend it—it's one heck of a return. Humor aside, if by some misfortune you were to pass on after opening your IUL LASER Fund—even within one day of making your first payment—your beneficiaries would receive your death benefit, income-tax-free. And depending on when you pass away during the span of your policy, your death benefit can blossom a little, or a lot (as much as two to three times what you put into the policy). No matter what the amount, that money becomes instantly liquid to your beneficiaries to use as they see fit, income-tax-free.

As a side note, compare that to money you might have in an IRA or 401(k). When you pass away, the money in your 401(k) will go to your beneficiary—but so will the tax liabilities. Unless it's rolled over to an IRA, with most 401(k) plans, the money is paid out as a lump sum to the beneficiary no later than December 31 of the year following your

death—with income taxes due that same year. (Note, if your beneficiary is your spouse, she or he will have the option of keeping it in your name or rolling it over to her/his own 401[k], but will need to make mandatory withdrawals after age 72, which then become taxable income.) With any IRA or 401(k) that is inherited, your beneficiaries are responsible for taxes on the account, whereas with life insurance, your heirs will not pay any income taxes on the tax-free death benefit you pass on.

We've had clients who experienced this very contrast between these two types of financial vehicles. Tragically, the husband died in a boating accident—leaving behind his widow and their six children. He had about $63,000 in his 401(k), but after his wife paid taxes on it, she only netted about $40,000. He also had about $40,000 in his life insurance policy that was designed to accumulate $1 million for future retirement income. When he passed away, that $40,000 blossomed immediately into a $1 million income-tax-free death benefit, which allowed his widow to educate her children, fund their church missionary service, and live with dignity. She was definitely grateful they had decided to go beyond the 401(k) and open a life insurance policy as part of their financial portfolio.

There are a few **Dumb Ways** to access money from your IUL LASER Fund. The first would be to surrender your policy, which would trigger taxes on any gains your policy has earned. What's more, if you surrender the policy within the first ten years, you would pay surrender charges (unless you had specifically purchased a rider to waive surrender charges).

Another dumb way would be to "withdraw" more money than you've put in (your basis). Life insurance policies are taxed FIFO (meaning the first money you put in, is the first money you take out, and that's the money on which you're taxed). The second? Once it's fully funded, if you were to continue withdrawing money after recovering your basis (rather than borrowing it from the policy in the form of a loan), you would incur taxes, as well. Again, this is where it's critical to work with an IUL specialist who is experienced with IUL LASER Funds to ensure you're accessing your money correctly.

And how do you access it correctly? **The Smart Way**. By taking a loan on your policy. First, you never want to pull out more than 80% to 90% of your cash value. Your cash value is the actual amount that is liquid, and it's based on your accumulation value minus surrender charges, or penalties for early cancellation and any outstanding loan balances on

the policy. (This is another reason you want an IUL specialist who can help ensure you leave minimum balances required by the policy to avoid creating a taxable event or surrender charges.)

If you choose to take withdrawals up to the basis, it is tax-free. But after recovering your basis, the Smart Way to access your money would be to begin taking out tax-free loans. Otherwise, you will trigger unnecessary tax.

We typically do not recommend taking withdrawals up to your basis, because withdrawals are permanent, and you cannot put the money back into your policy. With a loan, however, you can always repay your loan by putting money back into your policy. Most people worry that because loans come with interest, that must mean they're a negative—but it's quite the opposite, as we'll illustrate below.

ZERO WASH LOANS VS. ALTERNATE LOANS

As we introduced in Section I, Chapter 5, loans are not due during the life of the policy. While you can choose to repay your loan, you can also decide not to—you simply need to keep the policy in force to avoid a taxable event. Should you decide not to repay your loan, any loan balances will be automatically paid off with the cash value / death benefit upon your passing.

Based on the insurance company you're using, loan provisions may slightly differ, but two common loan provisions are the Zero Wash Loan (also known as a Standard Loan or a Declared Rate Loan) and the Alternate Loan (which some companies call an Alternative Loan, Participating Loan, Indexed Loan, Variable Loan, or Spread Loan).

A Zero Wash Loan allows you to borrow money out of your policy at a fixed rate set by the insurance companies, typically 2% to 4%. (Remember every insurance company is slightly different with the rates charged and the features of each policy.)

Let's look at an example of a Zero Wash Loan. Let's say you have $1 million in cash value inside your policy. You would like to borrow $100,000. Since you don't want to do it the Dumb Way (by taking out withdrawals), you do it the Smart Way to keep it tax-free—you borrow the $100,000,

in this case as a Zero Wash Loan. Your loan is being charged a fixed interest rate of, let's say 3% in this example.

Since it's a loan and not a withdrawal, you still have $1 million in cash value inside your policy. But keep in mind, $100,000 of that $1 million is not earning indexed returns any longer. It is now working as the collateral for the loan, so it earns a different rate, and in this example, it is earning a fixed rate of 3%.

In summary, in this example, you have $1 million in cash value in your policy; $900,000 of that $1 million is earning the indexed returns (which average 5% to 10%); and the $100,000 that is acting as collateral is earning a fixed return of 3%. So the 3% charged in interest and the 3% earned in interest essentially becomes a zero wash, thus the name: Zero Wash Loan.

While you still have $1 million in cash value in your policy, you have a $100,000 debt as well, leaving you a net cash value of $900,000. As we've mentioned, this loan is not due until you die, at which point it would be paid off by your policy's cash value and death benefit before the remaining death benefit transfers income-tax-free to your heirs. (Of course, you may also choose to repay the loan at any time, thus adding money back into your policy that can go to work earning indexed returns, tax-free.)

Now let's compare Zero Wash Loans to Alternate Loans. With Alternate Loans, you borrow at a rate set by the insurance companies. This rate is often variable—for reference, it's currently around 4.4% to 5%. This rate also often has a cap of around 7.5% to 8%, which is the highest rate the insurance company would charge. Keep in mind, this rate would likely only go this high if the economy were experiencing a general environment of sky high interest rates—and on the reverse side, this would likely mean your indexed returns are earning much higher rates as well, helping offset the impact of your loan's interest rate.

Unlike Zero Wash Loans, with Alternate Loans, the cash value acting as collateral for the loan will continue to earn the indexed returns. This is a significant benefit, as it allows the full $1 million in cash value to continue to grow at your indexed return rate (rates that historically average around 5% to 10% tax-free).

As an example, let's say you have $1 million of cash value in your policy. You want to borrow $100,000 (which again, is the Smart Way, as it allows you to access your money tax-free).

Let's say the borrowing rate on your Alternate Loan is 5%. While $100,000 of your $1 million cash value is acting as collateral for the loan, the entire $1 million in cash value continues to earn the indexed returns (in this example, we'll say that's an average of 7%). This yields you an average positive spread of 2%.

This might not seem like much at first glance, but that 2% spread is on money you've borrowed. Over time, that spread can generate a lot more income than the Zero Wash Loan.

DIVING DEEPER INTO THE COMPARISON

Now let's say your goal with your IUL LASER Fund is to borrow money from your policy for annual income (which many of our clients do). Let's compare the two types of loans in this scenario (with a $1 million in cash value in the policy).

With the Zero Wash Loan, let's say your policy is earning average indexed returns of 7%. You could borrow around $70,000 of tax-free income per year at 3%, while the cash value that is collateral for that annual loan is earning 3%. This way you maintain that "zero wash" impact on your policy.

Compare that to an Alternate Loan, where your policy is earning that same average indexed return of 7%. You could borrow $100,000 per year at, say, 5%, and the cash value that is collateral for that annual loan continues to earn the indexed return of 7%. This way you create a 2% positive spread (by borrowing at 5%, with the cash value earning 7%).

This is a $30,000 a year difference in your annual tax-free income. Just think of what more you could do with $30,000 a year!

Now before you think Alternate Loans are the end-all, be-all, it's important to consider the risks to determine which type of loan is better for you.

Even though IUL LASER Funds have historically earned 5% to 10% in indexed returns, some years, they have earned 0% (due to market

volatility). With an Alternate Loan, it is possible that you could earn 0% to 4.9%. In years where you're seeing a 0% indexed return, your loan balance is still being charged 5% interest. In a year like this, you would see a negative 5% spread. Your policy will be fine as long as you have enough cash value working as collateral for your current loan balance. If you find yourself in a situation where your loan balance is almost the same as your cash value (for example, if your loan balance were $950,000 and your cash value is $1 million), your policy could be in danger of lapsing and triggering a taxable event. In this case, you would want to initiate your Loan Protection Rider to safeguard your policy from lapsing.

Basically, Zero Wash Loans provide a more conservative approach. However, most of our clients have opted for the Alternate Loans, because they feel the gains outweigh the risks. Keep in mind that you have flexibility—most insurance companies allow you to switch between the types of loans from year to year.

THE ADVANTAGE OF LOANS VS. TRADITIONAL RETIREMENT VEHICLES

People sometimes think that these loans are negative, because you have to pay interest to access money in your policy tax-free. And interest is always bad, right? Wrong. Not when you put interest to work for you. The light bulbs really come on when you consider that Alternate Loans have advantages over traditional retirement vehicles.

Not only is this approach tax-free when you access money in your policy for things like annual income, but your money is still in the policy earning interest. Contrast this with other financial vehicles, like a 401(k).

Let's say you want to withdraw $100,000 a year from your 401(k) for income. Not only will you pay income tax on that $100,000, that money is no longer in your 401(k) account earning interest. Your account value has decreased by that $100,000 withdrawal, and that cycle will continue each year you withdraw income.

To underscore the comparison: When you borrow $100,000 from your IUL LASER Fund using an Alternate Loan, not only can you access that money income tax-free, but that money is still in the account, with the opportunity to earn interest. As mentioned above, you're typically

borrowing at an average of 5%, but the money in the policy is still earning an average of 7%, giving you that powerful 2% spread.

You might be thinking, Wait, what if I take money out of a Roth IRA? Isn't that tax-free income? Yes, absolutely. But the advantages stop there. The money you take out is no longer in your Roth IRA. It can no longer go to work for you earning interest.

With The IUL LASER Fund, on the other hand, when you borrow money, it's still technically in your policy, able to earn interest. And you can pay the loan back, which only adds money back into your policy. With a Roth IRA, your annual contributions are limited (currently $6,000 under age 50, $7,000 age 50 or older). Thus, you could never repay the entire $100,000 into your Roth IRA in any given year.

Imagine borrowing $100,000 a year for many years, and then you receive a large inheritance or you sell a property. You have the option to throw that huge chunk of change back into your policy and pay back your loans. If you had a Roth IRA, you could only deposit $6,000 or $7,000 (depending on your age) back into your account.

HOW TO AVOID OVER-BORROWING & CAUSING YOUR POLICY TO LAPSE

Let's pause for a moment to discuss the importance of avoiding taking too much out of your policy—and the value of Loan Protection Riders.

Consider this: No one knows when they are going to die. No one wants to outlive their money. And most people want to leave money to their heirs. So how do you ensure your IUL LASER Fund lasts as long as you do? You want to avoid draining your policy too quickly by working with a qualified IUL specialist as you go.

But let's say you are living longer than anticipated, or the annual Alternate Loans you're taking for income are causing the net cash value (cash value net of your loan balance) to rapidly deplete. If you find that your loan balance is coming close to 95% of your accumulation value, you're in danger of your policy lapsing. Fortunately with IUL LASER Funds, there's a safety valve in place. It's called the Loan Protection Rider.

What's wrong with the policy lapsing? This would be like killing the goose that lays the golden eggs.

The minute your policy lapses, you would no longer have a tax-protected life insurance policy. "No life insurance" means no tax-deferred accumulation, no tax-free income, and no income-tax-free death benefit. You would owe taxes on all of your gains. As in a lot of taxes. And the worst part is, you would have probably already spent the money you borrowed.

So rather than your policy providing a regular income every year and a valuable income-tax-free death benefit to your heirs, you could run your policy into the ground AND owe Uncle Sam a lot of money.

To help you avoid inadvertently lapsing your policy, you can opt to include something called a Loan Protection Rider.

This rider is available if and when the loan balance equals or exceeds about 95% of the policy's cash value. It essentially protects the remaining account value as death benefit. This balance remains in place until you as the policyholder pass on, at which time it passes on to your heirs income-tax-free.

Keep in mind there are certain eligibility conditions policyholders must meet; there's a rider fee assessed once you implement it; and it's not automatically triggered—you do have to opt to use it once you're notified.

Of course, if you're working with IUL specialists who meet with you every year, you can avoid coming close to needing the Loan Protection Rider. But if you're working with someone who doesn't know enough to keep you from this kind of freefall? It could spell retirement disaster.

MORE ON IUL LASER FUND LOANS

Essentially, how you access your money could be the difference between liquidation and liquidity. Withdrawals can trigger partial surrender charges, taxes, and, if continued unchecked, could eventually deplete the money in your policy. By contrast, loans provide liquid access to your money throughout the life of the policy.

Remember IUL LASER Funds allow you to add lump sums into your policy to pay off loans. For example, let's say you're age 85 when your spouse passes, and you suddenly receive a lump sum of a $1 million income-tax-free death benefit. Not only are you grieving, but you've got to figure out how best to utilize this $1 million.

You'd love to open a new IUL LASER Fund to accommodate the million dollars. But you are suffering from health setbacks and can't qualify for a new policy. Now what about your existing IUL LASER Fund policy? It's been in place since you were age 60, when you easily qualified with good health. Could you use that policy for your million dollars? You wonder if it's possible, because you maximum funded it with $500,000 in the first five years. You know that once maximum-funded, the premium bucket of IUL LASER Fund policies can't be increased, so you worry that idea is a bust, too.

However, your IUL specialist explains to you that because you've been taking out loans over the past ten years, you have another option. When you take tax-free income in the form of loans from an IUL LASER Fund, you have the option of never repaying the loan during your lifetime (your loan balance and fees are deducted from the death benefit upon your passing), or you can repay the loans in part or full at any time. In this example, let's say you've been taking out loans of $100,000 a year in tax-free income on that policy. You can simply "repay" the $1 million in loans you've taken out with that $1 million lump sum you received from your spouse's income-tax-free death benefit.

Now that $1 million lump sum is tucked inside a financial vehicle that provides safety of principal, predictable rates of return, tax-deferred growth, the opportunity for tax-free income, and an income-tax-free death benefit to your posterity. This is much more advantageous than dumping the million into something like a mutual fund where you would be taxed on the distributions, and your heirs would have to pay taxes on any gains or dividends as it passes to them.

In summary, you can see how loans are a positive, not a negative. Whether you choose a Zero Wash Loan or an Alternate Loan, IUL LASER Funds give you the ability to borrow money tax-free. And if you go with Alternate Loans, you have the added advantage of arbitrage (earning a spread on the money you borrow). These are critical benefits that can empower you to move forward toward your financial and retirement goals.

LIQUIDITY FOR LIFE'S IMPORTANT MOMENTS

With our years of experience helping clients benefit from The IUL LASER Fund's advantages, we've seen its impact in real-life situations

time and again. The liquidity it offers can provide much-needed access to cash in a variety of situations.

Take a healthcare emergency, for example. We had a client, whom we'll call Beth, who put $200,000 into her policy and made an oath, "I will not touch this for twenty years."

Not long after, she was involved in a horrific car accident on a trip to California. Beth called from the hospital and said, "Remember I told you I wouldn't touch it for twenty years? I'm going to be in critical care for a while; I almost died. I need $120,000 right now to cover all of this medical care."

Doug said, "Beth, I'm so glad you survived! Okay, you need $120,000? No problem."

About five days later, she called to ask how long it would take to get that $120,000. Doug replied, "Oh, that's right, you're stuck in the hospital. You wouldn't know—it's probably already in your mail box." She called her son to check, and sure enough it was right there, in her mail box.

She couldn't believe it was that easy, and that it was income-tax-free. If her money had been in another type of vehicle, things would have been much more difficult. If she had invested that $200,000 in a piece of real estate, she would have had to put the property up for sale (which would have taken much longer than a few days to access for liquidity) and pay capital gains on any profit.

If she'd had her money in a 401(k), she could have had relatively quick access to her money, but she would have paid a 10% penalty for withdrawing her money before age 59½, and she would have owed income taxes on that $120,000 (and the additional income could push her into a higher tax bracket).

The IUL LASER Fund's ability to provide liquidity without taxes is huge—it can make a big difference in your overall financial well-being. Then there's also the fact that with an Alternate Loan, your money is still working for you, even when you take out a loan on your policy.

In this example Beth used an Alternate Loan, so technically, Beth's $120,000 was still IN the policy. She simply took out a loan, and the original $120,000 was acting as collateral for that loan. The $200,000

she had put into the account a few months earlier was still earning the current interest rate, say 7% on average. The $120,000 loan was being charged interest, say 5%. So let's say she was averaging 7% on $200,000; was being charged 5% on $120,000; then she she was averaging a 2% spread on that $120,000. All of her money was still at work in the account. Contrast that with other types of financial vehicles, where whatever she withdraws would be deducted from the account value and would no longer be capable of earning interest.

We had another client, whom we'll call Dave, who demonstrated the value of an IUL LASER Fund's liquidity for temporary income replacement. Dave was a partner in a medium-sized business that was looking to sell in the next year or two. To become more financially attractive to prospective buyers, the company was preparing to cut back on expenses. That meant part of Dave's salary was going to be reduced.

He knew when the sale went through he'd stand to make a large sum, but he needed a stop gap for the next twelve to twenty-four months. He had a daughter getting married, a healthy mortgage on a nice home, and plenty of other expenses.

Luckily for Dave, he had an IUL LASER Fund to turn to. He decided to take out Alternate Loans on his policy to make up for the lost income until the company sold. He knew his money in the policy would still be working for him, and once the company sold he could pay back the loan into his policy if he wanted to. He wouldn't miss a beat moving toward his goals for retirement—and he could enjoy income-tax-free access to his money to bridge the short-term income gap.

Aside from these big life-changing moments, you can also use an IUL LASER Fund for everyday situations—like buying a car. Say it's time to get a new car—you have your eye on a $50,000 beauty. Typically, people think they have two options: pay cash for it, or take out a loan and pay a significant amount in interest over the life of the loan.

The upside of using cash to buy it outright? You won't be paying interest on a loan. But the downside is you'll also be out $50,000 that could have gone toward your future, earning interest in a financial vehicle. Over the next thirty years, that $50,000 could have become as much as $350,000. So essentially, that car didn't cost you $50,000—it cost you $350,000.

What if instead you borrowed that $50,000 from your IUL LASER Fund with an Alternate Loan, and because the money is still technically in your IUL LASER Fund, it's still able to earn a spread? You can pay it back into the policy if you choose, that way your full $50,000 will be working for you. You'll have a car AND still benefit from your money having the opportunity to grow.

This is exactly how each of us has purchased cars, motorcycles, ATVs, and every other kind of vehicle you can imagine over the past several years—and it's proven to be an excellent way to get in motion (literally ... and financially).

S: SAFETY

Warren Buffett has two simple rules of investing. Rule number one: don't lose money. Rule number two: never forget rule number one. To avoid losing money, your financial vehicle should provide as much safety as possible.

In Chapter 4 of this section, we introduced two critical components of safety: 1) the safety of the financial institution you're entrusting with your money, and 2) the safety of your principal within your financial vehicle.

Let's start with the safety of the institution—how does The IUL LASER Fund fare on delivering on that component? It's virtually unparalleled. When you open an IUL LASER Fund, you're typically opening a policy with insurance companies that have been around since the 1800s.

During the Great Depression, more than 9,000 banks failed. Americans lost a total of $140 billion of their money deposited in banks in 1933 alone. What about the insurance industry? It fared relatively well. During the Great Recession, nearly 500 insured financial institutions failed—even titans like Lehman Brothers and Bear Stearns. But again, the insurance industry came through largely unscathed, with just eleven small insurance companies facing insolvency.

While nothing can ever be guaranteed against failure, if history says anything, it's fair to say that insurance companies are likely to be the

last of the dominoes to fall during major economic crises. They're the kind of institutions that can provide peace of mind when the financial winds start to howl.

Even with the industry's record for strength, it's important to note that not just any insurance company can provide the right combination of service and know-how to properly structure, fund, and manage an IUL LASER Fund policy properly. Often people—and even financial professionals—will assume they can open an IUL LASER Fund with just any insurance company, but that's simply not the case. Tier 2 and Tier 3 insurance companies are not up to the task. Out of thousands of companies, there are just a handful we recommend. They're Tier 1 companies, which means they have distinct qualifications, including:

- They are financially sound, with superior ratings.
- They maintain competitive internal costs, which helps policyholders make the most of their IUL LASER Funds for living benefits, as well as the death benefit.
- They have a good long-term track record in regard to cost structure (unlike other companies that have increased their cost of insurance or other fees on policies that are in force).
- They treat all policyholders well—offering improved features not just for new policies, but for those that have been in place for years.

As for safety of principal, The IUL LASER Fund delivers safety better than most financial vehicles. As discussed in Section I, Chapters 5 and 6, because your IUL LASER Fund is indexed, the money in your policy has the protection of at least a 0% floor—and zero is the hero. Your policy will not lose any money due to market volatility. As mentioned, even when the market took a nose dive in 2008 (with traditional accounts losing as much as 40%), our clients didn't lose any of their gains from 2007 or other previous years due to market volatility.

Keep in mind, however, when the markets drop that it's possible for your policy to go down in value due to policy charges. These are the fees that are required for the account to be classified as life insurance and provide tax-free income and a death benefit. These can include cost of insurance charges, asset based charges, premium charges, policy fees,

per unit charges, and rider charges. For example, while our clients' policy values didn't lose any value due to market volatility in 2008, they did go down slightly that year because of the policy charges.

In 2009 when the market started to revive, our clients' policies started making money again right away. How? Because of the annual reset on their policies. They didn't have to wait for the market to come back up to where it had been before the crash, like those with stocks, bonds, IRAs, and 401(k)s invested in the market had to do.

This brings up another component of safety, one that's rarely available in most common financial vehicles: the safety of your gains. With an IUL LASER Fund, you can benefit from a strategy called "lock-in and reset." During every one-year segment (or two years or five years, depending on the index strategies on your policy) that a gain is realized, that gain is locked in. The starting point for the next segment is then reset at endpoint of the previous segment.

For example, say your policy has $1 million in cash value at the start of the segment. During that segment it gains 5%. At the end of that cycle, your cash value is now $1,050,000, and that $50,000 gain is locked in. During the next segment, let's say the market goes down 20%. At the end of the segment, you would gain 0%. Your policy would incur some fees, but at least you would not lose any cash value due to market volatility. This is a powerful strategy that can help your money grow much faster in an IUL LASER Fund than other vehicles.

To explain this principle further, in Figure 8.1 we'll compare putting $100,000 into an IUL LASER Fund versus a market-based financial vehicle. We'll look at a ten-year period in which the market goes up 10% the first year, followed by a 10% decrease the next year, and the market continues that pattern of 10% fluctuation each year for the entire decade. In this example, we would have five 10% gain years and five 10% loss years.

Looking at The IUL LASER Fund, after a 10% gain in the first year, your $100,000 is worth $110,000. Remember with indexing, that gain becomes newly protected principal, and you reset for the next year. The following year, the market goes down 10%. With your floor of 0%, your $110,000 balance would remain the same. Your IUL LASER Fund resets at the beginning of the third year, during which the market goes up 10%. Your $110,000 balance then grows to $121,000.

FIGURE 8.1

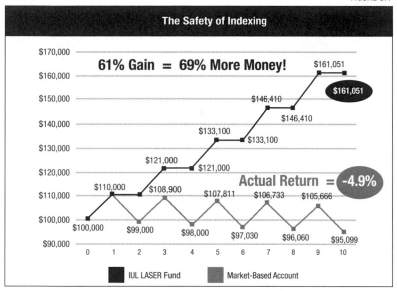

The Safety of Indexing

61% Gain = 69% More Money!

Actual Return = -4.9%

IUL LASER Fund   Market-Based Account

Let's compare this to having your money actually invested IN the market. After the first year, your balance is the same as the indexed policy: $110,000. However, during the next year when the market goes down 10% (10% of $110,000 is $11,000), you don't result in a net of zero. You find yourself below your beginning point: your account value is only worth $99,000. In the third year, your $99,000 balance earns 10% and comes back to a total of $108,900.

Remember, many financial professionals will tell you that if the market goes up 10%, down 10%, up 10%, down 10% you are experiencing a zero rate of return. However, as you have seen, when your money is invested directly in the market and your account value goes up 10% then down 10%, you lose some of your original principal. So at the end of this ten-year period, your $100,000 would only be worth $95,099. You would have actually experienced a 4.9% overall loss.

With indexing, each year that you made 10% you would have locked in that gain. So during your five gain years, you would have experienced a 10% increase. During each of the five loss years, you would not have earned anything, but you also would not have lost what you had made the year before due to market volatility. Look at the dramatic difference

in the result at the end of the decade. Using indexing, your final account balance would be $161,051, or a 61% overall gain, during that decade. Compare that to the 4.9% loss with your money *in* the market. By using indexing, you would have had 69% more money at the end of the decade than you would have had by having your money exposed in the market.

Looking back at real-life situations, many Americans who had IRAs and 401(k)s in the market suffered up to a 40% loss in 2008. That was followed by years of financial stress, as it took many of them until the year 2012 to return to a break-even point (to their pre-crash account values). By contrast, many of our clients were calm—they did not suffer those kinds of losses in 2008. What's more, during the next year, many locked in double-digit gains.

Whether you're setting money aside for retirement income, working capital, kids' education, or business ventures, that money is important. Protecting your money from unnecessary loss in the market can make the difference in reaching your objectives, or watching it all go up in smoke. This is why the safety provided by IUL LASER Funds is so critical.

SAFETY FROM THE STORM

If seeing is believing, then many of our clients became even more devoted believers of The IUL LASER Fund when the market melted down in 2008. For example, one couple we'll call the Hansens, had moved most of the money out of their 401(k) into an IUL LASER Fund through a strategic rollout prior to the market crash. While they didn't get all of it out before the downturn, they had transferred at least 90% of their money in the nick of time.

When the economy tanked, they watched the last 10% that was still in their 401(k) go up in smoke, and they couldn't believe how grateful they were that they'd been able to protect most of their money from the market inferno. Over the next several months, Mr. Hansen, who works in the healthcare industry, heard several colleagues complain about how much they lost in the market crash. While he felt badly for them, he couldn't help but breathe a sigh of relief. He told us, "I'm so glad I'm not dealing with that chaos right now."

Conversely, we have another client (we'll call Keith) who came to us *after* the crash, having just lost a significant amount of money. Keith had put

more than $3 million in a Real Estate Investment Trust, and when real estate took a nosedive in 2008 and 2009, he lost more than $2 million of that money. He was able to salvage about $600,000 and was looking for a much safer place to put it. We introduced him to The IUL LASER Fund.

Keith's IUL LASER Fund has been growing since, and it's currently valued at more than $1 million. He said, "I can't tell you how refreshing this is. I have confidence now that for the first time in my life, I know my money is safe. I can't lose it again due to another market crash—plus I have a death benefit along for the ride."

Just as Keith described, The IUL LASER Fund's indexing provides powerful safety—and confidence. As we've mentioned, thousands of people we've worked with not only weathered the Lost Decade—but actually thrived in it. When the market plummeted (twice, between 2000 and 2003, and again in 2008), their IUL LASER Funds didn't lose a dime due to market volatility. Many experienced double-digit gains over that ten-year period, with their financial futures looking as bright as ever. Similarly, our clients didn't lose anything due to market volatility during the 2020 pandemic.

R: RATE OF RETURN

When we presented rate of return in Section I, Chapter 4, we explained that the goal is to earn a **competitive rate of return** that historically has beaten inflation. And if your rate of return is under **tax-favorable circumstances**, you can dramatically increase not only the end result, but also the net spendable income available during your harvest years.

We also looked at predictability. Just as Deming proved the power of predictability in the manufacturing industry, predictability with the rate of return on your money can bring you greater peace of mind. It can help you look to achieving your future financial goals.

While nothing is guaranteed, gauging history can help you get a good idea of how likely your financial strategies are to yield the results you're aiming for. IUL LASER Funds have demonstrated a strong track record for predictable, solid rates of return. Here's a look at historical index performance for the NYSE Zebra Edge, provided by one of the insurance companies we recommend, with a 125% current participation rate, a 0% floor, and no cap guaranteed. (See Figure 8.2. Keep in mind past performance is not a prediction of future results.)

FIGURE 8.2

Index Strategy	Cap	Participation Rate	5 Years	10 Years	15 Years	20 Years
NYSE Zebra Edge	N/A	125%	9.11%	8.93%	8.02%	7.18%

Overall, when it comes to rate of return, you want a vehicle that can get you to your desired destination with the most predictability as possible. It's kind of like a cross-country road trip.

Do you want a vehicle that races ahead, speeding down the road some years, until (SLAM!) it hits the brakes and slows to a crawl? And if road conditions really go south, this kind of vehicle can send you backward, requiring you to make up the distance once things clear up? (This is like many traditional accounts, such as IRAs and 401[k]s invested in the market.)

Or would you rather have a vehicle that's more reliable, one you know that is likely to maintain a predictable average speed? And even if it encounters big traffic jams or bad weather, it will stay put until conditions improve and it can move forward again?

Traditional accounts tend to be like the first vehicle, and IUL LASER Funds can be like the second. Predictable rates of return are yet another reason The IUL LASER Fund has earned our esteem.

Keep in mind, your rate of return can get an extra boost from multipliers. As explained in Section I, Chapter 6, the historical returns for the last forty years could have been around 11% to 15% (see Section I, Figure 6.4). Don't forget these gains are tax-free. When compared to other retirement vehicles, it's hard to find another that can give you those kinds of gains, tax-free.

AT ANY RATE

When a client we'll call Tom Russo opened an IUL LASER Fund, he couldn't express how relieved he was. He explained that he had attended one of our seminars ten years earlier, and he was intrigued by the advantages of an IUL LASER Fund, particularly with indexing's ability to protect his money from losses due to market volatility.

He had invited his current financial professional to join him at the seminar, who was skeptical because he wasn't familiar with the strategies.

The professional eventually dissuaded Tom from opening a policy. He convinced Tom there was just no way he would want to be limited by average gains of 5% to 10% in an IUL LASER Fund, when he could have possible gains of 20% with his money directly in the market.

Well, Tom did experience some 20% gains in the coming years, but those years also included the economic storms between 2000 and 2008, when he lost 40% of his money, twice. His accounts were just returning to break-even when he decided to finally pull his money out of the market and put it in an IUL LASER Fund. He was looking forward to indexing, where he could enjoy the upside of the market, without the painful downsides. He told us he had learned the hard way, that he had repented, and that he was ready for predictable rates of return.

FLEXIBILITY FOR THE UNEXPECTED

In addition to liquidity, safety, rate of return, and tax advantages, another IUL LASER Fund advantage is flexibility. Life rarely follows down planned paths. Twists and turns often take us in unexpected directions, and that's when having a nimble financial vehicle can become critical.

One of our clients (we'll call Sarah) opened an IUL LASER Fund policy that she planned on funding up to $2 million. By the time Sarah had funded it halfway—up to $1 million—sadly, Alzheimer's began setting in. Because her life expectancy was now going to be shorter than anticipated, we worked with Sarah's family to minimum fund the account, rather than maximum fund it. Why? The death benefit became the primary objective instead of the secondary objective.

Her IUL LASER Fund goals went from having income during retirement to having the best death benefit possible for her heirs. This flexibility was crucial for her and her family, who could benefit from her income-tax-free death benefit when she passed on.

This would not have been possible if Sarah had been putting her money into a vehicle like an IRA. There would have been no death benefit attached, and while her family would have inherited the account, they likely would have lost a significant amount to taxes.

Flexibility also comes into play if you open an IUL LASER Fund policy, but hit a rough patch during the funding phase. While it's always best to

fully fund your policy within those first five years on average, there are times when our clients have had emergencies and had to take a temporary break from funding the policy.

If the setback occurs in the later years, say when the policy is funded 80%, as long as it's structured properly, the interest the policy is earning can typically cover the policy charges for a while. If the shortfall takes place earlier, say when it's only funded 20%, it's even possible to hit pause on making payments then. It does mean the policy value will be draining a bit—the insurance company will likely need to take a portion of the interest and principal to cover the policy charges—but at least you would have that flexibility to get through a tough time. And once your financial life is back on track, you can return to fully funding the policy, without having to give up on your financial goals.

If your money were in a different kind of vehicle, such as real estate, you wouldn't find yourself in as flexible a position. If you miss mortgage payments, the mortgage company doesn't say, "That's okay, you've made 80% of your payments so far, you can coast for a while. Don't bother paying every month." Nope, they'll likely get ready to foreclose.

As mentioned in Section I, Chapter 7, beginning in 2021 with the passage of H.R. 133, Section 7702 of the Internal Revenue Code was adjusted. Essentially, the change allows you to purchase less insurance than before. For example, before the bill passed, a male age 60 who wants to put $500,000 in to an IUL LASER Fund would have to purchase about $1.3 million of death benefit. After the bill, he would only have to purchase about $1 million of death benefit. This significantly reduces policy expenses and commissions, saving you money and giving you more flexibility.

JUST PLAIN SMART

Here's a question for you: what would you be willing to pay to hire some of THE best money managers in the world—money managers that have proven themselves for, say, over one hundred years?

That's exactly what you're getting with The IUL LASER Fund, for a fraction of what you would spend to be in premier managed money accounts. The life insurance companies we work with are among those who have

demonstrated financial strength, integrity, and acumen for more than a century. And all you're paying for are policy charges, which become relatively nominal over time. In this context, leveraging an IUL LASER Fund for your future is cost-effective, savvy money management, and it's just plain smart.

TOP 5 TAKEAWAYS

1. Get "LASER-focused" on your financial future by identifying strategies that can deliver as much liquidity, safety, rates of return, tax advantages—and flexibility—as possible.

2. The IUL LASER Fund offers superior liquidity via Zero Wash Loans and Alternate Loans, with the ability to access your money tax-free for a variety of reasons (retirement income, helping with education, business planning, etc.).

3. The IUL LASER Fund's safety is one of its most compelling advantages. With index strategies that provide a 0% floor, you will not lose anything due to market volatility, even during tumultuous economic times.

4. The IUL LASER Fund has historically offered competitive average rates of return of 5% to 10%, and multipliers could have historically boosted those rates to as high as around 11% to 15%. With indexing strategies, our clients' IUL LASER Funds have seen rates of return as high as 10.5% to 60% in one-year accounts, 19% to 41% in the two-year account (with a two-year return), or 60% to 110% in the five-year account (with a five-year return), depending on their index performance year-to-year (and that's without multipliers). And even when borrowing money from your policy, your cash value can continue to grow with an Alternate Loan.

5. The IUL LASER Fund's tax advantages are nearly unparalleled, with after-tax contributions, tax-deferred growth, tax-free access to money in the policy, and an income-tax-free death benefit for your heirs.

9

LASER Fund Scenarios

Seeing is understanding. Understanding—when put into action—is power. In this chapter, we'll give you the power of comprehending how The IUL LASER Fund's miracle solution applies in real life. (As a reminder, we use the terms IUL LASER Fund and LASER Fund interchangeably throughout the book.)

In the following examples, we'll examine how The IUL LASER Fund can be used in different ways, for different objectives:

- For a sixty-year-old non-smoker setting aside $500,000 over five years as a tax-advantaged way to grow wealth, then pass that wealth along to heirs, income-tax-free

- For a sixty-year-old non-smoker setting aside $500,000 over five years as a tax-advantaged way to grow wealth; provide annual tax-free income during retirement; and ultimately transfer money to heirs (income-tax-free)

- For a forty-year-old non-smoker setting aside just $24,000 a year for twenty-five years (for a total of $500,000) as a tax-advantaged way to grow wealth; provide annual tax-free income during retirement; and provide an income-tax-free death benefit for beneficiaries

- For a fifty-year-old non-smoker setting aside $500,000 over five years as a tax-advantaged way to grow wealth using high-impact multipliers; provide annual tax-free income during retirement; and provide an income-tax-free death benefit for beneficiaries someday

- For a seventy-year-old non-smoker setting aside $1,000,000 over five years as a tax-advantaged way to grow wealth; provide annual tax-free income during retirement; and ultimately transfer money to heirs (income-tax-free)

Note that while we are using examples of policies funded with $500,000 to $1,000,000, you can set aside more or less. On the lower end, we have clients who set aside as little as $50,000, $100,000 or $200,000 over the life of the policy.

Remember with these policies, you must demonstrate the need for the life insurance death benefit (for things such as income replacement, estate preservation, wealth transfer, etc.). As you read on, simply extrapolate the numbers and scenarios for your own financial circumstances. And please note these examples are based on theoretical scenarios and are not guarantees of future performance. Note that these illustrations have been created using a hypothetical Indexed Universal Life Simulator Calculator.[1]

---

[1] The IUL Simulator Calculator is an educational tool intended to help you understand how differing assumptions may affect the potential for index credits and theoretically an Indexed Universal Life Insurance policy's cash value. By using different floors, accounts, growth caps, participation rates, multipliers, and threshold rates through different historical market periods, the calculator can help you better determine what might be reasonable assumptions to use within a complete personalized illustration provided by an insurance company, within the guidelines set forth by the current National Association of Insurance Commissioners (NAIC) illustration regulations. The calculator is not intended to represent a specific insurer's IUL product or indexed account nor predict or guarantee actual or future results. This calculator is designed to help you better understand how the different accounts, cap rates, participation rates, threshold rates, floors, and multiplier rates and associated charges affect the potential credits in Indexed Universal Life insurance policies. By varying the percentage allocation of total assets in each account, the participation features (accounts, floors, threshold rates, growth caps, multipliers and participation rates) or by varying the calendar years presented you can see how aggregated growth rates would vary based on the performance of the S&P 500 index or other indexes as noted. The growth rates illustrated here are hypothetical and not representative of an Indexed Universal Life insurance policy, as they do not consider the actual insurance policy charges of any product. Please request a personalized basic life insurance illustration from your life insurance producer to help you understand an Indexed Universal Life policy. Policy fees and expenses vary by product, and some fees and expenses such as cost of insurance will vary according to the insured's age, sex distinct or unisex rates, smoking status, face amount and any applicable substandard rating. All charts/figures in this chapter are hypothetical and do not represent any insurance company or actual IUL product. This content is intended for educational use only. Please consult with a licensed IUL specialist to acquire actual illustrations from insurance companies.

DEFINITION OF TERMS

Before we dive into our examples, let's talk about the terms you'll see throughout this chapter. Here's a quick look at general usage:

- **Premiums** - Any money put into an insurance policy is considered a premium. (Some people think the word premium means "the policy costs and fees," but this is not correct. The premium is the after-tax money you actually put into the policy).

- **Policy Charges** - Includes all policy costs, such as premium charges, admin fees, expense charges, and cost of insurance.

- **Interest Rate** - The annual rate of return credited to the accumulation value of your policy at the end of each year, based upon the index return. (In most of this chapter's examples, we are using a gross average rate of return of 7.5%.)

- **Index Credit** - The dollar amount credited to your policy's accumulation value (based on the interest rate).

- **Interest Bonus** - Bonus interest credited to your policy, as defined in Section I, Chapter 6. This bonus interest differs based on the type of policy and insurance company.

- **Tax-Free Income via Policy Loans** - This refers to any loans you choose to take against your policy's cash value. In this chapter's illustrations, the policyholders are all taking Alternate Loans (see Section I, Chapter 8 for more details).

- **Policy Loan Balance** - This is the total loan balance of any and all loans you've taken over the life of the policy for tax-free income, including the loan interest.

- **Accumulation Value** - This term is essentially your policy's cash value balance. It includes premiums paid, minus any charges, plus interest earned.

- **Net Annual Accumulation Value Rate of Return** - This is the net rate of return in a given year after fees, index credit, and bonus. (See Figure 9.1 for an illustration of how this applies.)

- **Surrender Value** (aka Net Surrender Value or Cash Surrender Value) – This term is based on the accumulation value minus surrender charges (penalties for early cancellation), and any outstanding loan balances on the policy.

- **Death Benefit** – The amount paid out to beneficiaries in the event of your passing. This amount includes the surrender value, minus any outstanding policy loan balances.

- **Cash Value** – We don't include this term in our illustrations, but you'll hear the term used often in discussions about policies. Generally, cash value is used as: 1) as an umbrella term for the cash build-up in the policy, or 2) the net surrender value. Throughout this book, we've used the term cash value to refer to both accumulation value and/or surrender value, depending on context.

- **Internal Rate of Return** – This is the average rate of return you would have earned in a given year, retroactive to Day 1, net of all fees and expenses. IRR is used to show the true return, net of policy costs. Because the fees in an IUL LASER Fund are not a typical 1% to 2% a year, IRR is a way to quickly gauge the impact of policy costs. (See Figure 9.2 to see how this applies.)

MORE ON SURRENDER VALUE

It's important to understand surrender value, as it relates to how you access the money in your policy. As noted above, the surrender value is the accumulation value minus surrender charges (penalties for early cancellation), and any outstanding policy loan balances.

As discussed in Section I, Chapter 7, there are much smarter ways to access money in the policy than withdrawing money through a partial or full surrender. If done properly, for example, you could access around 80% to 90% of your surrender value in the form of a policy loan without surrendering or canceling the policy. (That 80% to 90% is the amount of money in the policy that's liquid.) Of course, a qualified IUL specialist can help you access your money in the best way possible.

As a side note on surrender charges: if you're not a fan of surrender charges, it may be helpful to know that they disappear after Year 10. However, before you're tempted to withdraw all of your money or cancel the policy after that time, be aware you would cause a taxable event, paying taxes on any gains above and beyond your initial premium payments. If potential surrender charges are something you want to avoid altogether, at the outset of your policy, some companies allow you to purchase a rider that waives all surrender charges from Day 1.

Let's pause for a moment to reiterate that IUL LASER Funds are designed as long-term financial vehicles, not short-term like CDs or money markets. The benefits of this vehicle are arguably unparalleled if you fund it and structure it properly over time. But if you're in a situation where you're looking for short-term financial strategies, it would be wise to choose another type of vehicle.

SURRENDER VALUE & DEATH BENEFIT OVER TIME

As you look at the surrender value and death benefit over time, you'll notice the death benefit is higher than the surrender value. That difference is necessary for the policy to be classified as life insurance. The difference between the surrender value and the death benefit is the net amount of insurance risk. Watch how this plays out in the following examples.

The death benefit will always be slightly higher than the surrender value, until age 96. At age 96, the tax code allows the surrender value and the death benefit to be the same (some companies follow this pattern, others choose to keep a small difference between the two). Your policy is still considered life insurance so it will still transfer income-tax-free upon your passing, but there is no longer any insurance risk because the surrender value and death benefit value equal one another. And remember the surrender value is already included in the death benefit.

STARTING AN IUL LASER FUND AT AGE 60 WITH NO INCOME TAKEN

In our first example (see Figure 9.1), we'll call our insured Larry. Here are the details:

- **Insured's description**: Larry is a sixty-year-old non-smoker.

- **Size of policy**: He's looking to put away $500,000 (after-tax money).

- **Required amount of insurance**: The required amount of insurance for Larry is nearly $930,000. (As mentioned, this amount is based on the desire to put in $500,000 at his age and gender. This amount could be slightly higher or lower, depending on the insurance company.)

- **Planned annual premiums**: He'll pay $100,000 a year, every year for five years until the policy is fully funded at $500,000 (to comply with TAMRA, as explained in Section I, Chapter 7).

- **Assumed average annual interest rate**: Based on historical rates, we'll assume the policy is earning an average gross annual interest rate of 7.5%.

- **Interest bonus**: This policy provides an interest bonus of thirty basis points starting in Year 11. (Thirty basis points would be 0.3% of the surrender value.)

- **Indexing strategy**: Larry wants to diversify his approach amongst the volatility control indexed accounts, which have historically averaged 6% to 10.5%. In this illustration, we'll assume his policy is earning an average of 7.5%. (Please refer to Section I, Chapter 6, for a refresher on volatility control indexed accounts.)

- **IUL LASER Fund objective**: Larry wants to use his IUL LASER Fund for a safe repository for his money, where it can grow tax-deferred and pass on someday as a robust, income-tax-free death benefit to his beneficiaries.

FIGURE 9.1

End of Year	Age	Premium	Policy Charges	Index Credit	Interest Bonus	Tax-Free Income via Policy Loans	Policy Loan Balance	Accumulation Value	Net Annual Accumulation Value Rate of Return	Surrender Value	Death Benefit
1	60	$100,000	$16,495	$6,627	-	-	-	$90,131	-9.87%	$60,753	$928,472
2	61	$100,000	$14,499	$13,536	-	-	-	$189,169	-5.42%	$159,609	$928,472
3	62	$100,000	$14,881	$20,952	-	-	-	$295,240	-1.59%	$264,357	$928,472
4	63	$100,000	$14,902	$28,906	-	-	-	$409,244	2.31%	$373,452	$928,472
5	64	$100,000	$14,877	$37,458	-	-	-	$531,825	4.43%	$493,761	$928,472
6	65	-	$8,829	$39,603	-	-	-	$562,598	5.79%	$530,589	$928,472
7	66	-	$8,952	$41,907	-	-	-	$595,552	5.86%	$569,715	$928,472
8	67	-	$8,994	$44,377	-	-	-	$630,935	5.94%	$611,380	$928,472
9	68	-	$9,008	$47,030	-	-	-	$668,958	6.03%	$655,805	$928,472
10	69	-	$9,020	$49,882	-	-	-	$709,820	6.11%	$703,184	$928,472
11	70	-	$1,611	$53,185	$2,110	-	-	$763,503	7.56%	$763,503	$928,472
12	71	-	$1,387	$57,218	$2,291	-	-	$821,625	7.61%	$821,625	$944,869
13	72	-	$620	$61,602	$2,465	-	-	$885,072	7.72%	$885,072	$1,000,131
14	73	-	$587	$66,362	$2,655	-	-	$953,502	7.73%	$953,502	$1,058,387
15	74	-	$550	$71,495	$2,861	-	-	$1,027,307	7.74%	$1,027,307	$1,119,765
16	75	-	$512	$77,032	$3,082	-	-	$1,106,908	7.75%	$1,106,908	$1,184,392
17	76	-	$464	$83,003	$3,321	-	-	$1,192,768	7.76%	$1,192,768	$1,252,407
18	77	-	$393	$89,445	$3,578	-	-	$1,285,398	7.77%	$1,285,398	$1,349,668
19	78	-	$424	$96,391	$3,856	-	-	$1,385,222	7.77%	$1,385,222	$1,454,484
20	79	-	$461	$103,877	$4,156	-	-	$1,492,794	7.77%	$1,492,794	$1,567,434
21	80	-	$507	$111,943	$4,478	-	-	$1,608,708	7.76%	$1,608,708	$1,689,144
22	81	-	$572	$120,635	$4,826	-	-	$1,733,597	7.76%	$1,733,597	$1,820,277
23	82	-	$645	$129,999	$5,201	-	-	$1,868,152	7.76%	$1,868,152	$1,961,559
24	83	-	$715	$140,088	$5,604	-	-	$2,013,129	7.76%	$2,013,129	$2,113,786
25	84	-	$822	$150,958	$6,039	-	-	$2,169,305	7.76%	$2,169,305	$2,277,770
26	85	-	$961	$162,667	$6,508	-	-	$2,337,519	7.75%	$2,337,519	$2,454,395
27	86	-	$1,149	$175,277	$7,013	-	-	$2,518,660	7.75%	$2,518,660	$2,644,593
28	87	-	$1,392	$188,855	$7,556	-	-	$2,713,678	7.74%	$2,713,678	$2,849,362
29	88	-	$1,679	$203,472	$8,141	-	-	$2,923,612	7.74%	$2,923,612	$3,069,793
30	89	-	$2,095	$219,203	$8,771	-	-	$3,149,492	7.73%	$3,149,492	$3,306,966
31	90	-	$2,625	$236,127	$9,448	-	-	$3,392,443	7.71%	$3,392,443	$3,562,065
32	91	-	$3,189	$254,331	$10,177	-	-	$3,653,761	7.70%	$3,653,761	$3,836,449
33	92	-	$3,981	$273,904	$10,961	-	-	$3,934,645	7.69%	$3,934,645	$4,092,030
34	93	-	$3,987	$294,970	$11,804	-	-	$4,237,432	7.70%	$4,237,432	$4,364,555
35	94	-	$3,598	$317,692	$12,712	-	-	$4,564,238	7.71%	$4,564,238	$4,655,523
36	95	-	$2,703	$342,231	$13,693	-	-	$4,917,458	7.74%	$4,917,458	$4,966,633
37	96	-	$1,461	$368,762	$14,752	-	-	$5,299,512	7.77%	$5,299,512	$5,299,512
38	97	-	$120	$397,460	$15,899	-	-	$5,712,750	7.80%	$5,712,750	$5,712,750
39	98	-	$120	$428,452	$17,138	-	-	$6,158,221	7.80%	$6,158,221	$6,158,221
40	99	-	$120	$461,863	$18,475	-	-	$6,638,438	7.80%	$6,638,438	$6,638,438
41	100	-	$120	$497,879	$19,915	-	-	$7,156,112	7.80%	$7,156,112	$7,156,112

On the row for Year 1, under the premium column, you can see that Larry put his first $100,000 into his policy. This is like leasing out the first floor of that apartment building we discussed in Section I, Chapter 5.

In the next column (policy charges), his Year 1 fees total $16,495. As we mentioned, policy charges include all policy costs, such as premium charges, admin fees, expense charges, and cost of insurance. Let's pause for a moment to look at the general trends for policy charges. While your IUL specialist can provide a detailed breakdown of fees over time for your age and the size of your policy, we want to give you a little preview here.

Policy charges are most expensive during the first five years. From Year 6 on, part of those charges—the premium charges—disappear (because you're no longer paying premiums into the policy).

Starting in Year 11, you'll see another drop in fees because some of the expense charges go away.

Now look further down Larry's illustration—at around Year 19, you'll see as he gets older, the policy charges start to increase again. Why is this? It has to do with the increasing risk of death as policyholders get older.

Let's look specifically at Larry's illustration at Year 21 (age 80). The cost of insurance at that time is $507. This charge pays for the net amount of insurance risk that is currently present. How is that risk calculated? By looking at the difference between: 1) the death benefit and 2) the surrender value (because the surrender value is already part of the death benefit).

So in Larry's case, the death benefit is $1,689,144, and his surrender value is $1,608,708. Doing the math, Larry's net amount at risk is $80,436. Keep in mind, the insurance company is not charging for $1,689,144 of insurance; they are charging for the net amount at risk.

With the net amount at risk for Larry's policy at age 80 being $80,436, Larry's policy is costing him just $507. To help cover that cost, in that same year Larry has $1,608,708 of accumulation value, and his policy earns $111,943 of index credit and $4,478 of interest bonus. Plus, don't forget those policy gains are tax-free.

(As a side note, you'll notice throughout the book that we refer to gains inside IUL LASER Funds as tax-deferred or tax-free. We use both of these terms, based on the assumption that policyholders will access their money the smart way—via loans—versus the dumb way—via withdrawals, or they will avoid creating a MEC. Please see Section I, Chapters 7 and 8 for more details).

Back to Larry's example, if he were to pass away at age 80, his heirs would receive a death benefit of $1,689,144, income-tax-free.

Looking at policy charges, in this particular illustration, you'll see the cost of insurance peaks at age 93 (since the risk of passing away continues to increase as Larry heads into his 90s). Notice that at age 96, there are still $1,461 in charges, and at age 97 those drop to $120, where they'll stay for the rest of the policy. Why is this?

By the end of age 96, going into age 97, the tax codes allow the surrender value and the death benefit to be the same. At this point, Larry is just paying for the administration fee; he's no longer paying for the cost of insurance. This policy design is common for many insurance companies—however as you'll see in Figure 9.5, some policy designs show continued fees up to age 100 and beyond.

According to the tax codes, your policy is still classified as life insurance and still transfers to your heirs income-tax-free, but the surrender value and death benefit will be the same all the way through the end of the policy (policies typically end at age 120—for brevity, in Larry's example we're only showing to age 100).

Let's look more closely at how index credit works. If you recall, index credit is the interest credited to the policy, based on the indexing strategy returns. In Larry's illustration, we're using an annual interest rate of 7.5%. In Year 1, it might be easy to assume that on the $100,000 Larry put into the policy, he would earn $7,500 ($100,000 multiplied by 7.5%). But keep in mind that policy charges impact how index credit is calculated.

When policyholders put in their premiums, the insurance company pays interest based on the average balance of the accumulation value throughout the year, with most fees applied monthly. For example, when Larry puts in $100,000 at the start of Year 1, the premium charge is deducted immediately. Over the course of the year, the rest of the charges are deducted monthly, for a total of $16,495. The insurance company pays 7.5% on the average balance of the accumulation value for that year, which comes to $6,627 for Year 1.

Notice that in Year 2, the index credit is $13,536, which is about $1,000 less than the policy charges of $14,499. In Year 3, the index credit is $20,952, and the policy charges are $14,881. Skip to Year 6, and you can see this trend continue: the index credit is $39,603, and the policy charges are $8,829.

Now look at Year 11, when the index credit is $53,185, and the policy charges are down to $1,611. Jump ahead to Year 21, when Larry is age 80, the index credit is $111,943, and the policy charges are only $507.

Keep in mind these gains are tax-free—imagine if Larry had to pay taxes on that $111,943! In a 30% federal and state combined tax bracket, Larry would have to pay $33,583. But because Larry's money is in an IUL LASER Fund rather than a taxable account, he gets to enjoy all of his annual gains tax-free.

Finally, let's examine the interest bonus. In Larry's example, the interest bonus starts in Year 11 (which is typical for most IUL LASER Funds). In this illustration, we're using a 0.3% interest bonus. The insurance company multiplies the surrender value by the interest bonus percentage each year moving forward for the life of the policy. You'll notice, the interest bonus is valuable in that it can often completely offset the policy charges. For example, look at Year 21 when Larry is age 80. The interest bonus is $4,478, compared to policy charges of $507.

You'll notice the next two columns in Larry's illustration, tax-free income via policy loans and policy loan balances, show $0. While Larry could borrow from his policy, in this example, Larry chooses not to do so. He wants to use this policy as a safe place for his money to grow and pass it along income-tax-free to his heirs. (In other examples in this chapter, you'll see how policy loans impact the illustration.)

Now let's look at the accumulation value, which is the current account value, minus policy charges, plus the index credit and interest bonus. In Year 1, Larry's accumulation value is $90,131 (which is $100,000 minus $16,495 of policy charges, plus the index credit of $6,627).

Look at Year 4, where Larry's accumulation value is $409,244. Larry has put in a total of $400,000 at this point, so he's essentially broken even by Year 4. Most policies break even around Year 3 through Year 8, based upon individual policy charges and index credits the first few years.

Notice in Year 10, Larry's accumulation value is $709,820, which is over $200,000 more than he put into the policy. By Year 30, Larry's accumulation value is upwards of $3 million—pretty impressive considering he only put in $500,000, and all of those gains have occured tax-free.

With a gross return of 7.5%, the next column, net annual accumulation value rate of return, shows the actual net return, net of fees, index

credit, and interest bonus for each year. For example, in Year 1, we see a -9.87% net annual accumulation value rate of return. This is because after Larry put in $100,000 that year, his accumulation value is $90,131 (after all the costs and interest are applied).

Now let's jump ahead to Year 9 (age 68), where the net annual accumulation value rate of return is 6.03%. That year, Larry's accumulation value is $668,958, which means his 7.5% gross rate of return was really a net of 6%, after the fees of $9,008 and the interest of $47,030.

You'll notice from Year 11 on, the net annual accumulation value rate of return is above 7.5%. How is this possible when we've stated the gross return is 7.5%? For one, the fees drop to an extremely low level after the initial ten years. And Larry is also benefiting from an annual interest bonus. These two benefits put him above the 7.5% gross rate of return throughout the rest of his policy years. (Another advantage of IUL LASER Funds? The growth is tax-free, whereas with managed accounts, the growth is taxable.)

The next column, the surrender value, is the accumulation value minus any surrender charges (which apply the first ten years for most policies) and minus the loan balance. In Year 1, you'll notice the difference between the accumulation value and surrender value is about $30,000. By Year 10, the difference is only $6,636. Larry's surrender charges decrease each year until Year 11, when they disappear.

Also, you can think of the surrender value as the liquidity value—the amount you would receive should you need to close the policy for any reason. That said, should you need to access the money in your policy, we can't stress enough the importance of working with an IUL specialist to access your money the smart way via loans, versus withdrawing money directly or worse, canceling the policy. Most insurance companies allow you to access 80% to 90% of the surrender value via loans, even in the early years.

Look ahead to Year 30, when Larry has over $3.1 million in surrender value. If Larry needed to access this money, even at this point he would want to do so via loans, rather than withdrawing money or canceling the policy. If he were to cancel the policy, he would pay taxes on roughly $2.6 million ($3.1 million minus the $500,000 after-tax money he put into the policy).

Now let's look at the last column, the death benefit. You'll notice in Year 1 the death benefit is $928,472. This amount would be paid out to your heirs income-tax-free if you passed away (even if you were to pass away during Year 1). In Year 12, you'll see Larry's death benefit start to increase automatically as the cash value grows (based on Larry's average rate of return of 7.5%).

For example, at age 85, Larry's surrender value is $2,337,519, and his death benefit is $2,454,395. If Larry were to pass away at age 85, since the surrender value is already included in the death benefit, his heirs would get the death benefit of $2,454,395.

You'll notice if he passes away at, say age 98, Larry would leave behind $6,158,221 that will pass along income-tax-free to his heirs.

Now let's look at Figure 9.2 to understand more about the internal rate of return. As noted above, IRR is the average rate of return you would have earned in a given year, retroactive to Day 1, net of all fees and expenses.

We use IRR to assess the true return, net of policy costs. Because the fees in an IUL LASER Fund are not a typical 1% to 2% a year, IRR is a way to quickly gauge the impact of policy costs. Many times we'll look at a span of the first thirty years to see the true net cost of an IUL LASER Fund (because the IRR tends to level off from that point forward).

It's helpful to look at how IRR applies to both the accumulation value and death benefit—to do so let's look at Figure 9.2, Year 1. The accumulation value IRR is -10.4%, due to the accumulation value of $90,131, after policy charges and interest are applied to the $100,000 Larry has put in that year). While that may seem like a negative, look at how the death benefit counterbalances things: That same year, the death benefit IRR is 828.5%.

To expound, if Larry were to pass away in Year 1, he would have only put in $100,000. That $100,000 would blossom in value to a death benefit of $928,472 income-tax-free, which is a return of 828.5%. (Keep in mind, an IUL LASER Fund is designed to be a long-term financial vehicle, but if by misfortune you pass away within the first ten years, the death benefit IRR is very high, which can be a comfort to your loved ones.)

So let's start by focusing on Year 30, where the accumulation value IRR is 6.5%. When you recall that our gross return in this example is 7.5%,

and our accumulation value IRR is 6.5%, the difference of 1% is the true net cost, averaged over the thirty years.

To explain, this shows that on average, the fees were 1% on average over the last thirty years. But in reality, as you saw in Figure 9.1, the fees are much higher in the beginning and much lower after Year 10. For example, compare this to the net annual accumulation value rate of return in Figure 9.1 for Year 30: 7.73%. That is the net return for that particular year, but the accumulation value IRR of 6.5% is the net return average over the last thirty years.

What about the death benefit IRR at Year 30? You'll see it's slightly higher (6.7%) than the accumulation value IRR (6.5%). So let's say Larry were to pass away at Year 30, his beneficiaries would receive the income-tax-free death benefit of $3,306,966, which is an IRR of 6.7% income-tax-free. With the gross return of 7.5%, this means his true net cost at that point is 0.8% average every year.

Now what if you're curious about the true net cost by, say, Year 20? Look at Figure 9.2, Year 20, where you'll see the accumulation value IRR is 6%. Since our gross return is 7.5% and the accumulation value IRR is 6% income-tax-free, the true net cost at that point is 1.5%. Larry's death benefit IRR is 6.3% income-tax-free, which means if he were to pass away that year, his true net cost would be 1.2%.

[FIGURE 9.2 ON FOLLOWING PAGE]

FIGURE 9.2

End of Year	Age	Premium	Accumulation Value	Surrender Value	Death Benefit	Accumulation Value Internal Rate of Return	Death Benefit Internal Rate of Return
1	60	$100,000	$90,131	$60,753	$928,472	-10.4%	828.5%
2	61	$100,000	$189,169	$159,609	$928,472	-3.8%	158.8%
3	62	$100,000	$295,240	$264,357	$928,472	-0.9%	68.3%
4	63	$100,000	$409,244	$373,452	$928,472	0.9%	36.7%
5	64	$100,000	$531,825	$493,761	$928,472	2.0%	19.5%
6	65	-	$562,598	$530,589	$928,472	2.9%	15.0%
7	66	-	$595,552	$569,715	$928,472	3.4%	12.1%
8	67	-	$630,935	$611,380	$928,472	3.8%	10.1%
9	68	-	$668,958	$655,805	$928,472	4.1%	8.7%
10	69	-	$709,820	$703,184	$928,472	4.3%	7.6%
11	70	-	$763,503	$763,503	$928,472	4.6%	6.8%
12	71	-	$821,625	$821,625	$944,869	4.9%	6.3%
13	72	-	$885,072	$885,072	$1,000,131	5.1%	6.2%
14	73	-	$953,502	$953,502	$1,058,387	5.3%	6.2%
15	74	-	$1,027,307	$1,027,307	$1,119,765	5.5%	6.1%
16	75	-	$1,106,908	$1,106,908	$1,184,392	5.6%	6.1%
17	76	-	$1,192,768	$1,192,768	$1,252,407	5.7%	6.1%
18	77	-	$1,285,398	$1,285,398	$1,349,668	5.8%	6.1%
19	78	-	$1,385,222	$1,385,222	$1,454,484	5.9%	6.2%
20	79	-	$1,492,794	$1,492,794	$1,567,434	6.0%	6.3%
21	80	-	$1,608,708	$1,608,708	$1,689,144	6.1%	6.4%
22	81	-	$1,733,597	$1,733,597	$1,820,277	6.2%	6.4%
23	82	-	$1,868,152	$1,868,152	$1,961,559	6.2%	6.5%
24	83	-	$2,013,129	$2,013,129	$2,113,786	6.3%	6.5%
25	84	-	$2,169,305	$2,169,305	$2,277,770	6.3%	6.5%
26	85	-	$2,337,519	$2,337,519	$2,454,395	6.4%	6.6%
27	86	-	$2,518,660	$2,518,660	$2,644,593	6.4%	6.6%
28	87	-	$2,713,678	$2,713,678	$2,849,362	6.5%	6.6%
29	88	-	$2,923,612	$2,923,612	$3,069,793	6.5%	6.7%
30	89	-	$3,149,492	$3,149,492	$3,306,966	6.5%	6.7%

Through Larry's illustration, you can see the many advantages of IUL LASER Funds:

- The index credit and interest bonus quickly offset policy charges, making this a cost-effective financial vehicle.
- You're protected by a 0% floor, which means that even in market downturns, you'll never see a negative index credit due to market volatility.
- All policy gains occur tax-free inside the policy.
- Your heirs will receive your death benefit income-tax-free, passing along a powerful financial legacy.

STARTING AN IUL LASER FUND AT AGE 60 WITH TAX-FREE ANNUAL INCOME

Now how would a similar IUL LASER Fund perform if someone wanted to take out regular, annual loans to use as income during retirement? Let's see how that would work, with a man we'll call John (see Figure 9.3). His scenario mirrors Larry's example, but this time we'll look at the impact of taking out tax-free income via loans.

- **Insured's description**: John is a sixty-year-old non-smoker.

- **Size of policy**: He's looking to put away $500,000 (after-tax money).

- **Required amount of insurance**: The required amount of insurance for John is about $930,000. (As mentioned, this amount is based on the desire to put in $500,000 at his age and gender. This amount could be slightly higher or lower, depending on the insurance company.)

- **Planned annual premiums**: He'll pay $100,000 a year, every year for five years until the policy is fully funded at $500,000 (to comply with TAMRA, as explained in Section I, Chapter 7).

- **Assumed average annual interest rate**: Based on historical rates, we'll assume the policy is earning an average gross annual interest rate of 7.5%.

- **Interest bonus**: This policy provides an interest bonus of thirty basis points starting in Year 11. (Thirty basis points would be 0.3% of the surrender value.)

- **Indexing strategy**: John wants to diversify his approach amongst the volatility control indexed accounts, which have historically averaged 6% to 10.5%. In this illustration, we'll assume his policy is earning an average of 7.5%. (Please refer to Section I, Chapter 6, for a refresher on volatility control indexed accounts.)

- **IUL LASER Fund objective**: John wants to set aside his money to provide annual tax-free income during retirement and to provide an income-tax-free death benefit for his beneficiaries someday.

FIGURE 9.3

End of Year	Age	Premium	Policy Charges	Index Credit	Interest Bonus	Tax-Free Income via Policy Loans	Policy Loan Balance	Accumulation Value	Surrender Value	Death Benefit
1	60	$100,000	$16,495	$6,627	-	-	-	$90,131	$60,753	$928,472
2	61	$100,000	$14,499	$13,536	-	-	-	$189,169	$159,609	$928,472
3	62	$100,000	$14,881	$20,952	-	-	-	$295,240	$264,357	$928,472
4	63	$100,000	$14,902	$28,906	-	-	-	$409,244	$373,452	$928,472
5	64	$100,000	$14,877	$37,458	-	-	-	$531,825	$493,761	$928,472
6	65	-	$8,829	$39,603	-	$50,634	$53,166	$562,598	$477,423	$875,307
7	66	-	$8,952	$41,907	-	$50,634	$108,989	$595,552	$460,725	$819,483
8	67	-	$8,994	$44,377	-	$50,634	$167,604	$630,935	$443,776	$760,868
9	68	-	$9,008	$47,030	-	$50,634	$229,150	$668,958	$426,655	$699,322
10	69	-	$9,020	$49,882	-	$50,634	$293,773	$709,820	$409,411	$634,699
11	70	-	$1,611	$53,185	$1,228	$50,634	$361,627	$762,621	$400,994	$566,845
12	71	-	$1,387	$57,152	$1,203	$50,634	$432,874	$819,590	$386,716	$444,723
13	72	-	$620	$61,449	$1,160	$50,634	$507,683	$881,580	$373,896	$422,503
14	73	-	$587	$66,100	$1,122	$50,634	$586,233	$948,214	$361,981	$401,799
15	74	-	$550	$71,098	$1,086	$50,634	$668,710	$1,019,848	$351,138	$382,740
16	75	-	$512	$76,472	$1,053	$50,634	$755,311	$1,096,861	$341,550	$365,458
17	76	-	$464	$82,250	$1,025	$50,634	$846,242	$1,179,672	$333,429	$350,101
18	77	-	$393	$88,463	$1,000	$50,634	$941,720	$1,268,742	$327,022	$343,373
19	78	-	$424	$95,142	$981	$50,634	$1,041,972	$1,364,441	$322,470	$338,593
20	79	-	$461	$102,318	$967	$50,634	$1,147,236	$1,467,266	$320,030	$336,032
21	80	-	$507	$110,029	$960	$50,634	$1,257,763	$1,577,748	$319,985	$335,984
22	81	-	$572	$118,313	$960	$50,634	$1,373,817	$1,696,448	$322,632	$338,763
23	82	-	$645	$127,213	$968	$50,634	$1,495,673	$1,823,984	$328,311	$344,726
24	83	-	$715	$136,776	$985	$50,634	$1,623,622	$1,961,029	$337,407	$354,277
25	84	-	$822	$147,051	$1,012	$50,634	$1,757,969	$2,108,270	$350,301	$367,816
26	85	-	$961	$158,089	$1,051	$50,634	$1,899,033	$2,266,450	$367,417	$385,788
27	86	-	$1,149	$169,947	$1,102	$50,634	$2,047,150	$2,436,350	$389,200	$408,660
28	87	-	$1,392	$182,681	$1,168	$50,634	$2,202,673	$2,618,807	$416,134	$436,940
29	88	-	$1,679	$196,356	$1,248	$50,634	$2,365,972	$2,814,733	$448,761	$471,199
30	89	-	$2,095	$211,038	$1,346	$50,634	$2,537,436	$3,025,022	$487,585	$511,965
31	90	-	$2,625	$226,792	$1,463	$50,634	$2,717,474	$3,250,652	$533,178	$559,837
32	91	-	$3,189	$243,696	$1,600	$50,634	$2,906,513	$3,492,758	$586,245	$615,557
33	92	-	$3,981	$261,829	$1,759	$50,634	$3,105,004	$3,752,364	$647,360	$673,254
34	93	-	$3,987	$281,299	$1,942	$50,634	$3,313,420	$4,031,618	$718,199	$739,745
35	94	-	$3,598	$302,256	$2,155	$50,634	$3,532,256	$4,332,431	$800,174	$816,178
36	95	-	$2,703	$324,845	$2,401	$50,634	$3,762,035	$4,656,973	$894,938	$903,888
37	96	-	$1,461	$349,226	$2,685	$50,634	$4,003,302	$5,007,422	$1,004,121	$1,004,121
38	97	-	$120	$375,553	$3,012	$50,634	$4,256,632	$5,385,868	$1,129,235	$1,129,235
39	98	-	$120	$403,936	$3,388	$50,634	$4,522,630	$5,793,071	$1,270,442	$1,270,442
40	99	-	$120	$434,476	$3,811	$50,634	$4,801,927	$6,231,239	$1,429,313	$1,429,313
41	100	-	$120	$467,339	$4,288	$50,634	$5,095,188	$6,702,746	$1,607,558	$1,607,558

As mentioned, you can see in Figure 9.3 that John's illustration mirrors Larry's exactly for Years 1 through 5. During this time, John max funds his policy with all $500,000. Each year the premium, policy charges, index credit, interest bonus, accumulation value, surrender value, and death benefit are the same as Larry's.

Where you'll start to see things diverge is in Year 6, because this is when John will begin to take out annual tax-free loans on his policy for retirement income. He's going to borrow an amount designed specifically to avoid draining the policy too quickly (to ensure he does not cause the policy to lapse). For John's specific policy, that is $50,634 (as a reminder this is just an illustration of how this type of policy would perform under these assumptions—not a guarantee of all similar policies).

As noted, his annual income is taken out as a loan, which means it is income-tax-free under Internal Revenue Code 7702. He can continue to take this amount every year for the life of the policy in this illustration (being careful not to exhaust his surrender value, which an IUL specialist can help him with).

Now can John live on just over $50,000 a year? Probably not, especially with the effects of anticipated inflation. But he isn't planning on living on this income solely. At age 66, he'll start taking Social Security, and he has other accounts, like a 401(k) he had through his employer for several years that will help provide supplemental income. This is why we recommend having a diversified approach to retirement, with different types of accounts and strategies coming together to ensure you have more than enough, and that you don't outlive your money during retirement.

Notice a few things happening in Years 6 through 10. His premium outlay—or the money he put into the policy—is still just $500,000. During Years 6 through 10, he has been able to receive loans totaling $253,170, which he uses as tax-free income.

Also, John's 7.5% index credit is increasing the accumulation value each year. On the other hand, now that he's taking annual Alternate Loans, his policy has started to accrue a loan balance, which is being charged, say a current rate of 5%.

Most people think of loans and loan interest as negative. But with an insurance policy, it's a positive. Loans (as opposed to withdrawals) are how you access your money income-tax-free. And typically with an Alternate Loan, while you're borrowing at one rate, your money can still earn at a higher rate. For example, with John's policy, he is borrowing that $50,634 and being charged a current rate of 5%. His accumulation value that is the collateral for this loan is still earning whatever the

index return is for that year. If he earns an average of 7.5% and is borrowing at 5%, he is averaging a 2.5% spread.

This is why you're able to take out significant amounts of money from your IUL LASER Fund policy. John's taking over $50,000 a year—that's about 10% of the total $500,000 he's put in. Alternate Loans allow you to take advantage of arbitrage (borrowing at one rate and earning at a higher rate), which can give you a very useful financial advantage, especially because it's tax-free.

Now let's pause for a moment to see what would happen if John had chosen to take income via Zero Wash Loans rather than Alternate Loans. As explained in Section I, Chapter 8, Zero Wash Loans are more conservative because you're not counting on the positive spread the Alternate Loan can have (but may not have if the policy average annual returns are lower than the loan rate due to lower index returns).

So in this example, the Zero Wash Loan might charge 2.25%, and the accumulation value (that is collateral for the loan) would no longer be earning the indexed return. It would earn the rate of 2.25%. So essentially John would be charged 2.25% for the loan, while the collateral for the loan would be earning the same rate, thus John would net 0% (that's why it's called a Zero Wash Loan). How would this impact his income? He would be receiving around $36,000 a year income-tax-free instead of the $50,634 with his Alternate Loan.

Getting back to John's example, let's take a look at the death benefit—in Year 6 it starts to decrease. Why? Because the loans can impact the death benefit, as the death benefit is net of any outstanding loan balances in the policy.

If John had opened this policy when he was younger, say at age 35, he could have funded his policy in as few as four years, and his death benefit would have started at around $2.2 million. If he had been older, at age 70, he could have funded his policy over six years, and his death benefit would have started closer to $700,000. Keep in mind that age, gender, and health impact the level of the death benefit, while the cost remains essentially the same at any age.

We point all of this out because understanding the ins and outs, ups and downs of this (or ANY) type of policy is invaluable for your future. Whatever you decide to do, it's important to partner with IUL specialists

who want to help educate you so you're making fully informed decisions about your money, acting as co-fiduciaries to pursue your best interests.

Notice the policy charges. They begin to drop significantly starting in Year 11. You'll notice the policy charges start to increase again at age 78, and they peak around Year 34 at age 93. At age 97, remember the policy charges drop to $120 a year for the remainder of the policy, because there is no longer any insurance risk (and the surrender value and the death benefit equal each other).

The reason the policy charges take this down-up-down trajectory? Remember that one of the main fees goes away after ten years. Beyond that, risk comes into play. Policy charges, or the cost of insurance, are based on the risk the insurance company is carrying at any particular point in time, determined by the insured's age. The risk, or amount of insurance, is determined by the difference between the surrender value and the death benefit.

Now let's look at John's accumulation value, which you can see continues to increase year-over-year. This is because he's not actually withdrawing his money—he's just borrowing against his accumulation value. Hence, his accumulation value keeps accruing interest. His surrender value (which is the net amount he has after the loan balance) is decreasing each year until Year 21 at age 80, due in part to the annual tax-free loan of $50,634. Notice how it starts to climb again at Year 22. While it's complicated, to put it simply, this is due to the arbitrage. He is borrowing at 5% and still earning higher rates on the accumulation value, all while the policy charges are very minimal.

In this illustration, we have shown that John is not repaying his annual loans. With IUL LASER Funds, you don't have to—the loans and loan charges can simply go against the accumulation value, and the death benefit when you pass on. That is why the surrender value and death benefit are lower, because that's the net value after the loans are paid off when you pass away.

(You can, however, repay loans if you choose. When you do, it will add more money to the surrender value and will lower the loan balance. This is powerful, because other financial vehicles don't allow you to add money back into the account, but with tax-free income via policy loans on life insurance, you can always repay those loans and put money back into the policy.)

At the end of Year 41 at age 100, John has still only paid $500,000 into the policy, and he's had the benefit of over $1.8 million in tax-free income over the past few decades. He and his children have peace of mind that this policy is helping ensure he has a good financial quality of life throughout his golden years. And it's still providing an income-tax-free death benefit of over $1.6 million when John's time is done at age 100.

This example has shown an annual income of over $50,000, but you may be wondering about inflation. We used this example to keep things simple, but you do have options in how much income you take over the years to counteract inflation. For example, rather than taking the same maximum amount of income each year, you can start with a lesser amount and increase the size of the policy loans over time.

Applying this approach to John's scenario, he could start taking $34,000 a year at age 66, then increase the loan amount 3% a year for the life of the policy. This means by age 80, his income would be over $50,000 a year; at age 90, it would be over $69,000; and by age 100, he would be taking out over $92,000 a year.

WHAT IF THERE'S A LOWER AVERAGE INTEREST RATE?

You might be wondering how John's scenario would look if the market conditions were different, and the average annual index returns were lower, say around 6%. Let's assume most of the parameters are the same (size of the policy, required amount of insurance, etc.), except for the 6% average annual interest rate. (See Figure 9.4)

Here, John would need to borrow less in annual tax-free income: around $37,000. Why? Because his policy is earning lower returns, and just like any other financial vehicle, he wants to avoid depleting the policy. By taking less in annual tax-free income, the policy can still last until age 100 without draining the policy and causing it to lapse.

FIGURE 9.4

End of Year	Age	Premium	Policy Charges	Index Credit	Interest Bonus	Tax-Free Income via Policy Loans	Policy Loan Balance	Accumulation Value	Surrender Value	Death Benefit
1	60	$100,000	$16,495	$5,301	-	-	-	$88,806	$59,860	$928,472
2	61	$100,000	$14,500	$10,749	-	-	-	$185,055	$156,138	$928,472
3	62	$100,000	$14,887	$16,514	-	-	-	$286,682	$256,695	$928,472
4	63	$100,000	$14,919	$22,611	-	-	-	$394,375	$359,883	$928,472
5	64	$100,000	$14,911	$29,073	-	-	-	$508,537	$472,140	$928,472
6	65	-	$8,896	$30,283	-	$37,095	$38,949	$529,924	$460,825	$889,523
7	66	-	$9,066	$31,562	-	$37,095	$79,846	$552,420	$448,607	$848,626
8	67	-	$9,168	$32,909	-	$37,095	$122,788	$576,162	$435,516	$805,684
9	68	-	$9,263	$34,331	-	$37,095	$167,877	$601,230	$421,532	$760,595
10	69	-	$9,394	$35,832	-	$37,095	$215,220	$627,668	$406,581	$713,252
11	70	-	$2,150	$37,605	$1,220	$37,095	$264,931	$664,343	$399,412	$663,542
12	71	-	$2,137	$39,806	$1,198	$37,095	$317,127	$703,210	$386,083	$443,995
13	72	-	$619	$42,177	$1,158	$37,095	$371,932	$745,926	$373,993	$422,612
14	73	-	$587	$44,740	$1,122	$37,095	$429,478	$791,201	$361,723	$401,512
15	74	-	$550	$47,458	$1,085	$37,095	$489,902	$839,194	$349,292	$380,729
16	75	-	$510	$50,339	$1,048	$37,095	$553,346	$890,070	$336,724	$360,294
17	76	-	$459	$53,392	$1,010	$37,095	$619,963	$944,014	$324,051	$340,253
18	77	-	$385	$56,631	$972	$37,095	$689,911	$1,001,232	$311,321	$326,887
19	78	-	$409	$60,063	$934	$37,095	$763,356	$1,061,820	$298,464	$313,387
20	79	-	$436	$63,698	$895	$37,095	$840,473	$1,125,978	$285,505	$299,780
21	80	-	$465	$67,547	$857	$37,095	$921,446	$1,193,915	$272,470	$286,093
22	81	-	$505	$71,622	$817	$37,095	$1,006,468	$1,265,850	$259,382	$272,351
23	82	-	$542	$75,937	$778	$37,095	$1,095,740	$1,342,023	$246,282	$258,596
24	83	-	$566	$80,507	$739	$37,095	$1,189,477	$1,422,702	$233,225	$244,886
25	84	-	$605	$85,347	$700	$37,095	$1,287,900	$1,508,143	$220,243	$231,255
26	85	-	$649	$90,472	$661	$37,095	$1,391,245	$1,598,627	$207,382	$217,752
27	86	-	$701	$95,900	$622	$37,095	$1,499,756	$1,694,448	$194,692	$204,426
28	87	-	$757	$101,647	$584	$37,095	$1,613,694	$1,795,923	$182,230	$191,341
29	88	-	$803	$107,735	$547	$37,095	$1,733,328	$1,903,402	$170,074	$178,578
30	89	-	$869	$114,182	$510	$37,095	$1,858,943	$2,017,225	$158,282	$166,196
31	90	-	$933	$121,009	$475	$37,095	$1,990,840	$2,137,777	$146,937	$154,283
32	91	-	$966	$128,242	$441	$37,095	$2,129,331	$2,265,493	$136,162	$142,970
33	92	-	$1,017	$135,903	$408	$37,095	$2,274,747	$2,400,788	$126,041	$131,082
34	93	-	$873	$144,025	$378	$37,095	$2,427,434	$2,544,318	$116,884	$120,391
35	94	-	$686	$152,641	$351	$37,095	$2,587,755	$2,696,624	$108,869	$111,046
36	95	-	$471	$161,785	$327	$37,095	$2,756,093	$2,858,265	$102,172	$103,194
37	96	-	$273	$171,489	$307	$37,095	$2,932,847	$3,029,787	$96,940	$96,940
38	97	-	$120	$181,784	$291	$37,095	$3,118,438	$3,211,742	$93,304	$93,304
39	98	-	$120	$192,701	$280	$37,095	$3,313,310	$3,404,603	$91,294	$91,294
40	99	-	$120	$204,273	$274	$37,095	$3,517,925	$3,609,030	$91,106	$91,106
41	100	-	$120	$216,539	$273	$37,095	$3,732,770	$3,825,722	$92,952	$92,952

You'll also notice that at age 100, the surrender value is $92,952, which is a lot less than John's previous example (where he was earning an average annual return of 7.5%). In this example, we see that John is earning a smaller spread on the loan. He is borrowing at 5%, and the collateral for the loan (the accumulation value) is earning 6%. That 1% spread is good, but it's not as impactful as the 2.5% spread in the earlier example.

Now what if John's policy were averaging even lower annual interest rates, say 5%? Assuming the interest rate on his loans averaged 4% (because when index rates are low, typically rates on loans are also lower), he would only be able to borrow about $31,000 a year in tax-free income to avoid lapsing the policy.

WHAT IF THERE'S A HIGHER AVERAGE INTEREST RATE?

Now what if the market conditions were stellar, and John were able to earn an average annual interest rate of 9%? Again, most of the other parameters are the same, but the biggest difference is the annual income John could borrow: over $70,000, tax-free!

These examples illustrate why it's important to work with an IUL specialist who knows how to manage your indexed accounts and how to monitor the amount of annual tax-free income you borrow (so you can enjoy the maximum amount of income while being careful to avoid lapsing your policy).

STARTING AN IUL LASER FUND AT AGE 40 WITH TAX-FREE ANNUAL INCOME AT AGE 65

Now what if family members might be interested in IUL LASER Funds, but they're younger and aren't sitting on $500,000 to set aside in just five years? Can this work for them? Absolutely.

Let's look at how an IUL LASER Fund might work for someone who's younger, setting aside a moderate amount every year leading up to retirement (see Figure 9.5). Here we'll call our policyholder Adhira, and she's putting away $24,000 a year for the next twenty-five years.

- **Insured's description**: Adhira is a forty-year-old non-smoker.

- **Size of policy**: She's looking to put away $24,000 a year for the next twenty-five years (after-tax money).

- **Required amount of insurance**: The required amount of insurance for Adhira is about $408,000. (As mentioned, this amount is based on the desire to put in $24,000 a year at her

age and gender. This amount could be slightly higher or lower, depending on the insurance company. Also note, this policy will require an increasing death benefit option. We use this option when structuring a policy for longer than a five-year contribution period—see below for more details.)

- **Planned annual premiums**: She'll pay $24,000 a year, every year for twenty-five years, with the flexibility to put in less if needed in any given year.

- **Assumed average annual interest rate**: Based on historical rates, we'll assume the policy is earning an average gross annual interest rate of 7.5%.

- **Interest bonus**: This policy has a complex interest bonus that runs from Year 11 through Year 45, providing additional interest for nearly thirty-five years. The interest bonus on this policy is more modest than others, based on Adhira's age and the insurance company she's working with.

- **Indexing strategy**: Adhira wants to diversify her approach amongst the volatility control indexed accounts, which have historically averaged 6% to 10.5%. In this illustration, we'll assume her policy is earning an average of 7.5%. (Please refer to Section I, Chapter 6, for a refresher on volatility control indexed accounts.)

- **IUL LASER Fund objective**: Adhira wants to set aside her money to provide annual tax-free income during retirement and to provide an income-tax-free death benefit for her beneficiaries someday.

[FIGURE 9.5 ON FOLLOWING PAGE]

FIGURE 9.5

End of Year	Age	Premium	Policy Charges	Index Credit	Interest Bonus	Tax-Free Income via Policy Loans	Policy Loan Balance	Accumulation Value	Surrender Value	Death Benefit
1	40	$24,000	$4,044	$1,609	-	-	-	$21,566	$16,316	$408,006
2	41	$24,000	$3,731	$3,237	-	-	-	$45,071	$40,325	$448,331
3	42	$24,000	$3,490	$5,007	-	-	-	$70,589	$66,370	$474,377
4	43	$24,000	$3,291	$6,928	-	-	-	$98,226	$94,555	$502,561
5	44	$24,000	$3,087	$9,007	-	-	-	$128,146	$124,606	$532,613
6	45	$24,000	$2,979	$11,254	-	-	-	$160,421	$156,984	$564,990
7	46	$24,000	$2,870	$13,679	-	-	-	$195,229	$192,190	$600,196
8	47	$24,000	$2,764	$16,293	-	-	-	$232,757	$230,417	$638,423
9	48	$24,000	$2,648	$19,111	-	-	-	$273,220	$271,890	$679,897
10	49	$24,000	$2,645	$22,146	-	-	-	$316,721	$316,721	$724,728
11	50	$24,000	$1,949	$25,431	$51	-	-	$364,253	$364,253	$772,260
12	51	$24,000	$1,935	$28,996	$106	-	-	$415,420	$415,420	$823,427
13	52	$24,000	$1,907	$32,835	$168	-	-	$470,516	$470,516	$878,522
14	53	$24,000	$1,971	$36,965	$236	-	-	$529,745	$529,745	$937,752
15	54	$24,000	$2,038	$41,405	$311	-	-	$593,424	$593,424	$1,001,430
16	55	$24,000	$2,163	$46,177	$395	-	-	$661,832	$661,832	$1,069,839
17	56	$24,000	$2,266	$51,304	$473	-	-	$735,343	$735,343	$1,143,349
18	57	$24,000	$2,382	$56,813	$574	-	-	$814,349	$814,349	$1,222,355
19	58	$24,000	$2,516	$62,735	$670	-	-	$899,238	$899,238	$1,307,244
20	59	$24,000	$2,675	$69,096	$776	-	-	$990,435	$990,435	$1,398,441
21	60	$24,000	$2,844	$75,930	$892	-	-	$1,088,414	$1,088,414	$1,496,420
22	61	$24,000	$3,038	$83,273	$1,020	-	-	$1,193,668	$1,193,668	$1,601,674
23	62	$24,000	$3,257	$91,160	$1,160	-	-	$1,306,730	$1,306,730	$1,714,737
24	63	$24,000	$3,500	$99,631	$1,295	-	-	$1,428,156	$1,428,156	$1,836,163
25	64	$24,000	$3,754	$108,730	$1,461	-	-	$1,558,593	$1,558,593	$1,901,484
26	65	-	$2,275	$116,821	$1,620	$150,728	$158,265	$1,674,759	$1,516,494	$1,819,793
27	66	-	$2,296	$125,533	$1,794	$150,728	$324,443	$1,799,790	$1,475,347	$1,755,663
28	67	-	$2,414	$134,907	$1,984	$150,728	$498,929	$1,934,267	$1,435,337	$1,693,698
29	68	-	$2,529	$144,989	$2,164	$150,728	$682,141	$2,078,890	$1,396,749	$1,634,197
30	69	-	$2,642	$155,832	$2,359	$150,728	$874,512	$2,234,438	$1,359,926	$1,577,514
31	70	-	$2,680	$167,497	$2,602	$150,728	$1,076,503	$2,401,857	$1,325,355	$1,524,158
32	71	-	$2,705	$180,052	$2,700	$150,728	$1,288,592	$2,581,904	$1,293,311	$1,461,442
33	72	-	$2,532	$193,561	$2,799	$150,728	$1,511,287	$2,775,732	$1,264,446	$1,403,535
34	73	-	$2,320	$208,105	$2,899	$150,728	$1,745,116	$2,984,417	$1,239,301	$1,350,838
35	74	-	$2,065	$223,765	$3,001	$150,728	$1,990,636	$3,209,118	$1,218,482	$1,303,776
36	75	-	$1,763	$240,627	$3,105	$150,728	$2,248,433	$3,451,087	$1,202,654	$1,262,787
37	76	-	$1,401	$258,786	$3,209	$150,728	$2,519,119	$3,711,682	$1,192,563	$1,252,191
38	77	-	$1,526	$278,327	$3,313	$150,728	$2,803,340	$3,991,795	$1,188,455	$1,247,878
39	78	-	$1,672	$299,331	$3,416	$150,728	$3,101,771	$4,292,869	$1,191,098	$1,250,653
40	79	-	$1,835	$321,906	$3,517	$150,728	$3,415,125	$4,616,458	$1,201,333	$1,261,400
41	80	-	$2,037	$346,169	$3,617	$150,728	$3,744,145	$4,964,207	$1,220,061	$1,281,065
42	81	-	$2,579	$372,233	$2,972	$150,728	$4,089,617	$5,336,832	$1,247,215	$1,309,576
43	82	-	$3,156	$400,161	$2,294	$150,728	$4,452,363	$5,736,131	$1,283,768	$1,347,957
44	83	-	$3,782	$430,088	$1,592	$150,728	$4,833,246	$6,164,029	$1,330,783	$1,397,322
45	84	-	$4,469	$462,158	$803	$150,728	$5,233,173	$6,622,521	$1,389,348	$1,458,815
46	85	-	$5,232	$496,521	-	$150,728	$5,653,096	$7,113,810	$1,460,713	$1,533,749
47	86	-	$6,129	$533,338	-	$150,728	$6,094,016	$7,641,019	$1,547,004	$1,624,354
48	87	-	$7,166	$572,846	-	$150,728	$6,556,981	$8,206,699	$1,649,718	$1,732,204
49	88	-	$8,376	$615,233	-	$150,728	$7,043,095	$8,813,556	$1,770,461	$1,858,984
50	89	-	$9,798	$660,701	-	$150,728	$7,553,514	$9,464,459	$1,910,945	$2,006,492

51	90	-	$11,479	$709,465	-	$150,728	$8,089,455	$10,162,445	$2,072,990	$2,176,640
52	91	-	$14,222	$761,726	-	$150,728	$8,652,192	$10,909,949	$2,257,757	$2,348,067
53	92	-	$13,959	$817,797	-	$150,728	$9,243,066	$11,713,786	$2,470,720	$2,544,842
54	93	-	$12,879	$878,119	-	$150,728	$9,863,484	$12,579,027	$2,715,542	$2,769,853
55	94	-	$10,478	$943,090	-	$150,728	$10,514,923	$13,511,638	$2,996,715	$3,026,682
56	95	-	$6,407	$1,013,167	-	$150,728	$11,198,934	$14,518,398	$3,319,464	$3,352,659
57	96	-	$7,952	$1,088,624	-	$150,728	$11,917,146	$15,599,070	$3,681,924	$3,718,744
58	97	-	$9,850	$1,169,613	-	$150,728	$12,671,268	$16,758,833	$4,087,565	$4,128,441
59	98	-	$12,247	$1,256,518	-	$150,728	$13,463,096	$18,003,104	$4,540,009	$4,585,409
60	99	-	$15,341	$1,349,739	-	$150,728	$14,294,515	$19,337,502	$5,042,987	$5,093,417
61	100	-	$19,163	$1,449,696	-	$150,728	$15,167,505	$20,768,035	$5,600,530	$5,656,535

One thing you'll notice right away is the death benefit does not remain level in the early years—it increases each year until Adhira stops paying premiums after Year 25. Why? This policy is structured differently than the others we have described: as an increasing death benefit, also known as Option B.

You can see in the premium column how Adhira is adding her $24,000 a year to the policy faithfully. She starts in Year 1 with a death benefit of just over $400,000 (not bad for just putting in $24,000), and it only goes up from there. In the first couple years, her policy charges do outweigh her interest credits, so she is not making money yet. But that changes in Year 3, when she starts to earn more in interest than she's paying in policy charges. By Year 4, her accumulation value is around $98,000, while her premium payments total $96,000, which means she's broken even.

In the next two decades, you can see how Adhira's policy continues with similar patterns. Her premium is consistently $24,000 a year. (As a side note, if during your prime earning years your income goes up, it's prudent to save more by opening another policy.)

Note that Adhira is still not taking out any loans. In this example, she is using her policy purely as an accumulation vehicle until later in retirement, however she could borrow up to 80% to 90% of her surrender value at any time.

During these years, her index credit (interest) continues to climb, as does every other category. By Year 25, she has over $1.5 million in accumulation value. She's ready to start taking retirement income from the policy soon, which we'll look at in the coming years.

At age 65, Adhira starts to take out annual loans of around $150,000, income-tax-free. That may sound like a lot, but with inflation, that $150,000 won't likely be doing much more than covering the basics twenty-five years from now (which is another reminder that you will likely need more than you think now to avoid outliving your money down the road).

At this point Adhira's IUL specialist also transitions her policy from an increasing death benefit to a level death benefit—this way she can minimize her fees. As Adhira takes her annual income, you can see her death benefit decrease slightly year-to-year.

What about her policy charges? You'll notice over the life of the policy they tend to fluctuate between about $2,000 and $4,500 until around her mid-80s, when they increase. Policy charges, or the cost of insurance, are based on the risk the insurance company is carrying at any particular point in time, determined by the insured's age.

The risk, or amount of insurance, is determined by the difference between the surrender value and the death benefit, and each company approaches how they handle risk differently (while complying with the law's minimum requirements). In this example, there is still insurance risk all the way to age 100, which we didn't see in the first couple examples of this chapter (Figures 9.1 and 9.3).

You'll notice in Year 39 (age 78), however, the surrender value and the death benefit start to climb again. Why? While it's complicated, to put it simply, this is due to the arbitrage. She is borrowing at 5% and still earning 7.5% on the accumulation value.

In this illustration, we have shown that Adhira is not repaying her annual loans. (Remember with IUL LASER Funds, you don't have to—the loans and loan charges can simply go against the accumulation value, and the death benefit when you pass on. That is why the surrender value and death benefit are lower, because that's the net value after the loans are paid off when you pass away. You can, however, repay loans if you choose. When you do, it will add more money to the surrender value.)

Her intention with this policy is ultimately to provide retirement income at this stage of her life so she won't be a burden on her family, and so that she can enjoy a decent quality of life during her golden years.

Also, she's getting older and she won't need as much death benefit. By the time she passes away (in our illustration, at age 100), she will have enjoyed nearly $5.5 million in total tax-free retirement income, and after paying off the Alternate Loans, her policy will transfer over $5.6 million in income-tax-free death benefit to her heirs. That's a pretty good return for just socking away $24,000 a year from age 40 to 64.

STARTING AT AGE 50 WITH MULTIPLIERS AND TAX-FREE ANNUAL INCOME AT AGE 65

In Section I, Chapter 6, we discussed how multipliers can be a powerful way to supercharge your returns. If you recall in Figure 6.4, without multipliers, average annual returns on a five-year index strategy were 9.14%; with multipliers, the same strategy averaged 15.32%. Similarly, with a two-year index strategy, the average annual return was 7.04% without multipliers, versus 11.35% with multipliers.

So let's take a look here at an in-depth example with multipliers (see Figure 9.6). We'll follow Nina, a fifty-year-old woman who starts an IUL LASER Fund at age 50 (see the Multipliers section below for the details on her multipliers).

- **Insured's description**: Nina is a fifty-year-old non-smoker.

- **Size of policy**: She's looking to put away $500,000 (after-tax money).

- **Required amount of insurance**: The required amount of insurance for Nina is about $1,356,076. (Remember, this amount is based on the desire to put in $500,000 at this age and gender; the amount could be slightly higher or lower, depending on the insurance company.)

- **Planned annual premiums**: She'll pay $100,000 a year, every year for five years until the policy is fully funded at $500,000 (to comply with TAMRA, as explained in Section I, Chapter 7).

- **Assumed average annual interest rate**: We are assuming the index strategies have their current caps, while we'll be using forty years of actual S&P 500 historical data, starting January 1, 1980.

- **Interest bonus**: This policy has a complex interest bonus that runs from Year 11 through Year 35, providing additional interest for nearly twenty-five years. (As a side note, this policy has slightly higher charges during the early years that enable the high-impact bonus, which can generate significantly more tax-free income during the retirement years—making the front-end costs worthwhile.)

- **Indexing strategy**: Nina is allocating 25% to the one-year S&P 500 high cap strategy, with a floor of 0%, a current cap of 10.5% for a fee of 0.8%, and a 100% participation rate; 25% to the one-year S&P 500 no-cap, with a spread / threshold rate of 8.5%; 20% to the two-year S&P 500 strategy, with a floor of 0%, a current cap of 19%, and with a 100% participation rate; and 30% to the five-year S&P 500 point-to-last-year-average strategy, with a floor of 0%, no cap, and with a participation rate of 110%. (Please refer to Section I, Chapter 6, for a refresher on these types of indexed accounts.)

- **Multipliers**: Nina is using a multiplier strategy that starts in Year 2 and charges 7.5% for Years 2 - 20. This charge gradually decreases to 3% over Years 21 - 25, at which point it remains at 3% for the duration of the policy. This charge provides an options budget, which gives her a multiplier of 2.7 times the index return for Years 2 - 20, based on Nina's indexing strategies indicated above. When the charge reduces to 3%, the multiplier is 1.69 times the index return. (Please refer to Section I, Chapter 6, for a refresher on multipliers.)

- **IUL LASER Fund objective**: Nina wants to set aside her money to provide annual tax-free income during retirement and to provide an income-tax-free death benefit for her beneficiaries someday.

FIGURE 9.6

End of Year	Age	Premium	Tax-Free Income via Policy Loans	Policy Loan Balance	Accumulation Value	Surrender Value	Death Benefit
1	50	$100,000	-	-	$82,620	$62,507	$1,356,076
2	51	$100,000	-	-	$185,054	$165,566	$1,356,076
3	52	$100,000	-	-	$249,378	$234,475	$1,356,076
4	53	$100,000	-	-	$373,555	$359,594	$1,356,076
5	54	$100,000	-	-	$529,634	$515,004	$1,356,076
6	55	-	-	-	$534,572	$523,119	$1,356,076
7	56	-	-	-	$606,492	$597,050	$1,356,076
8	57	-	-	-	$758,010	$750,388	$1,356,076
9	58	-	-	-	$777,929	$774,143	$1,356,076
10	59	-	-	-	$867,121	$867,121	$1,356,076
11	60	-	-	-	$1,027,193	$1,027,193	$1,356,076
12	61	-	-	-	$1,025,081	$1,025,081	$1,356,076
13	62	-	-	-	$1,269,456	$1,269,456	$1,599,515
14	63	-	-	-	$1,325,519	$1,325,519	$1,643,644
15	64	-	-	-	$1,445,056	$1,445,056	$1,762,969
16	65	-	$151,066	$157,713	$1,425,151	$1,267,438	$1,520,926
17	66	-	$151,066	$322,365	$1,747,555	$1,425,190	$1,695,976
18	67	-	$151,066	$494,262	$2,109,204	$1,614,942	$1,905,632
19	68	-	$151,066	$673,723	$2,592,393	$1,918,671	$2,244,845
20	69	-	$151,066	$861,079	$3,358,909	$2,497,829	$2,897,483
21	70	-	$151,066	$1,056,680	$4,150,448	$3,093,768	$3,557,833
22	71	-	$151,066	$1,260,886	$4,307,018	$3,046,131	$3,442,128
23	72	-	$151,066	$1,474,078	$4,271,626	$2,797,547	$3,105,277
24	73	-	$151,066	$1,696,651	$4,116,693	$2,420,042	$2,637,846
25	74	-	$151,066	$1,929,016	$4,372,595	$2,443,579	$2,614,630
26	75	-	$151,066	$2,171,606	$4,341,261	$2,169,655	$2,278,138
27	76	-	$151,066	$2,424,869	$4,369,773	$1,944,904	$2,042,149
28	77	-	$151,066	$2,689,277	$4,544,780	$1,855,503	$1,948,278
29	78	-	$151,066	$2,965,318	$4,638,385	$1,673,067	$1,756,720
30	79	-	$151,066	$3,253,505	$4,524,722	$1,271,217	$1,334,778
31	80	-	$151,066	$3,554,372	$5,086,854	$1,532,483	$1,609,107
32	81	-	$151,066	$3,868,477	$5,230,984	$1,362,507	$1,430,633
33	82	-	$151,066	$4,196,403	$5,079,657	$883,255	$927,417
34	83	-	$151,066	$4,538,758	$5,244,210	$705,453	$740,725
35	84	-	$151,066	$4,896,176	$6,236,914	$1,340,738	$1,407,775
36	85	-	$151,066	$5,269,320	$6,710,595	$1,441,275	$1,513,338
37	86	-	$151,066	$5,658,883	$6,806,364	$1,147,480	$1,204,854
38	87	-	$151,066	$6,065,587	$7,509,984	$1,444,397	$1,516,617
39	88	-	$151,066	$6,490,186	$8,409,191	$1,919,005	$2,014,955
40	89	-	$151,066	$6,933,467	$8,744,182	$1,810,715	$1,901,251
41	90	-	$151,066	$7,396,252	$9,988,830	$2,592,578	$2,722,206
42	91	-	$151,066	$7,879,400	$10,954,286	$3,074,886	$3,197,881
43	92	-	$151,066	$8,383,807	$11,786,560	$3,402,753	$3,504,836
44	93	-	$151,066	$8,910,407	$11,631,823	$2,721,415	$2,775,843
45	94	-	$151,066	$9,460,178	$13,266,839	$3,806,661	$3,844,728
46	95	-	$151,066	$10,034,139	$14,717,140	$4,683,001	$4,729,831
47	96	-	$151,066	$10,633,354	$15,079,820	$4,446,466	$4,490,930
48	97	-	$151,066	$11,258,934	$16,424,020	$5,165,086	$5,216,737
49	98	-	$151,066	$11,912,041	$19,241,021	$7,328,981	$7,402,271
50	99	-	$151,066	$12,593,883	$21,182,790	$8,588,907	$8,674,796
51	100	-	$151,066	$13,305,727	$23,376,090	$10,070,363	$10,171,067

As you review Nina's illustration, let's look at a few things. First, to focus on how multipliers affect policies, you'll notice we've condensed the illustration to minimize the number of columns (not shown: policy charges, index credits, and interest bonus). If we had included that information, it would have required multiple columns accommodating the one-year, two-year, and five-year indexing strategies, as well as the multiplier charges and credits. If interested, an IUL specialist can walk you through those details in a similar policy illustration.

As noted in the bullet points above, in this example we're using forty years of actual S&P 500 historical data, starting January 1, 1980 (projecting those rates as if you could have had this policy back then).

We're doing this so you can see how the natural ups and downs of the market can impact a policy, especially with the impact of multipliers (as opposed to the flat average annual return we used in this chapter's previous examples).

You'll also notice the accumulation values start off a little lower in this policy when compared to our other examples. Why? Because some of the accumulation value is allocated to two-year and five-year indexing strategies, so you won't see that interest credited until the end of each of those periods.

There's another factor impacting the accumulation values: Policies like these tend to have higher charges in the first few years—but keep in mind these kinds of policies can also empower significant growth thanks to the multiplier strategy.

The advantages of diversifying between one-year, two-year, and five-year indexing strategies creates the potential for more stability (as opposed to having all the money in a single strategy).

Other highlights to note: You'll notice the surrender value and accumulation value are the same in Years 10 through 15, because the surrender charge only lasts for a ten-year period. The surrender value and accumulation value diverge in Year 16 because at that point Nina begins to take out loans for tax-free income (and not because there is a surrender charge—as there was in Years 1 through 9).

Also, in Year 13 at age 62, the death benefit starts to increase. This is because the surrender value and accumulation value are at a point where

they require the death benefit to increase to cover the insurance risk in the policy. (Remember the difference between the surrender value and the death benefit is the net amount at risk.) This enables the policy to continue to qualify as life insurance and maintain its tax-free benefits.

At Year 15, the accumulation value and surrender value are at $1,445,056, and the death benefit is $1,762,969. At this point, Nina (who is age 65 now) starts taking tax-free income via Alternate Loans in the annual amount of $151,066.

You'll also notice some significant variations in the surrender value. Why is this? With the ups and downs of the market, the policy is earning more in some years, less (or a 0% floor) in others. In the years with a more pronounced drop in the market, such as Years 33 and 34, the surrender value dips below $1 million. The market drops in those years, while the policy is still incurring the multiplier charge, which the surrender value reflects.

Since market conditions will naturally fluctuate, an experienced IUL specialist can help you make wise decisions about how much money to borrow from your policy to avoid depleting the policy. In Nina's case, this is why she is only borrowing just over $151,000 a year. This is still a huge amount, roughly 10% of her accumulation value, which is made possible by the power of the multipliers impacting her returns.

By way of comparison, it's helpful to see what Nina's tax-free income would look like if she did not have multipliers on her policy. Without the multipliers, her policy would be earning less. This means she would need to borrow less for tax-free annual income to avoid lapsing her policy—more in the range of $115,000.

Let's compare what her policy would look like in Year 15 (age 64 in Nina's example). As mentioned above, the policy with multipliers would have a surrender value of $1,445,056. Without the multipliers, her surrender value would be $1,048,916.

If we jump ahead to Year 26 (age 75), the policy with multipliers has a surrender value of $2,169,655. The policy without multipliers' surrender value is $1,116,322. Don't forget with the multipliers, her policy is generating $36,000 more in tax-free income a year, which can make a difference in Nina's lifestyle.

Back to Nina's illustration with multipliers, you'll notice by age 100, the policy is up to a nearly $10.2 million death benefit. This is a result of arbitrage (borrowing at 4.4% in this example), while the policy's accumulation value of $23.3 million continues to earn indexed returns with the multipliers. (Also note the nearly $10.2 million death benefit is net of the $13.3 million policy loan balance.)

With this example, you can see the pros and cons of multipliers. They can provide a significant benefit, generating more tax-free income than policies without multipliers. On the other hand, multipliers can be a risk in the down years, where the multiplier fee still applies (for example up to 7.5%). That said, many of our clients have found that multipliers' benefits vastly outweigh the negatives, currently choosing to go with multipliers about 90% of the time.

STARTING AN IUL LASER FUND AT AGE 70 WITH TAX-FREE ANNUAL INCOME

What if you have more to set aside for retirement—and you're already into retirement age? Let's look at an example where our policyholder is a bit older, and she has $1 million to set aside. Sometimes additional funds come from a sudden windfall, like an inheritance or sale of properties, or it could be from a strategic rollout from IRAs, 401(k)s, or other non-qualified investments.

In this example, we'll call our policyholder Marie, and we'll see how an IUL LASER Fund can perform when it's started at age 70. Marie will begin taking out tax-free income immediately after the policy is funded with a maximum premium over five years. (See Figure 9.7)

As a side note, keep in mind that IUL LASER Funds can be customized to your situation, including age, size of the policy, income objectives, etc. As with any of these examples, feel free to extrapolate for your circumstances as you envision what an IUL LASER Fund can do for you.

- **Insured's description**: Marie is a seventy-year-old non-smoker.

- **Size of policy**: She's looking to put away $1,000,000 (after-tax money).

- **Required amount of insurance**: The required amount of insurance for Marie is about $1.37 million (As mentioned, this amount is based on the desire to put in $1,000,000 at her age and gender. This amount could be slightly higher or lower, depending on the insurance company.)

- **Planned annual premiums**: She'll pay $200,000 a year, every year for five years until the policy is funded with a maximum premium of $1,000,000 (to comply with TAMRA, as explained in Section I, Chapter 7).

- **Assumed average annual interest rate**: Based on historical rates, we'll assume the policy is earning an average gross annual interest rate of 7.5%.

- *Interest bonus*: This policy provides an interest bonus of thirty basis points starting in Year 11. (Thirty basis points would be 0.3% of the surrender value.)

- **Indexing strategy**: Marie wants to diversify her approach amongst the volatility control indexed accounts, which have historically averaged 6% to 10.5%. In this illustration, we'll assume her policy is earning an average of 7.5%. (Please refer to Section I, Chapter 6, for a refresher on volatility control indexed accounts.)

- **IUL LASER Fund objective**: Marie wants to optimize her money to provide annual tax-free income during retirement and to provide an income-tax-free death benefit for her beneficiaries someday.

[FIGURE 9.7 ON FOLLOWING PAGE]

FIGURE 9.7

End of Year	Age	Premium	Policy Charges	Index Credit	Interest Bonus	Tax-Free Income via Policy Loans	Policy Loan Balance	Accumulation Value	Surrender Value	Death Benefit
1	70	$200,000	$36,112	$13,153	-	-	-	$177,041	$119,335	$1,369,585
2	71	$200,000	$33,431	$26,688	-	-	-	$370,297	$312,435	$1,369,585
3	72	$200,000	$34,408	$41,151	-	-	-	$577,040	$516,680	$1,369,585
4	73	$200,000	$34,535	$56,653	-	-	-	$799,158	$729,264	$1,369,585
5	74	$200,000	$33,941	$73,331	-	-	-	$1,038,547	$964,216	$1,369,585
6	75	-	$20,665	$77,226	-	$98,560	$103,488	$1,095,108	$929,314	$1,266,098
7	76	-	$20,583	$81,471	-	$98,560	$212,150	$1,155,997	$893,694	$1,157,435
8	77	-	$20,530	$86,039	-	$98,560	$326,245	$1,221,505	$857,401	$1,043,340
9	78	-	$20,055	$90,967	-	$98,560	$446,045	$1,292,418	$820,962	$923,540
10	79	-	$19,157	$96,315	-	$98,560	$571,835	$1,369,576	$784,938	$797,750
11	80	-	$1,020	$102,706	$2,355	$98,560	$703,915	$1,474,254	$770,340	$808,857
12	81	-	$1,040	$110,536	$2,311	$98,560	$842,598	$1,586,060	$743,462	$780,635
13	82	-	$1,184	$118,916	$2,230	$98,560	$988,216	$1,706,023	$717,807	$753,697
14	83	-	$1,307	$127,910	$2,153	$98,560	$1,141,114	$1,834,779	$693,664	$728,348
15	84	-	$1,505	$137,560	$2,081	$98,560	$1,301,658	$1,972,915	$671,257	$704,820
16	85	-	$1,722	$147,913	$2,014	$98,560	$1,470,228	$2,121,119	$650,891	$683,436
17	86	-	$2,026	$159,019	$1,953	$98,560	$1,647,228	$2,280,065	$632,837	$664,479
18	87	-	$2,312	$170,930	$1,899	$98,560	$1,833,077	$2,450,582	$617,505	$648,380
19	88	-	$2,554	$183,711	$1,853	$98,560	$2,028,218	$2,633,592	$605,373	$635,642
20	89	-	$2,886	$197,427	$1,816	$98,560	$2,233,117	$2,829,948	$596,831	$626,673
21	90	-	$3,267	$212,141	$1,790	$98,560	$2,448,261	$3,040,612	$592,352	$621,969
22	91	-	$3,603	$227,930	$1,777	$98,560	$2,674,161	$3,266,717	$592,555	$622,183
23	92	-	$4,073	$244,873	$1,778	$98,560	$2,911,357	$3,509,294	$597,937	$621,854
24	93	-	$3,714	$263,078	$1,794	$98,560	$3,160,413	$3,770,451	$610,038	$628,339
25	94	-	$3,074	$282,685	$1,830	$98,560	$3,421,921	$4,051,892	$629,971	$642,570
26	95	-	$2,154	$303,823	$1,890	$98,560	$3,696,505	$4,355,450	$658,945	$665,535
27	96	-	$1,108	$326,623	$1,977	$98,560	$3,984,818	$4,682,943	$698,125	$698,125
28	97	-	$120	$351,217	$2,094	$98,560	$4,287,547	$5,036,134	$748,587	$748,587
29	98	-	$120	$377,706	$2,246	$98,560	$4,605,412	$5,415,966	$810,554	$810,554
30	99	-	$120	$406,194	$2,432	$98,560	$4,939,170	$5,824,471	$885,301	$885,301
31	100	-	$120	$436,832	$2,656	$98,560	$5,289,616	$6,263,838	$974,222	$974,222

In Figure 9.7, you'll notice that this is similar to other examples we've seen in this chapter, with the biggest differences including: 1) the starting age of 70, 2) the higher maximum premium amount of $1 million, and 3) the age she starts taking out income (at Year 6, which in this case is age 75).

Even though Marie is age 70 when she starts her IUL LASER Fund, the strategy works well because the TEFRA/DEFRA laws allow her to get away with less insurance at this age. Furthermore, the recent changes to Internal Revenue Code 7702 allows an even lower death benefit than ever before, which saves on fees and expenses.

Note that like many of our other examples, Marie funds her policy over five years—in this case with $200,000 a year. By Year 5, you'll see the policy has over $1 million in accumulation value, and her surrender value is $964,216, with a death benefit of about $1.37 million.

If she were to pass away at any point during the first five years, her beneficiaries would receive that death benefit of $1.37 million income-tax-free, regardless if it were Year 1 or Year 5. In other words, say she passed at age 72, she would have only put $400,000 into her policy, but her family would receive $1.37 million. This can bring peace of mind when starting a policy at that point in life.

As we've noted, IUL LASER Funds are not a get-rich-quick strategy They are a long-term prudent approach to accumulating money tax-free, accessing money tax-free, and passing along money to beneficiaries income-tax-free. As you can see by Year 5, her $1 million has only grown to $1,038,547. That may not provide a wow factor, but here's where things get exciting when it comes to tax-free income.

In Year 6, Marie starts to take out $98,560 income-tax-free with an Alternate Loan. She continues to take out that amount until she passes away. And even if she lives until age 100, she would leave behind just under $1 million income-tax-free to her beneficiaries.

Let's look at fees for a moment. Much like our other examples, her fees drop in Year 6, after she finishes funding the policy. The fees drop again in Year 11 and slightly increase through Year 23 (age 92), after which they go back down. As we've explained, the fees rise and drop according to the net amount of insurance risk (which is based on the difference between the surrender value and the death benefit).

Notice the surrender value dips to its lowest point in Year 21 (age 90), after which it starts to climb. If you recall, this is due to the accumulation value continuing to earn 7.5%, while the loan balance is being charged 5%. That arbitrage makes a bigger impact as the balances increase, reaching its highest level by age 100, with an accumulation value of about $6.3 million earning 7.5% and a loan balance of about $5.3 million being charged 5%. The accumulation value minus the loan balance equals the surrender value of about $1 million (note the death benefit is

the same amount at this age). As you might recall, when policyholders pass away, beneficiaries receive the death benefit (which includes the surrender value).

To summarize, even with starting an IUL LASER Fund at age 70, the advantages are significant. Marie is able to take out nearly $100,000 in tax-free income every year starting at age 75. Her money is safe, liquid, and is earning predictable rates of return tax-free (with a 0% guaranteed floor should the market drop). When she passes away, her beneficiaries receive her death benefit, income-tax-free. If she has other sources of retirement income such as pensions, Social Security, IRA and 401(k) distributions that are all taxable, she will be able to enjoy income from her IUL LASER Fund income-tax-free, which can make a significant difference for her quality of life, aging care, etc.

IUL LASER FUND – SO MANY WAYS TO BENEFIT YOUR LIFE

Whatever your financial objectives, as you can see, The IUL LASER Fund is a flexible financial vehicle that can help you reach your desired destination. In all, let's recap these typical IUL LASER Fund benefits:

- Typically for The IUL LASER Fund, by the end of Year 5, the policy has paid for itself.

- While we're using an average annual interest rate of 7.5% in many of these illustrations, the year-to-year interest rate depends on the indexing strategy you choose and how the market impacts that index.

- If the economy soars, if your policy has a cap, your rate of return will essentially have a "ceiling" on the highest percentage you can earn that year. If the economy were to experience a downturn, because IUL LASER Fund policies have a guaranteed 0% "floor," you won't lose any principal due to market volatility. Whatever your policy has previously earned becomes newly protected principal and you would simply earn 0% that year.

In our next chapter, we'll look at examples of how The IUL LASER Fund compares to other common financial vehicles, to better understand your financial portfolio options.

TOP 5 TAKEAWAYS

1. To understand how The IUL LASER Fund works, we've illustrated different scenarios in this chapter.

2. First, we explored the ins and outs of an IUL LASER Fund created primarily for tax-deferred financial growth and income-tax-free wealth transfer, with no intention to access income from the policy, tax-free. Next, we looked at a LASER Fund where the policyholder takes the maximum income allowed based on policy assumptions starting at age 66.

3. We also examined an IUL LASER Fund where the policyholder contributes annual amounts starting at age 40, and then begins taking tax-free retirement income from age 65 on.

4. Then we looked at an IUL LASER Fund that leverages multipliers with indexing strategies, using historical market returns, which demonstrate down years with a 0% return and multiplier charges, as well as up years with significant gains, accelerated by the multipliers.

5. Finally, we explored what would happen when starting an IUL LASER Fund at age 70, with a higher maximum premium of $1,000,000, and taking income starting at age 75.

10

Comparing Different Vehicles

Imagine you're finishing up a lovely meal at a fine dining restaurant. The last morsels of grilled Niman flap steak are melting in your mouth as the server appears to inquire about dessert. Your dinner party looks at each other—no one can resist, so you tell your server, "Yes, we'd like dessert." She asks, "Salted caramel pudding? Coconut semifreddo? Vanilla bean mousse?" You shrug and say, "Whatever. They cost about the same, so they all taste the same, right?"

Of course not. We all know no two desserts on the menu will deliver the same experience. But for some reason the same doesn't always hold true when people consider different financial vehicles. Many people assume they all deliver about the same benefits, so they figure it doesn't really matter which ones they choose.

But they are all different. And it's helpful to see how the approaches compare to one another to analyze what you're getting, what you're paying for (in costs and taxes), and what works best for you. (And remember, it's wise to have a mix of financial vehicles in your portfolio to provide balance, just like it's always nice to order different desserts to get the best of all worlds.)

A NOTE ON TAX BRACKETS

Throughout much of this book we've been examining The IUL LASER Fund, which can provide tax-free access to your money, with a death benefit that transfers income-tax-free to your heirs. So the impact of taxes hasn't been a factor in our illustrations yet—but it will now as we explore scenarios with taxable and tax-advantaged vehicles.

Before we dive into the illustrations, let's take a quick moment to understand tax brackets. Keep in mind when analyzing the actual benefit of a tax deduction or comparing financial vehicles, you should use your marginal tax rate rather than your effective tax rate.

Here's why: there's a significant difference between your **effective** tax rate and your **marginal** tax bracket.

- **Effective Tax Rate** - Your effective tax rate is the tax percentage you pay when compared to your total income.

- **Marginal Tax Bracket** - Your marginal tax bracket is the highest tax bracket into which your taxable income falls.

For example, let's say we have a married couple filing jointly whose combined income is $180,000. If they take the standard deduction, which is $25,100 for tax year 2021 and $25,900 for tax year 2022, their taxable income then is about $155,000, which puts them in a marginal federal tax bracket of 22% and a state tax bracket of 5%—for a combined bracket of 27%. (Keep in mind, some people have no state taxes, others will have state taxes as high as 10% or more, which is why we're going with a median of 5% for this example.)

It's important to remember that not all income is taxed at the highest bracket. This is a concept that is often confusing for people. They can grow alarmed when their financial professional alerts them that they're close to moving into the next tax bracket (from 24% to 32%, for example). They fear that all their income will be taxed at the higher rate. This is not true. You only pay the higher rate on dollars earned in excess of each tax threshold.

To explain, for our couple in the example, at 2021 tax rates, they would pay federal income tax of only 10% on the first $19,900 (which is $1,990); 12% on $19,901 to $81,050 ($7,338); and 22% on the remain-

ing $73,950 ($16,269). To explain the math above, we started with their taxable income of about $155,000 and do the multiplication for each tax bracket as we go. Their total taxes would add up to $25,597, which is 14.2% of their $180,000 gross income. So their effective tax bracket is 14.2%, while their marginal bracket is 22%. (Keep in mind this simple example does not include FICA, Medicare, or state income tax.)

For the sake of simplicity, the examples in this chapter will assume a combined federal and state income marginal tax bracket of 27%. Because the principles here remain the same regardless of changes that determine the precise tax bracket, it's easier mathematically to say that just under one-third of income is allocated for taxes. Feel free to extrapolate any illustrations for your personal income tax bracket.

IUL LASER FUND VS. AFTER-TAX ACCOUNT WITH TAX-DEFERRED GROWTH

For our first comparison, let's borrow an example from Section I, Chapter 9. We'll go with Nina, who is age 50. She has $500,000 after-tax money she wants to set aside in a financial vehicle that will allow her to take regular annual income during retirement.

To recap the highlights of Nina's IUL LASER Fund, she is choosing a policy with multipliers. We are assuming the index strategies have their current caps, while we'll be using forty years of actual S&P 500 historical data, starting January 1, 1980.

For her indexing strategy, she is allocating 25% to the one-year S&P 500 high cap strategy, with a floor of 0%, a current cap of 10.5% for a fee of 0.8%, and a 100% participation rate; 25% to the one-year S&P 500 no-cap, with a spread / threshold rate of 8.5%; 20% to the two-year S&P 500 strategy, with a floor of 0%, a current cap of 19%, and with a 100% participation rate; and 30% to the five-year S&P 500 point-to-last-year-average strategy, with a floor of 0%, no cap, and with a participation rate of 110%. (Please refer to Section I, Chapter 6, for a refresher on these types of indexed accounts.)

Nina is using a multiplier strategy that starts in Year 2 and charges 7.5% for Years 2 - 20. This charge gradually decreases to 3% over Years 21 - 25, at which point it remains at 3% for the duration of the policy.

This charge provides an options budget, which gives her a multiplier of 2.7 times the index return for Years 2 - 20, based on Nina's indexing strategies indicated above. When the charge reduces to 3%, the multiplier is 1.69 times the index return. (Please refer to Section I, Chapter 6, for a refresher on multipliers.) Once Nina begins accessing money, she does so via an Alternate Loan, with a current rate of 4.4%.

Now what if Nina chooses an after-tax account with tax-deferred growth and LIFO distribution instead of an IUL LASER Fund? This could be a vehicle such as a brokerage account or a managed money account. Since this type of account grows tax-deferred, she won't pay any taxes on annual gains.

To explain the LIFO distinction, this means when she goes to withdraw money, the account is taxed LIFO—last-in, first-out. In other words, she's taking out interest first (which is taxable) before she dips into the principal (which is not taxable, because she contributed after-tax dollars in the beginning). In this example, we are assuming long-term capital gains taxes, which would be lower than short-term capital gains taxes.

What would Nina's scenario look like if she put her $500,000 into an after-tax brokerage account rather than an IUL LASER Fund? Here's a comparison of the account versus policy details as a quick overview:

- **Funding - After-Tax Account**: Nina will fund her brokerage account with $500,000 after-tax dollars that will grow tax-deferred. (Taxes on the gains will be paid when distributions are taken.)

- **Funding - IUL LASER Fund**: Nina will fund her IUL LASER Fund with $500,000 after-tax dollars that will grow tax-free (and can be accessed tax-free and passed along to her heirs income-tax-free).

- **Assumed average annual interest rate - After-Tax Account:** To keep things as "apples to apples" as possible with this comparison, we'll say her after-tax brokerage account is earning the actual historical S&P 500 returns, starting January 1, 1980 (excluding dividends).

- **Assumed average annual interest rate - IUL LASER Fund**: As a reminder, Nina's IUL LASER Fund is also using the same S&P 500 historical returns (excluding dividends), and is impacted by multipliers (which can significantly increase returns), caps, and a guaranteed floor of 0% that impact her returns; whereas Nina's after-tax account follows the S&P 500 returns and is impacted by the ups and downs of the market. Her policy will also earn index credits and interest bonus, which is not shown in Figure 10.1. We did this for simplicity, as it would have required multiple columns accommodating the one-year, two-year, and five-year indexing strategies, as well as the multiplier charges and credits. (If interested, an IUL specialist can walk you through those details in a similar policy illustration.)

- **Expenses - After-Tax Account**: We'll also say Nina's after-tax brokerage account is being charged the industry average of 1.5% in annual expenses with no up-front sales charge.

- **Expenses - IUL LASER Fund**: Like all IUL LASER Funds, Nina's policy will incur costs, including premium charges, admin fees, expense charges, and cost of insurance. Because her policy includes multipliers, she will also incur multiplier charges.

- **Tax Rate - After-Tax Account**: We are assuming a long-term capital gains tax of 15% and a state tax of 5%, for a combined federal and state tax rate of 20%.

- **Tax Rate - IUL LASER Fund**: As you know, The IUL LASER Fund allows money to grow tax-free, access money tax-free, and transfer money upon death income-tax-free—so there are no taxes that will be assessed on Nina's IUL LASER Fund.

[FIGURE 10.1 ON FOLLOWING PAGE]

FIGURE 10.1

End of Year	Age	Premium	IUL LASER Fund Policy Using Indexing Strategies and Multipliers Based on the S&P 500 Historical Returns				After-Tax With Tax-Deferred Growth Based on S&P Historical Returns 1.5% Management Fees			
			Tax-Free Income via Policy Loans	Accumulation Value	Surrender Value	Death Benefit	After-Tax Withdrawal	S&P 500 Returns	Gross Balance (Before Tax)	Net After-Tax Balance
1	50	$100,000	-	$82,620	$62,507	$1,356,076	-	10.46%	$108,800	$107,040
2	51	$100,000	-	$185,054	$165,566	$1,356,076	-	20.92%	$248,692	$243,137
3	52	$100,000	-	$249,378	$234,475	$1,356,076	-	-13.43%	$297,322	$299,354
4	53	$100,000	-	$373,555	$359,594	$1,356,076	-	26.93%	$496,739	$484,273
5	54	$100,000	-	$529,634	$515,004	$1,356,076	-	14.00%	$670,074	$645,741
6	55	-	-	$534,572	$523,119	$1,356,076	-	2.09%	$673,814	$648,733
7	56	-	-	$606,492	$597,050	$1,356,076	-	21.19%	$804,343	$753,156
8	57	-	-	$758,010	$750,388	$1,356,076	-	27.10%	$1,006,987	$915,271
9	58	-	-	$777,929	$774,143	$1,356,076	-	-6.38%	$928,586	$852,551
10	59	-	-	$867,121	$867,121	$1,356,076	-	12.73%	$1,031,108	$934,569
11	60	-	-	$1,027,193	$1,027,193	$1,356,076	-	18.72%	$1,205,732	$1,074,268
12	61	-	-	$1,025,081	$1,025,081	$1,356,076	-	-8.07%	$1,091,776	$983,103
13	62	-	-	$1,269,456	$1,269,456	$1,599,515	-	34.55%	$1,446,898	$1,267,200
14	63	-	-	$1,325,519	$1,325,519	$1,643,644	-	3.69%	$1,477,736	$1,291,871
15	64	-	-	$1,445,056	$1,445,056	$1,762,969	-	8.94%	$1,585,688	$1,378,232
16	65	-	$151,066	$1,425,151	$1,267,438	$1,520,926	$151,066	-1.16%	$1,359,881	$1,197,587
17	66	-	$151,066	$1,747,555	$1,425,190	$1,695,976	$151,066	28.73%	$1,484,821	$1,297,539
18	67	-	$151,066	$2,109,204	$1,614,942	$1,905,632	$151,066	27.76%	$1,630,892	$1,414,396
19	68	-	$151,066	$2,592,393	$1,918,671	$2,244,845	$151,066	24.59%	$1,769,744	$1,525,477
20	69	-	$151,066	$3,358,909	$2,497,829	$2,897,483	$151,066	26.54%	$1,970,499	$1,686,081
21	70	-	$151,066	$4,150,448	$3,093,768	$3,557,833	$151,066	20.87%	$2,121,163	$1,806,612
22	71	-	$151,066	$4,307,018	$3,046,131	$3,442,128	$151,066	-9.45%	$1,723,423	$1,488,420
23	72	-	$151,066	$4,271,626	$2,797,547	$3,105,277	$151,066	-13.66%	$1,305,061	$1,153,731
24	73	-	$151,066	$4,116,693	$2,420,042	$2,637,846	$151,066	-18.16%	$899,804	$829,525
25	74	-	$151,066	$4,372,595	$2,443,579	$2,614,630	$151,066	21.34%	$849,786	$789,510
26	75	-	$151,066	$4,341,261	$2,169,655	$2,278,138	$151,066	4.78%	$682,136	$655,391
27	76	-	$151,066	$4,369,773	$1,944,904	$2,042,149	$151,066	8.31%	$538,031	$531,290
28	77	-	$151,066	$4,544,780	$1,855,503	$1,948,278	$151,066	11.21%	$416,489	$409,236
29	78	-	$151,066	$4,638,385	$1,673,067	$1,756,720	$151,066	-1.01%	$251,724	$251,724
30	79	-	$151,066	$4,524,722	$1,271,217	$1,334,778	$59,745	-40.50%	$59,745	$59,745
31	80	-	$151,066	$5,086,854	$1,532,483	$1,609,107	-	36.30%	-	-
32	81	-	$151,066	$5,230,984	$1,362,507	$1,430,633	-	12.61%	-	-
33	82	-	$151,066	$5,079,657	$883,255	$927,417	-	0.03%	-	-
34	83	-	$151,066	$5,244,210	$705,453	$740,725	-	14.09%	-	-
35	84	-	$151,066	$6,236,914	$1,340,738	$1,407,775	-	25.04%	-	-
36	85	-	$151,066	$6,710,595	$1,441,275	$1,513,338	-	9.37%	-	-
37	86	-	$151,066	$6,806,364	$1,147,480	$1,204,854	-	-4.45%	-	-
38	87	-	$151,066	$7,509,984	$1,444,397	$1,516,617	-	20.61%	-	-
39	88	-	$151,066	$8,409,191	$1,919,005	$2,014,955	-	22.06%	-	-
40	89	-	$151,066	$8,744,182	$1,810,715	$1,901,251	-	-7.31%	-	-
41	90	-	$151,066	$9,988,830	$2,592,578	$2,722,206	-	27.13%	-	-
42	91	-	$151,066	$10,954,286	$3,074,886	$3,197,881	-	15.61%	-	-
43	92	-	$151,066	$11,786,560	$3,402,753	$3,504,836	-	20.92%	-	-
44	93	-	$151,066	$11,631,823	$2,721,415	$2,775,843	-	-13.43%	-	-
45	94	-	$151,066	$13,266,839	$3,806,661	$3,844,728	-	26.93%	-	-
46	95	-	$151,066	$14,717,140	$4,683,001	$4,729,831	-	14.00%	-	-
47	96	-	$151,066	$15,079,820	$4,446,466	$4,490,930	-	2.09%	-	-
48	97	-	$151,066	$16,424,020	$5,165,086	$5,216,737	-	21.19%	-	-
49	98	-	$151,066	$19,241,021	$7,328,981	$7,402,271	-	27.10%	-	-
50	99	-	$151,066	$21,182,790	$8,588,907	$8,674,796	-	-6.38%	-	-
51	100	-	$151,066	$23,376,090	$10,070,363	$10,171,067	-	12.73%	-	-

Note the actual historical S&P 500 returns start January 1, 1980; thus Year 1 reflects the historical S&P 500 returns for 1980, Year 2 reflects 1981, etc.

In Figure 10.1, you'll see how Nina's after-tax brokerage account compares to her IUL LASER Fund. (Note that to keep the chart on a single page, we did not show the following in Figure 10.1: expenses for both types of accounts, and on the IUL policy, multiplier charges, index credits, and interest bonus.)

Comparing activity between The IUL LASER Fund and the after-tax account, at the end of Year 5, Nina's IUL LASER Fund accumulation value would be $529,634. Now let's look at her after-tax account values. Her gross balance (before tax) at the end of Year 5 would be $670,074, and the net after-tax balance would be $645,741.

What's the distinction between the two values? The gross balance indicates the account value before any taxes are incurred (which makes sense because this is a after-tax account, where the gains are not taxed, and the account is not taxed until withdrawals are taken). The net after-tax balance illustrates what the real-world account value would be at that point in time, if taxes were incurred. This helps you get an idea of the after-tax account value at any point in time.

So comparing the two vehicles at the end of Year 5, why are the after-tax account's values higher than The IUL LASER Fund's?

There are a couple reasons: first, IUL LASER Fund policies tend to have higher policy charges during those early years (remember, IUL LASER Funds are long-term financial vehicles). Also, since some of the funds are allocated to two-year and five-year indexing strategies, Nina will not realize some of those returns by the end of Year 5. For example, the $100,000 premium she puts in during Year 5 will not receive returns until Year 7 (for the two-year strategy) and Year 10 (for the five-year strategy).

If by some misfortune Nina were to pass away during Year 5, her designated beneficiary would inherit the after-tax account with a gross balance of $670,074 (we're using the before tax amount because her beneficiary would receive the gross balance and a step-up in basis under current tax law). With The IUL LASER Fund, Nina's heirs would receive over $1.3 million in death benefit from The IUL LASER Fund, income-tax-free.

Now let's look at big-picture comparisons. Nina's LASER Fund will generate $151,066 of tax-free income until she passes away, and still leave behind anywhere from $740,000 (at age 83) to over $10 million (at age 100) income-tax-free to her beneficiaries.

Compare this to the after-tax account, which would generate $151,066 in after-tax income until age 78 (with a nominal $60,000 in after-tax income at age 79) before the account is depleted. Her beneficiaries would receive nothing if she were to pass away after age 79. If she were to pass away before the account runs out of money, they could receive anywhere from about $59,000 (at age 79) to over $2.1 million (at age 70).

Let's dive a little deeper into the details. At age 66, Nina begins withdrawing an annual income of $151,066. By the end of Year 21 (when she's age 70), Nina's income from both vehicles would be the same: a total of $906,396 to-date.

Let's break things down on the income comparisons. The annual income from the after-tax account is $151,066 net after tax (as mentioned above, which is comprised of a long-term capital gains tax of 15% and a state tax of 5%, in this example). Nina is really withdrawing about $189,000 to net $151,066 after the 20% during the first eleven years of income, after which she begins to tap into principal (which is not taxed).

Compare that to the annual income from The IUL LASER Fund, where the $151,066 is completely income-tax-free.

As a side note, we'll use The IUL LASER Fund's surrender value rather than the accumulation value for comparisons from here on out because the surrender value reflects the actual liquid cash available to the policyholder if she surrendered the policy at that point. Remember, surrender value is the accumulation value, minus any outstanding loan balances and surrender charges (and surrender charges disappear after Year 10).

The accumulation value, on the other hand, reflects the total growth of the policy, with the incremental changes year-over-year. This is because annual loans aren't technically withdrawn from the account; they're just borrowed, meaning the policyholder's money is still in the policy, earning interest.

Back to our example, by the end of the Year 21 (at age 70), Nina would have a surrender value of $3,093,768 in her IUL LASER Fund; the after-tax account's gross balance would be $2,121,163 and the net after-tax balance would be $1,806,612. The IUL LASER Fund has about $1 million more in value. Why?

There are a few factors, including the increasing impact of after-tax account expenses and taxes (versus the diminishing costs of The IUL LASER Fund, especially after five to ten years). For example, both accounts saw good returns from age 66 to age 70, but The IUL LASER Fund experienced even better returns, thanks to the multipliers. Also, you can see the advantage of the Alternate Loan on Nina's IUL LASER Fund. She is borrowing at 4.4% while her accumulation value is still earning great returns in those years.

Now let's look at what happened during age 71 to 73, when the market saw a downturn with the dot-com crash and 9/11. Before the downturn, at age 70, Nina's after-tax account net after-tax balance is over $1.8 million. By 73, the net after-tax balance has dropped significantly—all the way down to $829,525 (due to market losses, in addition to her annual income withdrawals).

Compare that to her IUL LASER Fund. At age 70, her surrender value is almost $3.1 million, and at age 73, the value is over $2.4 million. That's a significant difference in not only dollars, but peace of mind.

Looking ahead, Nina's annual income withdrawals quickly deplete the after-tax account. By age 78, Nina has just $251,724 left. She withdraws the final amount of $59,745 the next year, after which her account will run dry, with a $0 balance from that point forward.

But Nina is just seventy-nine years old. What if she lives beyond that (which, according to current longevity trends, she's likely to)? What if Nina makes it to age 90? She would have another eleven years to go.

Going the after-tax account route, she'd need other significant sources of income just to make ends meet, let alone have anything to pass along to her heirs. And even if she did plan ahead with other sources of income, when 2008's big downturn hits market-based vehicles again, what would happen to Nina?

Looking at the big picture, by the time Nina is age 79, her initial $500,000 placed into the after-tax account would have enabled her to realize a total of $2,174,669 in after-tax income.

Over those same years, that same $500,000 put into her IUL LASER Fund would have yielded slightly more in income, $2,265,990, but what's more, Nina could have continued taking out an annual income of $151,066 tax-free for the remainder of the policy.

In the same year her after-tax account runs out of money, her IUL LASER Fund still has over $1.2 million in surrender value. That's a big difference.

By the time she passes away (we'll say that's at age 90), she would have realized a total income of over $3.9 million, tax-free.

Now let's look at how the two accounts impact her heirs. With Nina's after-tax account, she will have nothing left to transfer to her heirs. However, with her IUL LASER Fund account, she would pass on a death benefit of over $2.7 million that would transfer to her heirs income-tax-free.

What if she were to live to age 100? Thanks to the arbitrage of borrowing at 4.4% and allowing the accumulation value to keep earning the amazing returns with the multipliers, she would pass on over $10.1 million to her heirs income-tax-free.

WHAT ABOUT NO-FEE ACCOUNTS?

While we're discussing taxed-as-earned accounts, you may be wondering about accounts that have no fees. That sounds like the ultimate financial vehicle, right? Let's look at this a little closer.

Take a no-load mutual fund, for example. A no-load fund is essentially a mutual fund that you purchase directly from the investment company. Since the arrangement is direct, you don't pay any expenses (commissions, fees, etc.).

No expenses—great, right? The caveat is this is a DIY (do-it-yourself) process. You save on those fees because now you're the one who selects which fund you'll go with—but you're making that choice without the expertise of a financial professional (for example, do you know if you want a bond fund or a stock fund?).

Still, you may be thinking, "Vehicles with no expenses have always got to be better than those with fees. Won't I get farther ahead with a no-fee account than if I had something like an IUL LASER Fund with fees?"

If you were only evaluating financial vehicles based on expenses, yes, something like a no-load mutual fund would be wonderful. But there's much more to consider. Take safety, for example. Your no-load fund is often subject to the whims of the market. If it goes up, great, you see gains. But if the market tanks, you can lose money. On the other hand,

an IUL LASER Fund guarantees you a floor of at least 0%—you can't lose any principal or subsequent earnings due to market volatility.

And then there's our old friend Uncle Sam. He loves no-load mutual funds as much as any other traditional account, because he's going to take a chunk out in taxes every time your fund realizes gains.

What about a different no-fee account, something like a savings account at your local bank? No fees there, so that sounds like it would be a superior vehicle, right? But consider this. Even if the bank were paying you a 1% to 3% interest rate for depositing your money with them, what would you be giving up? The opportunity to earn more.

If your money were in an IUL LASER Fund, for example, you could be earning 7% on average, versus the bank's 1%. Essentially, the bank is costing you 6% in possible returns. That "opportunity cost" of 6% can make a dramatic difference in how much you can earn over time. And it's not just rate of return you're giving up for that "no-fee" bank account.

In summary, no-fee accounts typically have drawbacks, which are important to weigh when comparing with other financial vehicles.

COMPARING THE IUL LASER FUND TO A 401(k)

Moving on to other comparisons, let's look at how a 401(k) would perform versus an IUL LASER Fund. We'll call our person in this example Miguel, and note that he's a sixty-six year-old non-smoker when he begins taking out income.

Before we get started, let's review the fundamentals of a 401(k). A 401(k) is an employer-provided traditional retirement account that puts a percentage of your salary (which you determine) directly into your account, through payroll deduction. It's administered through an outside company (a mutual fund company or brokerage firm), and while the money in your fund can be put to work in a variety of financial vehicles, typical 401(k)s hold an assortment of five or more mutual funds. Often, employers will match contribution funds, up to a certain percentage (up to 3% to 6% of your salary).

One of the major differences between 401(k)s and IUL LASER Funds is the way they can be funded. If you remember, with an IUL LASER Fund, you

can structure the size of the policy to accommodate whatever amount you'd like to put in, and then fund the policy over five to seven years to remain in compliance with TEFRA, DEFRA and TAMRA (such as $10,000 a year, or $100,000 a year like with Miguel's example below, etc.).

With a 401(k), however, you're limited on annual contributions. Currently, the Internal Revenue Code has set the maximum annual contribution at $20,500 a year, or $27,000 if you're age 50 or older.

With the 401(k)'s annual funding limitations, we can't compare apples to apples when it comes to how a 401(k) and IUL LASER Fund are funded. For our illustration, we'll just assume that Miguel has been funding his 401(k) for the past thirty years to arrive at an account value of over $770,000 before taxes, and about $565,000 after-tax value, based on a 27% tax rate. (This after-tax value is comparable to the about $575,000 Miguel has in his IUL LASER Fund's accumulation value.)

When it comes to accessing money from a 401(k), if done before age 59½ you'll likely incur penalties, and currently, you must take Required Minimum Distributions after age 72 (RMDs are based on life expectancy). To access your money, you can choose to withdraw money (which means you'll pay taxes on the money you pull out), or you can borrow from a 401(k) (up to $50,000 maximum a year, with a strict forced repayment plan of five years—or less if you leave your current employer.) For all the rules and regulations related to 401(k)s, be sure to consult an experienced financial professional.

Now before we dive into our illustration, let's take a quick look at comparisons of Miguel's 401(k) versus IUL LASER Fund details, some of which we'll see in Figure 10.2:

- **Assumed average annual interest rate – 401(k)**: We'll assume Miguel's 401(k) earns a 7% average annual rate of return.

- **Assumed average annual interest rate – IUL LASER Fund**: Miguel's IUL LASER Fund is likewise earning a 7% average annual rate of return

- **Expenses - 401(k)**: In this illustration, we'll assume Miguel's fees are 1.5% a year. As a side note, 401(k) fees can vary, and they're often unnoticed or misunderstood by investors. They can include plan administration fees, investment fees, and individual service fees. Since high 401(k) fees can take a bite out of overall returns, it's important to investigate account's fees to see if there are ways to minimize them.

- **Expenses - IUL LASER Fund**: Like all IUL LASER Funds, Miguel's policy expenses include all policy costs, such as premium charges, admin fees, expense charges, and cost of insurance.

- **Taxes - 401(k)**: Miguel puts pre-tax dollars into his 401(k), and his money will grow tax-deferred while in the account. He will be taxed on any withdrawals he makes—we'll assume that he's in a 27% marginal tax bracket. (As a side note, in our example Miguel does not withdraw money before age 59½, but if he did, he would be at risk of incurring a 10% penalty on top of the taxes.)

- **Taxes - IUL LASER Fund**: Remember that The IUL LASER Fund is funded with after-tax dollars, and it allows money to grow tax-free, access money tax-free, and transfer money upon death income-tax-free—so there are no taxes that will be assessed on Miguel's IUL LASER Fund.

Figure 10.2 provides a snapshot of how the two financial vehicles will provide for Miguel during retirement. We'll also examine how taxes (or the lack thereof) will impact his ability to avoid outliving his money. Finally, we'll see how both strategies will impact his beneficiaries when he passes away.

[FIGURE 10.2 ON FOLLOWING PAGE]

FIGURE 10.2

End of Year	Age	Premium	IUL LASER Fund Policy Using Indexing Strategies Based on 7% Growth				401(k) Based on 7% Growth With 1.5% Fees			
			Tax-Free Income via Policy Loans	Accumulation Value	Surrender Value	Death Benefit	Pre-Tax Withdrawal	After-Tax With-drawal	Gross Balance (Before Tax)	Net After-Tax Balance
6	66	-	$51,156	$575,904	$493,621	$1,252,286	$70,077	$51,156	$773,615	$564,739
7	67	-	$51,156	$613,470	$475,689	$1,195,887	$70,077	$51,156	$741,494	$541,291
8	68	-	$51,156	$653,429	$461,039	$1,136,667	$70,077	$51,156	$707,640	$516,578
9	69	-	$51,156	$695,840	$445,879	$1,074,487	$70,077	$51,156	$671,960	$490,531
10	70	-	$51,156	$740,725	$430,091	$1,009,197	$70,077	$51,156	$634,355	$463,079
11	71	-	$51,156	$788,230	$413,653	$940,643	$70,077	$51,156	$594,721	$434,147
12	72	-	$51,156	$841,889	$399,940	$513,996	$70,077	$51,156	$552,949	$403,653
13	73	-	$51,156	$902,730	$389,811	$489,111	$70,077	$51,156	$508,923	$371,514
14	74	-	$51,156	$967,681	$375,402	$462,494	$70,077	$51,156	$462,522	$337,641
15	75	-	$51,156	$1,037,061	$361,454	$434,049	$70,077	$51,156	$413,618	$301,941
16	76	-	$51,156	$1,111,131	$348,030	$403,587	$70,077	$51,156	$362,076	$264,315
17	77	-	$51,156	$1,189,935	$334,965	$394,462	$70,077	$51,156	$307,752	$224,659
18	78	-	$51,156	$1,273,768	$322,336	$386,025	$70,077	$51,156	$250,498	$182,864
19	79	-	$51,156	$1,362,950	$310,233	$378,381	$70,077	$51,156	$190,155	$138,813
20	80	-	$51,156	$1,457,819	$298,752	$371,643	$70,077	$51,156	$126,557	$92,386
21	81	-	$51,156	$1,558,711	$287,978	$365,913	$70,077	$59,527	$59,527	$43,455
22	82	-	$51,156	$1,665,922	$277,938	$361,234	$59,527	$43,455	-	-
23	83	-	$51,156	$1,779,784	$268,686	$357,675	-	-	-	-
24	84	-	$51,156	$1,900,618	$260,252	$355,283	-	-	-	-
25	85	-	$51,156	$2,028,702	$252,604	$354,039	-	-	-	-
26	86	-	$51,156	$2,164,222	$245,605	$353,816	-	-	-	-
27	87	-	$51,156	$2,307,688	$239,426	$354,811	-	-	-	-
28	88	-	$51,156	$2,459,374	$233,986	$356,955	-	-	-	-
29	89	-	$51,156	$2,619,429	$229,057	$360,029	-	-	-	-
30	90	-	$51,156	$2,788,000	$224,397	$363,797	-	-	-	-

Miguel wants to realize an annual income of $51,156 from his financial vehicle. With The IUL LASER Fund, he can take that income in the form of a tax-free Alternate Loan. With the 401(k), however, his money in the account is tax-deferred. When he withdraws it, he must pay income tax. So he would need to withdraw $70,077 and pay taxes in his 27% tax bracket to net that desired $51,156 a year.

Look at age 66, where Miguel's 401(k) account value is shown in both pre-tax, $773,615, and after-tax terms, $564,739. In the early years, the 401(k)'s after-tax account value would be higher than his IUL LASER Fund's surrender value, but this will shift over time.

Look at what happens at age 81 through 83. At age 81, Miguel would take his last year of full income from his 401(k). By age 82, he would only be

able to take the remainder of what's in the account, or $59,527 in pre-tax dollars (which would be $43,455 after taxes). Then at age 83, his account would be zeroed out.

For total income over the years, he would have netted over $870,322 in after-tax income. But at age 83, he'd need other sources of income to get through his final years, and he'd have nothing to pass on to his heirs from this account.

By contrast, with The IUL LASER Fund, Miguel would still be taking his full $51,156 tax-free annual income from age 83 to age 90. When he passes away at age 90, his total income would be $1,278,900 tax-free, and he'd have that death benefit of $363,797 to pass along to his heirs, income-tax-free.

Let's pause for a moment to consider Miguel's heirs—how do the two vehicles impact the amount they receive if Miguel were to pass away earlier? As you look at the chart, in every year except Year 13, The IUL LASER Fund's death benefit is higher than the 401(k)'s before-tax balance. With 401(k)s, it's important to note that while beneficiaries receive the before-tax balance, they are responsible for paying taxes on that amount over the next ten years (under current laws). Looking at this example, we can see heirs still come out ahead in most years when money is in an IUL LASER Fund.

As you can see, 401(k)s have some advantages—tax-deferred growth and employer matching. Thus, they can play a role in a balanced approach to financial planning, but it's wise to note they do have some disadvantages, such as they:

- Are taxed on the back end, which can be costly for retirees, many of whom find themselves in a tax bracket that's as high as or higher than their working years

- May have costly expenses

- May provide little to no safety (remember the millions of Americans with 401[k]s invested in the market who lost up to 40% of their account values—twice—between 2000 and 2010?)

- Offer limited liquidity (removing money before age 59½ usually incurs a 10% penalty on top of the taxes)

- Have current contribution limits of $20,500 a year, or $27,000 if you're age 50 or older—if you want to set aside more money annually (due to high income or lump sums), other vehicles like The IUL LASER Fund are more flexible in the contribution amount they can accommodate

WHAT ABOUT A ROTH IRA?

You may be wondering about a comparison between The IUL LASER Fund and a traditional financial vehicle that gets a lot of praise: the Roth IRA. People often notice Roth IRAs and IUL LASER Funds have similar advantages. And they're right. You fund both vehicles with after-tax dollars, and the popular benefits for both are tax-deferred growth on the money in the account/policy and tax-free income on the back end.

But that's where the similarities stop, like in how you can access your money. With a Roth IRA, you can only withdraw money under very specific rules, including:

- After age 59½ (or you may incur a 10% tax on your withdrawal) or after five years

- For the purchase of a first home with a limit of $10,000

- In the case of the owner's death or disability

As for putting money into your Roth IRA, there are severe annual maximum contribution limits: $6,000 a year for those age 49 and under, or $7,000 if you're age 50 or older (which, by the way, are the same contribution limits as a traditional IRA).

With these low maximums, it would be impossible for you to use a Roth IRA to set aside an amount as high as $500,000. (Doing the math, even if you had started setting aside $6,000 a year in your Roth IRA from age 20 to 49, that would subtotal just $180,000. At $7,000 a year from age 50 to 65 ($105,000), you would have put in an overall total of $285,000 by age 66.

Plus, your income could be too high to participate in a Roth IRA. Currently, Roth IRA contributions are limited after a certain threshold for modified adjusted gross income, and at a certain income point, they are completely off limits.

This is why a lot of our clients can't participate in a Roth IRA, and why many CPAs call The IUL LASER Fund the "rich person's Roth." Why? Because both use after-tax money and provide income-tax-free advantages.

But where the Roth limits contributions, The IUL LASER Fund has no cap on your income level, or the amount you'd like to contribute—thus it has all the advantages of a Roth, but it's available to those with higher net worth. Plus, Roths do not have an income-tax-free death benefit that can leave a slightly higher amount than the surrender value to your heirs.

We like to point out, however, that The IUL LASER Fund isn't just for the wealthy. You can fill a policy with as little as $500 a month. So, it could be said instead, The IUL LASER Fund is "Everyone's Strategy."

Also, Roth IRAs can be invested in anything from a CD to money in the market, and most are in the market. The challenge here is it puts you at risk of losing money due to volatility in the market. As you know, The IUL LASER Fund has the reassurance of "zero's the hero"—with a guaranteed floor or 0% in down years and locked-in gains (see Section I, Chapter 6 for a refresher if needed). You can also choose to supercharge your returns on your IUL LASER Fund with multipliers.

The other huge advantage of an IUL LASER Fund over a Roth IRA is the opportunity to borrow money from your IUL policy with Alternate Loans. Let's say you borrow money at 4.5%, the money in your policy continues to earn indexed returns, which has historically been 5% to 10%. This way you're earning on that spread, benefiting from arbitrage.

And you can also choose to repay your loans on your policy, which you cannot do with a Roth IRA. Let's say you borrowed $500,000 tax-free from your policy to remodel your house. A couple years later you came into a windfall of $500,000—you could immediately drop all of that $500,000 into your policy to repay the loan. You could not do the same with a Roth IRA, due to contribution limits.

Even with all of Uncle Sam's strings attached to a Roth, there may be times when it makes sense to have one within your balanced portfolio—particularly because its tax advantages are noteworthy.

(As a side note, it's helpful to keep in mind tax laws may change. It has been rumored that a tax on Roth IRAs may be in the offing, with a possible

"excess tax" on Roth IRAs with high account values. Just a caution: always keep an eye on Uncle Sam.) Like we keep saying, it all comes down to staying informed so you can make educated decisions and create the best overall financial strategy for your individual situation and goals.

WHAT ABOUT A TAX-FREE BOND FUND?

Another financial vehicle that delivers tax advantages is a tax-free bond fund. In short, a tax-free bond fund is a fund comprised of several different municipal bonds. It offers typically conservative fixed rates of return and is exempt from federal income tax.

While it can play a tax-advantaged role in a diversified portfolio, a tax-free bond fund is often outpaced by The IUL LASER Fund in two areas: rate of return and continued growth during the distribution phase.

The IUL LASER Fund often provides higher average rates of return in any given market. And when you access money during the distribution phase, The IUL LASER Fund gives you a greater advantage because of the arbitrage on your IUL LASER Fund loans (see Section I, Chapter 8 for more details).

Furthermore, upon your passing, this type of bond fund may transfer tax-free, but like the Roth, it does not provide an income-tax-free death benefit that can leave a slightly higher amount than the surrender value to your heirs. Again, your financial professional can run a comparison between these two vehicles to help you make choices that are best for you.

BUYING TERM & INVESTING THE DIFFERENCE ... ON STEROIDS

We've also had professionals say The IUL LASER Fund approach is like "buying term and investing the difference, but on steroids." To explain what they mean, let's start with buying term and investing the difference—this is a strategy that has been used in the financial industry for decades. (In fact, when Doug started his career, that's often what he helped his clients do—until IUL LASER Funds came along.)

Buying term and investing the difference starts with the premise that you're buying term life insurance solely for the death benefit. Term insurance typically has a specific time limit on the policy: you buy it for a five-, ten-, or twenty-year period. It has no cash accumulation value or living benefits. Coverage lapses the moment premiums are no longer paid into the policy.

While it has these restrictions, the appeal of term insurance is that it's less expensive than many other types of life insurance. Thus the strategy goes, if you buy term, you're saving money on life insurance. You then take the rest of your money earmarked for savings and put it into another financial vehicle. This way you've got your death benefit covered, and you're taking steps to (hopefully) accrue retirement income down the road.

You could draw the analogy that buying term and investing the difference is kind of like knowing you ultimately want to go on fabulous vacations, but for now you spend as little as you can on "staycations" around town. You continue to stash the rest of your would-be vacation money in a financial vehicle so it can grow. Eventually, you use it to pay for that amazing four-week trip to Europe.

Well, with The IUL LASER Fund, you get the best of both worlds. You get the death benefit AND you get the opportunity for cash accumulation, tax advantages, and the ability to take money out in the form of loans. This is why it's been described as "buying term and investing the difference, but on steroids."

Let's take a quick look at a broader comparison, examining how even more financial vehicles deliver on different aspects of financial advantages. There are a few things to note in Figure 10.3 below. In the far left column, you'll see features, including:

- **Liquidity** - How easily can you access your money at any time?

- **Safety** - How safe is the institution and how safe is your principal from downturns in the market?

- **Rate of Return** - How predictable are the rates of return?

- **Tax-Free Access to Money** - Can you access your money tax-free?

- **Tax-Deferred** - Can the account grow tax-deferred or tax-free?

- **Tax-Deductible Payments** - Do you fund the account with pre-tax dollars?

- **Tax-Free Wealth Transfer** - Can you transfer your money to your heirs income-tax-free?

- **Penalty-Free** - Can you access your money without incurring penalties (like those levied by the IRS or the financial institutions)?

- **Leverage** - Can you earn more money than the financial institution is earning (for example, with The IUL LASER Fund, you have leverage because you're linking your return to an index, as explained in Section I, Chapter 6)? Also, can you access your money by borrowing at a lower rate than your financial vehicle is being credited?

- **Collateral** - When borrowing money from the vehicle, can you use the financial vehicle's account value to collateralize a loan from the same financial institution (or another)?

- **Disability Benefit** - If you suffer from a critical/chronic illness or need long-term care, can your financial vehicle offer the opportunity to access additional money to cover related expenses?

FIGURE 10.3

Comparing Financial Vehicles

OPTIMAL FEATURES	IRA/401(K) IN THE MARKET	MUTUAL FUNDS	HOME	CDs & BANK SAVINGS	ANNUITIES	REAL ESTATE	IUL LASER FUND
Liquidity - Use & Control	Possible w/Loan or Surrender	Yes	Yes with Equity Line	Yes	Yes, Possible Penalties	Yes with Equity Line	Yes
Safety - Protected from Market Loss	No	No	No	Yes	Possible	No	Yes
Predictable Rates of Return	No	No	No	Yes	Possible	No	Yes w/0% Floor
Tax-Free Access to Money	No	No	To IRS Limitations	No	No	To IRS Limitations	Yes
Tax-Deferred	Yes	No	Possible	Possible	Yes	Possible	Yes
Tax-Deductible Payments	Yes	No	Interest Portion Only	Possible	Possible	Possible	No
Tax-Free Wealth Transfer	No	No	To IRS Limitations	No	No	Possible	Yes
Penalty-Free	No	Possible	Yes	No	No	Yes	Optional
Leverage	No	No	Possible	No	No	Possible	Yes
Collateral	No	Yes	Yes	Yes	No	Yes	Yes
Disability Benefit	No	No	No	No	No	No	Yes

If you glance at the chart, you'll see several of the financial vehicles with "No" in their columns. Now look at the column for The IUL LASER Fund, where you see "Yes" after "Yes", with just one "No" and one "Optional" (which we'll get to). This underscores how many critical features The IUL LASER Fund offers your financial future:

- **Liquidity** - The IUL LASER Fund allows you to access your money tax-free via loans within the first or second year of the policy (typically up to 80% to 90% of the surrender value).

- **Safety** - IUL LASER Funds are maximum-funded IUL policies with insurance companies, companies that have historically been among the safest financial institutions in America. Many of these companies have been around for over 100 years and sailed through the Great Depression and Great Recession. They also have high ratings with A.M. Best and other rating agencies. As for safety of principal, The IUL LASER Fund protects you with a 0% guaranteed floor during market downturns.

- **Rate of Return** - IUL LASER Funds can provide predictable rates of return, historically averaging 5% to 10%.

- **Tax-Free Access to Money** - When you borrow from your IUL LASER Fund, you can access your money tax-free. This is possible because it's via a loan, which is not subject to tax (as long as the policy is not a MEC and remains in force until death).

- **Tax-Deferred** - The accumulation value in The IUL LASER Fund grows tax-deferred, which is why we refer to its capability for tax-free growth. (Note—Your policy's growth would only be taxable if you accessed money the Dumb Way—see Section I, Chapter 8.)

- **Tax-Deductible Payments** - Here's the only place you'll see a "No" on the chart—which is actually a positive, not a negative. We actually like that this one is a No because with The IUL LASER Fund, you pay your taxes up front before you put money into your policy. This allows your money to grow tax-free, and with loans you can access your money tax-free, and transfer income-tax-free to your heirs upon your passing.

- **Tax-Free Wealth Transfer** - As mentioned above, when you pass away, the available money in your policy will transfer to your heirs income-tax-free, in the form of a death benefit. Note that if you have any outstanding loans, those will be deducted from the death benefit, as shown in the illustrations in Chapters 9 and 10.

- **Penalty-Free** - You'll see "Optional" here, which is also a good thing. Most policies include a surrender charge during the first ten years. The surrender charge is a penalty that's incurred if you happen to cancel or surrender the policy in the first ten years. As you can see in the illustrations in Chapter 9, the surrender charge decreases each year until it disappears after Year 10. It's possible to pay an extra cost to exclude the surrender charge, but most people opt to include this optional penalty to enjoy lower fees. They want The IUL LASER Fund for long-term goals, so they don't anticipate canceling their policy during the first ten years.

- **Leverage** - As we've mentioned with loans, you can borrow from your policy with an Alternate Loan, which allows your accumulation value to continue earning interest and enjoy the opportunity for arbitrage—borrowing at a lower rate while potentially earning a higher rate of return with your index strategies.

- **Collateral** - With The IUL LASER Fund, your money technically remains in the policy as collateral when you borrow via a Zero Wash Loan or Alternate Loan. Some policyholders also use the accumulation value in their policy as collateral for loans with external financial institutions, such as banks or credit unions.

- **Disability Benefit** - Some policies offer riders that can allow you to accelerate your death benefit to access money for expenses related to critical/chronic illness or long-term care. To illustrate, let's say you need long-term care, and the rider on your policy allows you to access up to 2% of your death benefit a month to go toward related expenses. Some of these riders are built into the policy; others require you to add the rider before you initiate the policy.

Clearly, there are a lot of differences in how the various financial vehicles can provide income during retirement; are impacted by the market; are subject to taxes; etc. But perhaps the most surprising difference is ... while you can refer to almost all of these and other popular financial vehicles as an investment, you can't call The IUL LASER Fund an investment.

Even though it's an excellent accumulation tool that provides safety for your after-tax dollars. Even though its rate of return performance can average 5% to 10% annually. Even though it provides liquidity, allowing you to take out money at any age, income-tax-free. Even though it can provide money that passes on to your heirs after you do, income-tax-free.

You still can't call it an investment.

Why?

We'll tell you in the next chapter (look for the Reason #10).

TOP 5 TAKEAWAYS

1. How does The IUL LASER Fund compare to other traditional financial vehicles? This chapter walked you through in-depth comparisons.

2. We kicked things off with a comparison to an after-tax account with tax-deferred growth.

3. Next, we put The IUL LASER Fund side-by-side with a 401(k).

4. We also discussed the difference between The IUL LASER Fund and other vehicles, like no-fee accounts, Roth IRAs, and tax-free bond funds.

5. We believe in the power that comes from making informed decisions about your own financial future. Comparisons like these help you weigh your options and make choices that are best for your financial situation.

Why Isn't Everybody Doing This?

By now you may be feeling like something of an IUL LASER Fund aficionado. You have a grasp of what the financial vehicle is, how it came about, and more important, how it can provide liquidity, safety, predictable rates of return, tax-free income, and a death benefit (not to mention capital accumulation that can be used for "living benefits"). With all its superior advantages, you may now be wondering, "Why isn't everybody doing this?"

Great question. In fact, we've had countless people who, once they understand the benefits of The IUL LASER Fund, ask us the same thing. One of our clients, for example, has been a successful consultant for nearly 40 years, and her husband a partner in a law firm. After her beloved husband passed away from cancer, she took over the reins of the family finances—and she realized how little she knew. It was about this time she happened to come across one of Doug's articles on The IUL LASER Fund and decided to attend a seminar. She was intrigued but hesitant, wondering why she (and her savvy husband and his colleagues) had never heard of these strategies before.

With deep curiosity (but residual skepticism), she decided to attend a more in-depth two-day seminar—and she brought along her estate

attorney, her CPA, and a trusted family friend (a CEO of a large company) to help her vet the strategies. When all three professionals found the strategies to be sound, prudent, IRS compliant, and advantageous, she decided she was all in. (So did her CPA, who opened an IUL LASER Fund shortly after). Our client is now on a path toward better liquidity, safety, predictable rates of return, and tax advantages.

We've heard the initial pushback on IUL LASER Funds enough over the years that we've compiled a list of why everybody isn't taking advantage of The IUL LASER Fund, and it includes:

The TOP 10 Reasons Your Financial Professional
Didn't Tell You About This

#1 – LACK OF AWARENESS

There's a story Author and Motivational Speaker Zig Ziglar told about a young wife who sends her husband to the butcher to buy a ham. When he returns, she asks why he didn't have the butcher cut the ends off of the ham. The husband, perplexed, asks why that would be necessary. The wife admits she doesn't know—but her mother always did it. They go to her mother to find out why, and her mother says that likewise, she doesn't know—her mother had always done it, too. Finally, the women ask Grandma, who explains she cut the ends off the ham because her roasting pan was too small.

In many aspects of life—from cooking to spirituality to communication to finances—we often repeat what we've been taught because, well, we never bother to question the practice or consider approaching it any other way. We get in line; we mimic patterns; we follow the crowd, often without even realizing it. We don't know what we don't know.

From the time they were introduced, traditional accounts like IRAs and 401(k)s were extremely popular—essentially "everyone was doing it." But over the past few years, more financial experts have been decrying the downsides of relying solely on IRAs and 401(k)s for retirement planning. Headlines reveal increasing industry caution regarding these financial vehicles devised by (and arguably for) Uncle Sam, with articles like, "The Champions of the 401(k) Lament the Revolution They Start-

ed" (*Wall Street Journal*, Jan. 2, 2017); "Think Twice Before You Open an IRA" (*Forbes*, Jan. 16, 2015); "This Is a Smart Reason Not to Save in a 401(k)" (*Time*, May 24, 2016); and "13 Reasons Why Your 401(k) Is Your Riskiest Investment" (*Entrepreneur*, May 12, 2015).

Despite the growing concern surrounding these vehicles, millions of Americans continue to follow their financial professionals' conventional advice. They're putting all their retirement eggs in these traditional accounts' baskets, hoping it will develop into a nice big nest egg someday. Why? They hear everyone else is doing it. They don't know (or don't bother) to look beyond the IRA or 401(k) for other solutions.

#2 - PATH OF LEAST RESISTANCE

Sometimes it's not ignorance that keeps people from the benefits of vehicles like The IUL LASER Fund; it's downright avoidance. In physical science, we learn that matter, energy, and objects often take the path of least resistance. When a stream flows down the mountain, for example, it will likely follow the path with soft silt rather than solid rock. We humans aren't much different. When life presents a challenge, all too often we opt for the easier solution, regardless of whether it's the best solution.

Looking at many traditional financial vehicles through this lens, there are many financial professionals who are aware there may be additional options. However, they would rather sidestep the extra effort and personal responsibility it would require to help clients pursue diversified financial strategies. It's much easier to follow the herd, to recommend clients sign up for whatever qualified plan is being offered at the office, or to let clients "turn things over to their financial guy so he can handle it."

But as countless Americans learned during what we call the Lost Decade, taking the supposed easy road can lead down rocky paths. Between 2000 and 2010, millions of Americans lost 40% of their IRA and 401(k) account values—twice. Compare that to our clients who owned IUL LASER Funds. Their principal was protected by a 0% guaranteed floor, which means they did not lose any money due to market volatility. They also earned significant returns during the up years, locking in those gains.

#3 – TOO MUCH WORK

Even as more financial experts have come to agree with The IUL LASER Fund and other sound but unconventional financial strategies, it doesn't mean the professionals always utilize them with their clients. Why? It isn't necessarily easy. It actually requires a lot of personal responsibility and focus from the financial professionals. These strategies necessitate ongoing professional education, staying abreast of the latest products, regulations, and industry changes. This approach demands ongoing attention to clients' needs, year-after-year, to make any necessary adjustments as life unfolds.

For several years we taught these principles to thousands of CPAs, tax attorneys, and financial professionals from around the country. They would come to our Educational Institute and invest several days in continuing professional education, learning how to properly structure and fund the financial vehicles we recommend. They would get an in-depth examination of the related tax laws. They would explore how to teach their clients about these strategies and work alongside them for years to come.

But what we found was only the truly motivated professionals would return and implement the principles, bringing all the benefits to their clients. More often than not, many of the financial professionals would go back to their companies and fall into their old routines, offering a narrower mix of less-than-optimal strategies. Why? Because it was easier. It was what they were used to. It required too much effort. Traditional investments only required the client's name, address, Social Security Number and a check. (The IUL LASER Fund often takes several weeks to establish, plus a minimum of five years to fund properly.)

In fact, we had an incident where a major credit union enlisted our team to train its staff from nine branches on how to utilize these strategies. Then they brought us in to present these principles to nearly 200 of their clients. The event was a success, and about three months later they asked us to come back to give another client seminar. When we asked how the strategies were going for the clients who had participated in the initial seminar, the credit union explained they hadn't actually implemented them with their clients. They admitted, "Your seminar was a really good way to get people in, get their info, and get them going on some of our other products. We don't have time to educate them on these strategies."

We asked, "But isn't it better for your clients in the long run to use The IUL LASER Fund strategies we've shared?" The credit union folks shrugged and said, "What the client doesn't know won't hurt them."

We believe in the opposite—what the client doesn't know can hurt them; and conversely, what the client does know can *empower* them. Needless to say, that was the last time we worked with this credit union.

#4 – SELLING CLUBS VS. TEACHING THE SWING

Let's say you were going to be playing in a golf tournament and you had the choice of using a professional golfer's swing, someone like Jordan Spieth or legends like Jack Nicklaus, or you could use his clubs. Which would you rather use?

The answer is obvious: the swing. Once you have a successful swing down, you're capable of maintaining success. But all too often people look to whatever clubs the pros are using. They'll buy the latest ones, designed with state-of-the-art technology and materials—rather than focus on adding to their knowledge and skill.

Applying this to financial strategies, many well-meaning financial professionals focus on selling the clubs, or commodities—they tell their clients to buy this mutual fund, or open that IRA, or invest in gold or silver. Their clients comply with their financial professional and hope for the best. But those clients may be facing the awful reality down the road of outliving their money due to the impact of increased taxes, inflation, and the volatility of the market.

And when it comes to passing along wealth after they pass away? Many tax attorneys tend to divide up the golf clubs and the trophies among the kids and grandkids, instead of helping their clients leave behind the wisdom of "how to swing."

#5 – NOT AS LUCRATIVE

All of us in the financial industry earn our living by selling our clients clubs (offering and/or managing financial vehicles). But some clubs are more lucrative to sell than others. And that's where you need to have

a bit of caution. Ask yourself what your financial professionals have to gain by selling you a certain set of clubs, or a new set of clubs every time the latest line is introduced. Do they have your best interest in mind?

If you're a golfer, you've probably been through this routine. You head to the golf store, where golf instructors will ask you to swing for them. They'll then sell you clubs that fit your swing ... or the line that offers them the biggest commission.

Traditional financial professionals are taught to recommend putting all your money in traditional financial vehicles like mutual funds, money market accounts, stocks, and bonds. Because that's where the big financial institutions make their money, off their management fees, that 1% to 2% assessed on your financial vehicles. These aren't one-time commissions; they're ongoing, annual fees charged against the money in your account.

While 1% to 2% fees aren't exorbitant, the biggest downside is that with many traditional accounts, your money is at risk in the market. They're encouraging you to use financial vehicles that simply can't provide you the level of safety you deserve, but often financial professionals will keep on recommending this approach because that's where they're positioned to make the most money.

#6 – ONLY SO MUCH IN INSURANCE

While 1% to 2% fees aren't exorbitant, the biggest downside is that with many traditional accounts, your money is at risk in the market. Financial regulations have set limits on how much of your money can go into life insurance. This is why "buy term and invest the difference" is such a common approach. After you've gotten your life insurance coverage, traditional financial professionals often encourage you to put the rest of your money in traditional vehicles (where those financial professionals stand to make more in management fees).

The rationale is they want you to be "diversified." Now diversification itself is something all of us experts agree with. But the danger comes when you have a significant portion of your money in the traditional vehicles—it's at risk in the market.

This approach is akin to telling the Three Little Pigs to diversify their money by spreading it among each of their three houses. After the big bad wolf comes along, huffing and puffing, only the money in the brick house remains. The rest is gone with the wind. And the Three Little Pigs are now forced to live out their retirement splitting what's left—which probably means their bacon is cooked.

Remember the Hansens, whom we described in Section I, Chapter 8? Fortunately they had moved about 90% of their money from their 401(k) to an IUL LASER Fund before the Great Recession began. The 90% was safe—they didn't lose any of this portion due to market volatility. The 10% that was still in their 401(k), however, blew away with the economic tornadoes of 2008 to 2009.

Diversification is great in theory, but we'd pose the question—why not diversify your money among vehicles that provide the blend of up to four different types of income we introduced in Section I, Chapter 2 (and that we'll explain further in Section I, Chapter 14):

- Investment income
- Real Estate income
- Guaranteed income
- Tax-Free income

#7 – ISN'T INSURANCE TOO EXPENSIVE?

The notion that insurance is too expensive to use as a capital accumulation tool is one of the biggest misperceptions. Many uninformed financial professionals repeat this myth, without stopping to really understand and compare the costs.

Yes, if you were to look at the first few years of an IUL LASER Fund, the costs are higher than many other financial vehicles during that time-frame. But as we illustrated throughout Section I, Chapter 9, The IUL LASER Fund is a long-term financial vehicle, and when you treat it as such (properly structuring and funding it over time), it can yield cost-effective results.

Once you get into Years 3 to 6, The IUL LASER Fund often begins to pay for itself. In the long run, it's among the least expensive vehicles. If you recall

in Section I, Chapter 9, in Figure 9.1, we provide an illustration of an IUL LASER Fund, and in Column 4, you can see details on the policy charges, or expenses. In that same chart, you can also see in the third to last column the net annual accumulation value rate of return. This shows the net rate of return after fees, in any given year.

In this IUL LASER Fund example, we used a gross average rate of return of 7.5%. Now in that third to last column, you'll see from Year 11 on, the net rate of return is higher than 7.5% (around 7.7%), because the interest bonus is significantly higher than the fees.

Also in Figure 9.2, we explain internal rate of return in detail. To summarize, over the life of the policy, the net rate of return was 6.5% average every year net of all fees and expenses (retroactive to Day 1). Because the gross rate of return was 7.5% and the net rate of return was 6.5%, the average cost over the life of the policy was 1%. When structured properly, The IUL LASER Fund clearly gives you more bang for your buck—not to mention liquidity, safety, tax-free income, and the death benefit.

When structured properly, The IUL LASER Fund clearly gives you more bang for your buck—not to mention liquidity, safety, tax-free income, and the death benefit.

#8 – ISN'T IT ONLY FOR THE WEALTHY?

It's true that IUL LASER Funds are ideal for high-net-worth individuals. When structured correctly, the policies can accommodate very large sums of money—you can put millions of dollars into a single policy in as few as five years. Compare that to a 401(k), where you're currently limited to annual contributions of $20,500 ($27,000 if you're age 50 or over), and IRAs, with annual contribution limits of $6,000 ($7,000 for age 50 and over).

Because they're a valuable vehicle for the affluent, many financial professionals assume IUL LASER Funds aren't a viable option for those of more modest means. But nothing could be farther from the truth.

We have many clients who open a "starter plan," an IUL LASER Fund designed for moderate contributions—say, just $500 a month. While this means they're only putting in $6,000 a year, over time (with the growth of the policy), IUL LASER Funds can grow significantly in value.

For example, if a policyholder put $500 a month in her policy from age 25 to age 65, she would likely have $1.3 million in her policy, and be able to take out $100,000 to $130,000 a year in tax-free income for the rest of her life. Of course, forty years down the road, $130,000 will not go as far as it would in today's dollars, but it's still a valuable addition to her retirement income. This is why people don't need to wait until they have a lot of money to begin utilizing IUL LASER Funds. They can begin with a starter plan, and as their ability to set money aside increases, they can open additional policies, fund them with larger amounts, and benefit from multiple IUL LASER Funds.

Now what if you have even less than $500 a month to set aside? When we Andrew children were born, our parents, Doug and Sharee, opened policies for each of us. They structured the policies for long-term contributions, and started by putting in just $25 a month. As we grew up, we'd add whatever we could to our policies, whether that was birthday money from grandparents, or money from our high school jobs. By the time we were in college, we could borrow from our own LASER Funds to pay for things like tuition and books.

That said, part of The IUL LASER Fund's "only for the wealthy" reputation comes from the fact that there are some financial professionals who prefer to only work with the wealthy. They tend to be smaller firms that don't have the infrastructure to teach and guide individuals who can only afford smaller policies. This is part of the reason we've focused so much on growing our business and implementing educational programs—to help as many people as we can along the financial spectrum to take advantage of The IUL LASER Fund.

The bottom line: IUL LASER Funds aren't just for the wealthy. They can provide equal-opportunity benefits for people of various financial means. And what's more, since you can own several policies, you can open additional policies as your ability to set more money aside increases. So it's the kind of financial option that you can leverage throughout your different stages of life.

#9 – HARDLY ANYONE'S DOING THIS, RIGHT?

There's a misperception that hardly anyone is utilizing The IUL LASER Fund approach, so wouldn't it be better to just follow the crowd with traditional accounts like IRAs and 401(k)s? However, industry statistics

prove that quite a good-sized crowd is gathering around the liquidity, safety, rate of return, and tax advantages of this vehicle.

As mentioned in Section I, Chapter 1, the IUL industry has grown nearly 20% year-over-year for the past several years. In addition to those insurance companies that have specialized in IULs for years, more of the nation's large financial planning companies are adding IULs to their offerings. This significant growth is evidence that more Americans are taking note of the powerful IUL policies' advantages.

#10 – IF IT'S SO GOOD, WHY DON'T YOU CALL IT AN INVESTMENT?

We've mentioned earlier that The IUL LASER Fund is not called an investment. That confuses some folks (even some financial professionals), because the general assumption is anything you would use to set aside money to prepare for retirement should be called an investment, right? Nope.

Financial regulators differentiate between traditional accounts, like IRAs, 401(k)s, and mutual funds—what they call "investments"—and other financial vehicles, such as insurance policies.

And truly, that makes sense. Because a financial vehicle like The IUL LASER Fund is at its core an insurance policy, the primary reason for the policy is INSURANCE. IUL LASER Funds provide a valuable death benefit—and it just so happens, living benefits, as well. Despite the multitude of benefits it can provide, it is called insurance, plain and simple. And that designation is what allows it to be tax-advantaged under the Internal Revenue Code.

YOUR OWN SOLE PROPRIETORSHIP

Since many financial professionals aren't recommending The IUL LASER Fund, we return to questions we posed earlier in the book. First, who really should be your fiduciary? YOU. You're the one who has the biggest stake in your financial future. You're the one who has your best interest in mind. You're the one who deserves to understand your options so you can make informed decisions on what will help you best achieve your goals.

In Section I, Chapter 2, we discussed the notion of partnership, asking if you'd want a business partner who demanded you do all the work in building the business. If the business struggled along the way, he wouldn't offer any financial protection. When you sold or liquidated the company, he'd plan on taking one-third of the profits—and he could reserve the right to increase that percentage at any time. If you decided to sell early, he'd charge a 10% penalty in addition to his third. And if you wanted to sell it later than he deemed appropriate, he'd force you to sell and pay his portion sooner than later. We revealed this is exactly how Uncle Sam approaches his partnership with you and IRAs and 401(k)s.

Now if you could guarantee that your financial strategy partner were a good one: providing predictability and safety, someone who had your back, you'd be all in. But since Uncle Sam isn't that kind of partner with traditional retirement accounts, it might be helpful to think of approaching your financial future as a "sole proprietor." In business, a sole proprietor runs her business on her own, making the decisions and taking on the responsibilities of growing the company as she sees fit.

Financial vehicles like The IUL LASER Fund provide opportunities to be your own sole proprietor. As you work with qualified experts as your guide in maximum funding your policy, you're essentially self-insuring yourself (we'll talk more about self-insurance in Section I, Chapter 13). You own your policy. You decide which indexing strategy you want. You get the benefits of safety, liquidity, and predictable rates of return. And you're guaranteed not to lose when the market goes down, along with significant upsides like the opportunity for tax-free income and income-tax-free to your heirs upon death.

GETTING IN THE SWING OF THINGS

Going back to our discussion on the clubs vs. the swing, we recommend you learn the best swing, then move forward in choosing your clubs. There was a Kevin Costner film in the 90s, *Tin Cup*, that illustrates the value of the swing point perfectly. In one scene, Costner's character, Former Golf Pro Roy McAvoy, is trying to play into the US Open. In the qualifying tournament, he and his caddy snap all but one of his clubs, the 7-iron, in frustration. McAvoy ends up having to hit the rest of the round with just that 7-iron—which he uses to drive, get to the green,

wedge, putt, and eventually par the back-nine. Everyone wonders how. But Costner's character has a pro's swing, and sure enough, that was more valuable than a bag full of the world's best clubs.

The swing is where it's at. That's why when planning for the financial future, we favor having the knowledge of how to optimize assets, minimize taxes, and live abundantly throughout retirement (rather than outliving our money) so we can choose which financial vehicles, or clubs, are best along the way. As for our posterity, we'd rather leave behind the ability to swing, rather than dumping the trophies in our posterity's laps. For Authentic Wealth that lasts, our children and grandchildren will need to be empowered and self-reliant for generations.

Because we believe so strongly in this approach for ourselves, we believe in sharing this approach with others—in one-on-one meetings with clients, in speaking engagements nationwide, in 3 Dimensional Wealth YouTube videos, radio shows, and books. We believe you should have every opportunity to understand what different financial vehicles offer (the clubs), and we believe you should be empowered to take accountability and responsibility for practicing wise financial and Authentic Wealth habits (the swing).

We truly believe in teaching the swing, and we're not afraid to tell you, "You really ought to change your swing." We may not make as much money on teaching the swing as other financial professionals do on selling the latest clubs, but we believe in it. Because we believe in you.

TOP 5 TAKEAWAYS

1. If The IUL LASER Fund concepts are new to you, you're not alone. Many experienced financial professionals, CPAs, and tax attorneys may not yet be familiar with the strategies (or may not be experienced in executing them). This chapter outlines the reasons your financial professional may not have told you about The IUL LASER Fund before.

2. The reasons range from a lack of awareness, to preferring to stick with traditional financial strategies that make their workdays easier.

3. Other reasons come down to money—other financial vehicles can be more lucrative for financial professionals, so that can be a deterrent.

4. Still, others succumb to assumptions, inaccurate assertions like thinking insurance must be expensive, or it's only for the wealthy.

5. By investigating for yourself how The IUL LASER Fund works, how it complies with tax citations, and how it provides greater liquidity, safety, rates of return, and tax advantages, you're learning the "swing" of creating a brighter financial future, not just picking up the "clubs" your financial professional handed over.

12

What Can Go Wrong
... And How To Prevent It

From the time we Andrew children were young, the great outdoors have been the destination for countless family getaways. From backpacking and hiking, to fishing and Jeeping, the rivers, mountains, and canyons of the Intermountain West have been the playground for unforgettable adventures. While the activities may change from trip to trip, one hallmark of every family outing has been the campfire.

We hover over the orange and red heat for cooking (there's nothing like lemon pepper trout grilled fresh out of the river, and Dutch oven cobbler simmering with peaches from roadside stands). We circle around the flickering light to share What Matters Most and I Remember When stories (these are 3 Dimensional Wealth tools included in Doug's book, *Entitlement Abolition*—you're invited to order a free copy of the book at www.entitlementabolition.com). All of these bonding moments are illuminated by the mesmerizing flames.

From an early age, each of us was schooled in how to start and maintain the campfire. We learned to place the tinder bundle of leaves, grass, and needles in the center, add fuel with small sticks for kindling, then feed the flames with firewood to keep the blaze going throughout the evening.

We were also taught about the hazards of mismanaging the fire. One wrong move with the matches or one misplaced piece of firewood, and a magical night could turn miserable, causing injury, or worse, sparking a wildfire.

Many things in life are a lot like fire. They have the capacity to benefit our lives when we manage them correctly, but they can also produce everything from disappointment to disaster if mishandled.

Like many financial vehicles, IUL LASER Funds fall in this same camp (no pun intended). When structured and funded properly, they can lend warmth to a family's life, fueling everything from providing tax-free income for retirement to business opportunities, emergency funds, education, and charitable giving. However, if they're not correctly structured, funded, or managed over the long-term, IUL LASER Funds simply won't be able to perform optimally, and in some cases, they may fail the objectives miserably.

Since we believe in financial empowerment through education, it's important to understand the upsides AND downsides of any financial strategy. As revolutionary as an IUL LASER Fund is in providing liquidity, safety, predictable rates of return, and tax advantages, it's not foolproof. There are ways both policyholders and financial professionals who aren't adept at IUL LASER Funds can go astray with this financial vehicle, taking detours that can derail the plan. So let's take a moment to map the potential pitfalls—and how you can avoid them.

NOT ENOUGH IN

IUL LASER Funds perform best when properly structured and fully funded. What happens if you get off course during the funding phase?

This can happen for various reasons, even seemingly good ones. It may be, for example, that you direct your money elsewhere, like your kids. It's natural for parents to want to help their children. It feels loving and noble. However it can lead to anything-but-noble consequences when money is given without requiring accountability and responsibility in return.

In Doug's book, *Entitlement Abolition*, he shares several stories of otherwise well-meaning parents giving away money to their children and

grandchildren that they had originally intended to go toward retirement. One couple, for example, had initiated an IUL LASER Fund, designed with a premium bucket of $500,000. The first year they dutifully funded it with $100,000, but Years 2 through 5 they failed to put the remaining $400,000 in the policy. Why?

One of their children had gotten divorced and asked for financial help. Another child saw that money going to the sibling and asked for money to fuel a business investment. The third child demanded his fair share, as well. Before they knew it, they could no longer fund their policy, and they chose to let it lapse.

Remember, funding your policy is like managing that apartment building. You buy the building to make money on it. The only way to make money on it is by doing what? Leasing it out, collecting those lease payments, over a long period of time. Just the same, funding your IUL LASER Fund is critical for getting the most out of your policy. If you do not fund your policy properly or make sufficient adjustments, your cash value can diminish over time, and, like the couple above, your policy could eventually lapse.

That said, The IUL LASER Fund is flexible. If you find yourself in unexpected circumstances and are not able to fund your policy according to the way it was structured, you can contact your IUL specialist to make adjustments to your policy.

Let's look at an example of how making adjustments can rescue an otherwise tough financial situation. Let's say Fred is a non-smoking sixty-year-old who has created an IUL LASER Fund with a $500,000 premium bucket and a death benefit of over $900,000. Fred is planning to maximum fund it in five years, putting in $100,000 a year. The first year, things go according to plan: he puts in $100,000. During his second year, something comes up and Fred is only able to put in $35,000.

Despite his best intentions, Fred's circumstances do not improve—over the coming years, he is not able to add any more. By putting only $135,000 into the policy, it remains just 27% funded. What can Fred do to make sure the policy does not lapse?

Fred meets with his IUL specialist to make adjustments. To save on policy charges, they decide to drop the death benefit after Year 8 to as close

to the accumulation value as possible. While he will no longer look to take tax-free income from the policy, he can at least keep it in force. The lower death benefit will also minimize the policy's fees.

Now what if the story is slightly different? What if Fred puts $300,000 into his policy before stalling out? In this case, his policy is 60% funded. Fred still meets with his IUL specialist to decrease charges by reducing his death benefit. But the great thing is, he can now take out tax-free income. (Typically, if an IUL LASER Fund is at least 50% to 70% funded, you can take out tax-free income—it won't be as much as if it were 100% funded, but you can still borrow money tax-free.)

Overall, keep in mind that if your financial situation changes, you should contact your IUL specialist right away. She or he can help you explore your options for making the most of your financial future. Just remember, The IUL LASER Fund works best when fully funded. It's a long-term vehicle that takes dedication, responsibility, and accountability. Those who want to drive it into the future should be committed for the long-haul.

TOO MUCH IN

Some of The IUL LASER Fund's most coveted benefits include the fact that policyholders can have an income-tax-free death benefit, while also accruing money in a safe, predictable environment, and enjoying the ability to pull out money for tax-free income.

However, these benefits can get stymied if policyholders don't adhere to funding regulations. If you remember in Section I, Chapter 7, we talked about TAMRA tax citations, which indicate that policyholders can't fund their insurance policies with one lump sum. Instead, they're required to spread out the Guideline Single Premium payments typically over four to seven years.

Now, remember why the government passed TAMRA back in 1988? To slow the flow of money leaving traditional, taxable accounts like mutual funds and 401(k)s as more Americans were turning to insurance contracts for financial planning. With that in mind, the government levied a pretty significant consequence for violation of TAMRA. If individuals

fully funded their policies sooner than four to seven years, the policy would now be deemed a Modified Endowment Contract, and any income taken from the policy thereafter would not be tax-free. And of course, Uncle Sam would get his share of that income, taxed LIFO.

If you recall, we illustrated this kind of scenario using a $500,000 policy with the required life insurance of $930,000 for a sixty-year-old male. If it were funded with that $500,000 all at once (rather than over five years), it would become a MEC, which means the money could accrue tax-deferred, the death benefit would pass along tax-free, but any income taken out of the policy would be taxed LIFO.

So if it triggers income taxes, why would anyone want to violate TAMRA? There are occasions where some of our clients have deliberately done so, simply because they didn't intend to use their policy for income. In other words, they weren't going to take any money out of the policy. Instead, they wanted to leave their money tucked in the policy for the life of the contract, taking advantage of The IUL LASER Fund's death benefit, safety, and predictable rates of return—and they preferred to fund the account in one fell swoop.

For example, say someone has $500,000 sitting in the bank earning next to nothing. They don't need the money; they have plenty elsewhere. They decide rather than having it earn less than 1% annually (with any growth being taxed as it accumulates), they can put it to work in an IUL LASER Fund and enjoy tax-deferred growth.

They put $500,000 all in at once, which creates a MEC. No problem; they don't plan on touching their money for income, so they won't be taxed on any withdrawals or loans. But just say they did have an emergency and needed to access money, say $50,000, from the account?

They still can; they'll simply pay taxes on the gains (as they would with any other investment, anyway). They've still benefited from indexing, which protects their money from market loss. They've still enjoyed tax-deferred growth to this point. And there's that valuable death benefit. If they die, their beneficiaries could receive a $930,000 income-tax-free death benefit (or more, depending on what the policy has accrued to that point)—far greater than the $500,000 plus nominal interest would have ever been.

Going back to the issue of violating TAMRA, while there are occasions where folks may intend to create a MEC like we just described, there are plenty of times when policyholders violate TAMRA without meaning to. They put too much in too fast. This isn't something we encounter often with our clients, because we educate them to ensure they understand how to properly fund their accounts. However, we've had some clients come our way who have been working with other firms or financial professionals who didn't explain TAMRA well (or who didn't understand it well themselves).

If the violation is recent enough (within sixty days following the next policy anniversary from the date TAMRA was violated), we can help them perfect their MEC. By doing so, the insurance company refunds their overpayment, and their policy returns to compliance with TAMRA. But if it's longer than the grace period allowed to perfect the MEC, we can only offer condolences on their new MEC. If they'd like, we can help them open a different IUL LASER Fund which they can fund correctly to achieve their income objectives. (Remember, you can hold numerous policies at once.)

TOO MUCH OUT

Putting too much in too quickly isn't the only way to disrupt an IUL LASER Fund. You can also take too much out of the policy, too quickly. Not only can this trigger a taxable event, but it can also take a toll on how the policy performs, and on your death benefit.

To understand this concept, let's first examine how a policy looks when everything is done right. Using one of our examples from Section I, Chapter 9, John is our sixty-year-old who put $500,000 into his policy, with about $930,000 in required insurance (See Figure 12.1):

FIGURE 12.1

End of Year	Age	Premium	Policy Charges	Index Credit	Interest Bonus	Tax-Free Income via Policy Loans	Policy Loan Balance	Accumulation Value	Surrender Value	Death Benefit
1	60	$100,000	$16,495	$6,627	-	-	-	$90,131	$60,753	$928,472
2	61	$100,000	$14,499	$13,536	-	-	-	$189,169	$159,609	$928,472
3	62	$100,000	$14,881	$20,952	-	-	-	$295,240	$264,357	$928,472
4	63	$100,000	$14,902	$28,906	-	-	-	$409,244	$373,452	$928,472
5	64	$100,000	$14,877	$37,458	-	-	-	$531,825	$493,761	$928,472
6	65	-	$8,829	$39,603	-	$50,634	$53,166	$562,598	$477,423	$875,307
7	66	-	$8,952	$41,907	-	$50,634	$108,989	$595,552	$460,725	$819,483
8	67	-	$8,994	$44,377	-	$50,634	$167,604	$630,935	$443,776	$760,868
9	68	-	$9,008	$47,030	-	$50,634	$229,150	$668,958	$426,655	$699,322
10	69	-	$9,020	$49,882	-	$50,634	$293,773	$709,820	$409,411	$634,699
11	70	-	$1,611	$53,185	$1,228	$50,634	$361,627	$762,621	$400,994	$566,845
12	71	-	$1,387	$57,152	$1,203	$50,634	$432,874	$819,590	$386,716	$444,723
13	72	-	$620	$61,449	$1,160	$50,634	$507,683	$881,580	$373,896	$422,503
14	73	-	$587	$66,100	$1,122	$50,634	$586,233	$948,214	$361,981	$401,799
15	74	-	$550	$71,098	$1,086	$50,634	$668,710	$1,019,848	$351,138	$382,740
16	75	-	$512	$76,472	$1,053	$50,634	$755,311	$1,096,861	$341,550	$365,458
17	76	-	$464	$82,250	$1,025	$50,634	$846,242	$1,179,672	$333,429	$350,101
18	77	-	$393	$88,463	$1,000	$50,634	$941,720	$1,268,742	$327,022	$343,373
19	78	-	$424	$95,142	$981	$50,634	$1,041,972	$1,364,441	$322,470	$338,593
20	79	-	$461	$102,318	$967	$50,634	$1,147,236	$1,467,266	$320,030	$336,032
21	80	-	$507	$110,029	$960	$50,634	$1,257,763	$1,577,748	$319,985	$335,984
22	81	-	$572	$118,313	$960	$50,634	$1,373,817	$1,696,448	$322,632	$338,763
23	82	-	$645	$127,213	$968	$50,634	$1,495,673	$1,823,984	$328,311	$344,726
24	83	-	$715	$136,776	$985	$50,634	$1,623,622	$1,961,029	$337,407	$354,277
25	84	-	$822	$147,051	$1,012	$50,634	$1,757,969	$2,108,270	$350,301	$367,816
26	85	-	$961	$158,089	$1,051	$50,634	$1,899,033	$2,266,450	$367,417	$385,788
27	86	-	$1,149	$169,947	$1,102	$50,634	$2,047,150	$2,436,350	$389,200	$408,660
28	87	-	$1,392	$182,681	$1,168	$50,634	$2,202,673	$2,618,807	$416,134	$436,940
29	88	-	$1,679	$196,356	$1,248	$50,634	$2,365,972	$2,814,733	$448,761	$471,199
30	89	-	$2,095	$211,038	$1,346	$50,634	$2,537,436	$3,025,022	$487,585	$511,965
31	90	-	$2,625	$226,792	$1,463	$50,634	$2,717,474	$3,250,652	$533,178	$559,837
32	91	-	$3,189	$243,696	$1,600	$50,634	$2,906,513	$3,492,758	$586,245	$615,557
33	92	-	$3,981	$261,829	$1,759	$50,634	$3,105,004	$3,752,364	$647,360	$673,254
34	93	-	$3,987	$281,299	$1,942	$50,634	$3,313,420	$4,031,618	$718,199	$739,745
35	94	-	$3,598	$302,256	$2,155	$50,634	$3,532,256	$4,332,431	$800,174	$816,178
36	95	-	$2,703	$324,845	$2,401	$50,634	$3,762,035	$4,656,973	$894,938	$903,888
37	96	-	$1,461	$349,226	$2,685	$50,634	$4,003,302	$5,007,422	$1,004,121	$1,004,121
38	97	-	$120	$375,553	$3,012	$50,634	$4,256,632	$5,385,868	$1,129,235	$1,129,235
39	98	-	$120	$403,936	$3,388	$50,634	$4,522,630	$5,793,071	$1,270,442	$1,270,442
40	99	-	$120	$434,476	$3,811	$50,634	$4,801,927	$6,231,239	$1,429,313	$1,429,313
41	100	-	$120	$467,339	$4,288	$50,634	$5,095,188	$6,702,746	$1,607,558	$1,607,558

His IUL LASER Fund objective is to take annual income during retirement and pass along a death benefit to his heirs. John structures and funds his policy properly, putting in $100,000 a year for five years. Notice his death benefit remains constant at about $930,000 during those first five years.

You can see that in Year 6, John starts to take his maximum income of $50,634 per year. Take a peek at his death benefit. As he pulls money out, his death benefit decreases each year. John is fine with that—one of his primary objectives is the annual tax-free income (as well as the death benefit, liquidity, safety, predictable rates of return, and tax advantages).

But what if John takes out more than that maximum income amount each year? He is in jeopardy of outpacing the interest his policy is earning. If he ultimately takes out too much money, his policy could lapse. That would be like killing the goose that lays the golden eggs.

The minute he caused his policy to lapse, he would no longer have a tax-protected life insurance policy. "No life insurance" means no tax-deferred accumulation, no tax-free income, and no income-tax-free death benefit. He would owe taxes on all of his gains—as in a lot of taxes. And the worst part is John would have probably already spent the money he took out. So rather than his policy providing a regular income of $50,634 every year and a valuable income-tax-free death benefit to his heirs, John could run his policy into the ground AND owe Uncle Sam a lot of money. That would not be smart, John.

To help policyholders like John avoid inadvertently slaying their golden-egg-laying goose, they can opt to include something called a Loan Protection Rider (which we explained in Section I, Chapter 8). If you recall, this rider is available if and when the loan balance equals or exceeds about 95% of the policy's cash value. It essentially protects the policy from lapsing and triggering the big taxable event described above. This is why John would want to work with an IUL specialist who can help him avoid taking too much out, or help him safeguard his policy with a Loan Protection Rider.

Of course, if you're working with IUL specialists who meet with you every year, you can avoid coming close to needing the Loan Protection Rider. But if you're working with someone who doesn't know enough to keep you from this kind of freefall? It could spell retirement disaster.

BAD INCOME STRATEGY

One stumbling block we've seen some people have is when they (or their financial professional) are not astute at accessing income from The

IUL LASER Fund. Everything else can be in place—acquiring the policy from a reputable top-tier insurance company, structuring the policy correctly, funding it fully—but when it comes to taking income a few years down the road, things can still go off track.

Here's how: it's in making assumptions about what the policy is earning in interest, versus what the loan is being charged. Say, for example, you have $1 million in cash value in your policy, and currently you're earning 7% average annual interest. The insurance company will be charging you 5% interest on the money you borrow for income. You assume you'll be getting a consistent 2% spread. So you start taking out your maximum allowable income. Market conditions change, however, and your policy (which is tied to the S&P 500 Index) goes down to earning 5% to 6% average. Now you're no longer getting that same spread, but you and your financial professional aren't bothering to check in on your policy, so you still go on borrowing at the original maximum amount.

The problem: you're pulling money out at a rate that is faster than what you're earning. Your loan balance is growing faster than your account value and will deplete your available cash value for future loans. If this behavior goes unchecked for an extended period of time, you're at risk of depleting your policy entirely.

This is one of the reasons we insist on meeting with our clients every year, to closely monitor the status of the policy and protect against mistakes that could lead to unintended misfortune.

IT'S NOT MAGIC

One of the reasons the astute turn to The IUL LASER Fund is its ability to continue accruing interest, even after you've taken income out of the policy. Let's say your IUL LASER Fund has a current cash value of $1 million, and it's growing at an average rate of 7%. You decide to take out an Alternate Loan of $70,000 from your IUL LASER Fund (remember, that's tax-free income). Sure, your surrender value (your accumulation value minus your loans) goes down to $930,000, but you have the advantage of earning a percentage spread on that $70,000 you borrowed. Your $1 million is still in there, averaging 7%. That $70,000 is merely collateral for your loan, which in this example the insurance company

charges you 5% interest to borrow. So you're averaging 7% on $1 million; you're being charged 5% on the $70,000; this means you're averaging a 2% spread on that $70,000.

Compare this to a traditional savings account or mutual fund. If you have an account with $1 million and you pull out $70,000, you'll only have $930,000 left in the account working for you, period. (For more comparisons between IUL LASER Funds and traditional accounts, see Section I, Chapter 10).

This is definitely an advantage The IUL LASER Fund has over traditional financial vehicles—and one of the reasons people have called it a miracle. And while we agree it is a superior vehicle, it is not magic.

In the musical, *Mary Poppins,* there's a famous scene where Mary opens her carpet bag and pulls out a bounty of items: a hat rack, a wall mirror, a houseplant, a lamp … and the supercalifragilistic list goes on and on.

One of the dangers we've seen is that sometimes people begin to think of The IUL LASER Fund as Mary Poppins' mystical bag. While it can provide so many things—liquidity, safety, predictable rates of return, income-tax-free death benefit, and more—it isn't supernatural. If structured and managed correctly, yes, it can offer tax-free access to money for things like retirement income, business capital, or children's educations, but it is not a bottomless supply of enchanted never-ending cash to use for anything and everything into perpetuity.

With that in mind, many of our clients have found it valuable to decide their primary objective for their IUL LASER Fund. If it's retirement income, they generally don't touch the money in the policy until they officially retire. If it's business capital, they focus on borrowing money solely for professional purposes. If it's funding education or charitable efforts, then they prioritize money borrowed from the policy for those causes. For clients who want to use The IUL LASER Fund for several things, they often open several policies, so they can dedicate each policy to a specific purpose. While it is possible to use one policy for different objectives, a multi-pronged approach can have its limits. It takes special attention and expertise to ensure you're not taking more than is prudent at any one time for your different endeavors.

So just keep in mind, while The IUL LASER Fund has inherent advantages over traditional accounts when it comes to maintaining a healthy cash value, it is still subject to the "laws of subtraction."

NOT JUST ANY COMPANY

Let's say you drive a Tesla. It's time for the next maintenance visit. Do you head to the lube shop on the corner? Our guess is: no. You take your finely-crafted electric car to the Tesla specialists, even if that means a forty-five-minute drive to get to the shop that can properly care for its intricacies.

When it comes to your future, financial vehicles like IUL LASER Funds are not unlike that Tesla. They require special expertise and care. You can't just pull up to any insurance company and say, "Give me the works."

Over the years, though, we've seen it time and time again. We've had people come to our seminars—often with their own financial professional in tow. They get a smattering of knowledge and rush out to whatever insurance company they're familiar with and order up a life insurance policy that can "do all the things 3 Dimensional Wealth talked about." However, without the proper approach and product features, the insurance company simply can't do what it takes. The policyholders often end up with a financial vehicle that can't provide the tax-free income and death benefit they were seeking.

Or they find themselves working with a reputable insurance company, one that can even offer an IUL LASER Fund that looks good on the surface, but ten to fifteen years down the road, they discover their policy has some limitations. Just like a car, sometimes what's under the hood isn't as good as the shiny exterior. And worse, the company isn't paying attention to customers with older policies. They offer improved features only to new policyholders—leaving older customers behind.

As we've mentioned, out of the thousands of insurance companies across America, there are only a handful that we recommend to our clients. They are well-versed in Indexed Universal Life policies. They understand how to structure and fund them properly. They are constantly working to innovate, adding features to improve policyholder benefits.

And for customers with older policies? They offer the latest, greatest benefits to them, as well. It's like if the car manufacturer came out with a better battery or software system—they'd automatically offer it to you, keeping your car up-to-date for as long as you own it. The insurance companies we recommend make it standard practice to offer the latest improvements to all of their policyholders, regardless of the age of the policy.

If you recall in Section I, Chapter 6, we mentioned the difference between a mutual holding insurance company and a publicly-traded insurance company. Traditionally, the mutual holding companies have better reputations for doing what's right for their policyholders than the publicly-traded companies. The publicly-traded companies often focus more on their responsibility to the stockholders, which can be disadvantageous to the policyholders.

This can't be overstated: working with the wrong insurance company can leave your future sputtering along the side of the road, with the hazard lights flashing.

NOT JUST ANY DESIGN

As you've likely gathered by now, there are numerous aspects to take into consideration when designing your IUL LASER Fund. You and your IUL specialist will want to make sure you cover all the critical bases before you implement your policy.

If you're hoping to take income from the policy down the road, for example, you need to structure your policy to put the most money in and take the least death benefit out. You also want to create a policy with commissions and fees that are as low as possible. When you start taking income, you need to make sure not to take too much out at any given time, in order to avoid lapsing your policy (and creating taxable events).

That said, a successful IUL policy needs to be designed for compliance with all related tax codes, as well as structured accurately for your specific policy size, death benefit level, funding cadence, your age and health, and many, many more details. Beyond that, you need to determine the best type of index strategies for you.

Which index strategy would you prefer—an S&P 500 one-year point-to-point, a two-year point-to-point, a five-year point-to-last-year-average, a one-year volatility control indexed account, or a two-year volatility control indexed account? And if available, would you like to add multipliers as well? In addition, you'll need to consider things like whether you prefer to make adjustments year-to-year, or leave indexing strategies in place for the life of the policy.

You'll also want to wisely—and realistically—address issues such as how likely you are to fully fund your particular policy over the next five to seven years. Say, for example, you are planning on funding the policy with $500,000 over the next five years. But that money is contingent on external circumstances (like an upcoming real estate or business deal). If there's a high potential you may not be able to fully fund it, your IUL specialist will show you options for protecting yourself, such as adding the "no surrender charge" rider we mentioned earlier.

This would allow you to avoid incurring the penalty that is normally assessed if you were to cancel your policy and pull all of your money out during the first ten years. There is a charge to add this rider, which only about 5% of our clients do. But it does provide peace of mind if you have concerns about funding your policy.

When you're working with IUL specialists, you're getting benefit of partnering with experts who can help you design an optimal IUL LASER Fund and manage or even negate potential problems upfront.

NOT JUST ANYONE LICENSED TO SELL IUL

Referring to the five-story building analogy, what would happen if you went to an architect who specializes in residential homes? She may be an expert in drawing up designs for a rambler, a multi-level, or a two-story house. But she may not understand all the complexities of creating the designs for your five-story office building, knowing how to avoid structural weaknesses (for local seismic and climate conditions), weight-bearing problems (for heavy office equipment), circulation and traffic jams (for larger numbers of occupants), building codes, etc.

Just the same, financial professionals who focus their attention primarily on traditional retirement accounts, or insurance professionals who

are immersed in life, auto, and property and casualty insurance, will likely not have the depth of experience to design a properly structured and maximum-funded IUL policy.

More than once, we've had people come to us (not clients of ours), frustrated that their policy isn't doing what it should be. We ask about their story, and they explain that they had attended one of our events years before, with their brother-in-law or nephew who's a financial professional. They listened to the strategies we presented, learned the names of the top-tier insurance companies we recommended, then had their relative set up their policy.

They assumed all would be well and good, but five to seven years down the road, the $500,000 they had funded the policy with hadn't grown. While our clients with a similar financial profile had seen their $500,000 policy increase in value in that time, theirs had dwindled to $250,000 in value. They ask, "Why are your clients' policies performing so much better than ours?" All we can do is ask again, "Now, who designed this for you?"

There's more to this whole strategy than having the right product and the right company. No matter how well-intentioned a brother-in-law or nephew may be, this approach requires very specific experience and know-how.

You're also better off with an independent IUL specialist, who can weigh the different benefits of the top companies for your particular situation—and it doesn't cost any more than going directly to the company. A financial professional who works for one specific insurance company can only sell for that company and may have blinders on when it comes to helping you find your optimal solution.

Remember that car analogy? You want to make sure the manufacturers and your auto service shop are working together to give your car the same upgrades as the latest model. Well, an independent IUL specialist can stay abreast of the latest products at each insurance company. For example, one of the companies we work with has been providing IUL policies since 2005. Since then, it's introduced over a dozen new features and indexed accounts, all in the clients' favor. Because we work closely with the insurance companies we recommend, we've been able to help our clients take advantage of new offerings with their existing policies—something that's helped make a difference in our clients' financial outcome.

You would also do well to look for IUL specialists who are with firms that have the size and the systems in place to support your success.

Smaller firms specializing in IUL policies can be great allies for you, however, since IUL LASER Funds require experts to devote a good amount of attention to each client's policies year-to-year, smaller firms can only afford to take on a few clients a year. When that's the case, which type of clients are they most likely to focus on? Yep, just the wealthiest of the wealthy. So if you're on the more moderate end of the financial spectrum, you may want to find a larger firm that can accommodate clients with a range of income. That way they can take care of you as you're starting out, and continue to support you if/when your income and financial goals increase.

No matter where you are on the financial spectrum, you also want to find a company that believes in partnering with you, that will invest the time and resources to help educate you on these complex strategies so you're in the know. When your financial professionals create educational and support systems, it empowers you to make wise decisions throughout the next few decades of managing your policy, which can save you time, energy, and money in the long-run.

LASER-READY TEST

If partnering with an expert IUL specialist is so critical to the success of your IUL LASER Fund, how will you know if a potential financial professional is up to the task? You can use the following "LASER-Ready TEST." You can ask your financial professional:

- What is TEFRA, DEFRA & TAMRA, and how do they impact my policy? *(Your IUL specialist should be able to answer this off-the-cuff. If they say "Let me check on that"—they're not likely prepared to help structure your policy correctly. Make sure to cross-check their response with information in Section I, Chapter 7.)*
- Explain to me Internal Revenue Code, Sections 72(e), 7702, and 101(a). And what changes to Section 7702 went into effect in January of 2021? *(Again, your financial professional should be able to easily explain this to you. If not, beware.)*
- What's a Guideline Single Premium? *(This is the total amount you will put in to fully fund, or self-insure, your policy.)*

- What factors will the insurance company consider when gauging the size of my policy, besides the Guideline Single Premium? *(This includes your age, gender, and health status.)*
- What size policy would someone have (on average) who is a non-smoking sixty-year-old with a GSP of $500,000? *(It's approximately a $930,000 to $1,050,000 death benefit.)*
- What are the rules for perfecting a Modified Endowment Contract? *(Compare the answer to information in this chapter.)*
- How can an insurance company earning 4% to 5% on their General Account Portfolio afford to credit a policy 5% to 10%? *(By linking to an index where the insurance company buys upside options with the interest on your principal—but your principal is preserved.)*
- How can policyholders experience 1% to 2% higher pay-outs than the average index that they are linked to? *(By using Alternate Loans where the interest charged might be 4% to 5% and the cash value is being credited a higher rate, such as 7%.)*
- Who runs your policy illustrations? *(Ideally it is your financial professional who designs your illustrations, not the third-party insurance company who hasn't met with you directly and who won't be familiar with your individual circumstances and objectives.)*
- If I maximum fund an IUL LASER Fund, over the life of the policy, what is the expected net internal rate of return likely to be—compared to the gross crediting rate—if the historical average were 7.5%? *(Usually around 1% different—which would be 6.5%. See Section I, Chapter 9, Figure 9.2)*
- How long have you been structuring these types of policies? Do you have access to several different types of IUL policies, and how many have you put in place? *(Hopefully they're not brand new to the strategies.)*
- Do you specialize in maximum-funded Indexed Universal Life policies, or do you handle other types of insurance, as well? *(Let's hope this is an experienced answer, or at least your financial professional is with an experienced firm who can support him/her in partnering with you.)*
- How many insurance companies do you represent? Do you work for only one company or are you an independent producer representing multiple companies? *(Remember, while not imperative, independent producers can have an advantage in*

ensuring you get the optimal policy for your situation, as well as upgrades down the road.)

- Is insurance your sole profession, or is it a part-time endeavor? *(Ideally you want someone who is dedicated to this full-time, not juggling it with other types of work.)*

If you're getting vague (or worse, incorrect) responses to the above, then it would be in your best interest (and your heirs' best interest) to explore working with a different, experienced IUL specialist. If your financial professional can answer these questions satisfactorily, then you're likely in good hands.

TOP 5 TAKEAWAYS

1. Even with its powerful upsides, The IUL LASER Fund is not foolproof, so it's important to understand what can go wrong and how to prevent it.

2. IUL policies perform best when they are structured correctly and funded properly. Avoid getting off course when funding your policy—and if circumstances change, you will want to meet with your IUL specialist to make adjustments to your policy as soon as possible.

3. IUL LASER Funds require critical knowledge and experience to structure properly—which means not just any financial professional, insurance company, or policy design will do. For optimal results, work with a financial professional who has expertise in designing and managing properly structured, maximum-funded IUL policies, and who has your best interests in mind.

4. While The IUL LASER Fund can provide several advantages for your financial future, it is not magical. It does have its limitations, and it requires everyone to assume responsibility and accountability in properly structuring, funding, and accessing money.

5. The LASER-Ready Test can help you identify financial professionals who will be valuable partners for you in creating a bright financial future.

The Self-Assurance
of Self-Insurance

Throughout Section I, we've explored The IUL LASER Fund from a historical perspective. We've looked at how properly structured, maximum-funded IUL policies provide the key elements of a prudent financial vehicle: liquidity, safety, predictable rates of return, and tax advantages. We've examined these policies in different scenarios, and we've compared them to other financial vehicles. Now we'll look at The IUL LASER Fund from one more vantage point—how, at its essence, it is "self-insurance." With a properly structured, maximum-funded IUL policy, you are essentially self-insuring your own death benefit.

And why is that death benefit so valuable? Thanks to certain Internal Revenue Codes, the death benefit gives you distinct advantages. As a reminder, Section 101(a) states that the death benefit in a life insurance policy is income-tax-free. Section 72(e) allows that any of the death benefit you own inside the insurance policy can be put to work for tax-deferred growth.

Section 7702 outlines perhaps the biggest plus—that you can manage the size of your own death benefit. If you follow Section 7702 correctly,

you can decrease your death benefit (because, for example, the needs for that benefit are no longer as great), and the surplus will be transferred to you. You can take that surplus out by way of withdrawal (which would incur taxes), or you can reduce that death benefit in the form of a loan, which is tax-free. That portion you take in the form of a loan is part of your cash value (which in turn is part of your death benefit). Essentially, this makes it possible for your policy to now be used for living benefits—which we'll explore through real-life scenarios in Section II.

So with all these benefits in mind, let's explore how assuring this concept of self-insurance can be.

THE EARLY BENEFITS

To begin, we'll focus first on a purely self-insured policy, the kind that was available before the 1980s. Back then, if you wanted to self-insure yourself for a half-million-dollar death benefit, you would put $500,000 into your policy. The policy would be entirely funded by you, without any risk on the part of the insurance company.

You might be wondering: if the insurance company wasn't at any risk in providing the death benefit, why would anyone have wanted to self-insure? The answers are compelling: 1) lowest-cost insurance, 2) liquidity, 3) safety, 4) tax-deferred accumulation, 5) tax-free access to your money, and 6) income-tax-free death benefit.

To expound, these policies cost the policyholder virtually nothing, because their cash value was equal to their death benefit. They provided liquid access to a policyholder's money. As for safety, an insurance policy has always been among the safest places to park the money you want to transfer to your heirs (safer than just about any other financial vehicle).

What's more, the money you put into your policy took on a new life. It was reclassified as death benefit, which means when you took it out—whether as income during your lifetime or as death benefit when you pass on—it was 100% tax-free. (Remember, this is possible through Internal Revenue Code Section 101[a], which identifies that the death benefit is not earned income, passive income, or portfolio income. Since these are the only types of income that are taxable, the money you or your heirs get from your policy—if structured properly—is completely tax-free.)

Furthermore, through Internal Revenue Code Section 72(e), the self-insured portion of your money would be put to work with the folks who have historically been the best money managers in the world, the insurance companies.

For example, let's say you had started with a $1 million-dollar self-insured policy, earning an average rate of return of 7%. According to the Rule of 72, in ten years your policy would have doubled to $2 million. In twenty years, it would have doubled again to $4 million in death benefit.

As the money continued to accrue, if you decided you wanted to reduce your death benefit (because, for example, as you aged you didn't need as much death benefit as before), could you reduce that death benefit before you passed on?

Yes, remember under Internal Revenue Code Section 7702, you can reduce your death benefit if your need decreases. So with that $1 million doubling twice to $4 million in twenty years, let's say in Year 20 you realized that at a 7% rate of growth, you were going to earn another $280,000 in interest that year. You were fine maintaining your death benefit at just $4 million, and you didn't think you needed another $280,000 added to the pile. So you decided to take out that $280,000 in the form of a loan now.

Where would that money have gone? Right into your pocket. It would still have been considered death benefit, which means it's tax-free. So now you could have had a tax-free supplemental income of $280,000. And you could continue doing that every year for the rest of your life by maintaining and managing your $4 million death benefit. Or what if you wanted to reduce that death benefit to just $2 million? Could you have taken $2 million out at once, rather than $280,000 a year? Absolutely.

As explained in Section I, Chapter 8, as long as you were accessing your money The Smart Way under Internal Revenue Code Section 7702, you could take your money out tax-free. It would still be considered death benefit, you were just accessing part of it prior to death because you determined a reduced need in your total death benefit. Not only were you benefiting from the tax-free income, but you were reducing your costs, because the lower the death benefit, the lower the policy charges. Thus, you were getting the best of all worlds: your money growing tax-deferred, unfettered by high charges, and the opportunity to access it tax-free.

THE IRS INTERVENES

By the early 80s, these self-funded insurance policies were growing in popularity. The IRS didn't love the increasing migration to this tax-free insurance solution, so it filed a lawsuit trying to shut it down. The IRS likely knew it wasn't going to win, but the lawsuit successfully halted the opening of any new policies and bought the IRS time to lobby Congress to draw up new legislation.

At the same time, the insurance industry (which has been bolstered by one of the largest lobbies for decades) counter-lobbied Congress to preserve the benefits of life insurance for Americans. Fortunately for America, Congress didn't just roll over for the IRS; instead, it struck a compromise.

The new law essentially defined "insurance" as "risk management." This clarification effectively put an end to purely self-funded policies. To explain, before the law passed, if you wanted a $500,000 policy, you would put the entire $500,000 into the policy. How much risk was there for the insurance company? Zero. With the new law, a policy with zero risk would not be considered insurance, and thus the death benefit would not qualify as tax-free under Section 101(a).

So the question became, how much risk was required for a policy to be deemed "insurance" under the law? In other words, what was the minimum amount, above what the policyholder put into his or her account, that must be met for the policy to qualify as insurance? Congress had to come up with a formula to determine that risk. They turned to the insurance industry to identify that algorithm, which it did, creating a formula that factored in age, gender, and health.

The change in law also necessitated a restructuring of how insurance companies made their money. Prior to the legislation, if you put $500,000 in to an insurance policy for a $500,000 death benefit, the insurance companies couldn't charge you for the risk, because there was no risk. Your policy was costing you $0.

So how were the insurance companies making money? Interest.

They were investing your money at a higher rate than what they were paying you. If they were investing your money at a 9% rate of return,

they would have passed on an 8% to 7% rate of return to you and kept the rest. Just like banks, all they needed was a 1% to 2% spread to be profitable.

But with the legislation, the insurance companies would now need to charge for the added risk. And guess how much the algorithm identified as the minimum risk you must pay for with your insurance? Yep, 1% to 2%. So today, you are paying 1% to 2% in policy charges, but the insurance company is giving you the entire rate of return. If your policy earned 9% last year, they would credit your policy the entire 9%, charge you 1% to 2%, and you would net at least 7%.

COMING OUT AHEAD

Did potential net earnings for the policyholder change with the legislation? No. And what's more, policyholders are now getting more in death benefit than when their policies were purely self-funded. Before, a $500,000 policy would have gotten a $500,000 death benefit.

But today? As illustrated in Section I, Chapter 9, for example, if you were a non-smoking sixty-year-old, you could put that Guideline Single Premium of $500,000 into your policy (spread out over five to seven years) and receive a minimum death benefit of about $930,000.

The difference between your $500,000 premium and the death benefit of about $930,000 is about $430,000 in minimum risk that you were required to purchase to comply with the law. (In other words, that $430,000 is what the insurance company is at risk for at the outset of the policy.)

In this post-TEFRA, -DEFRA, and -TAMRA era (and with recent changes to Internal Revenue Code 7702), today's IUL LASER Funds are essentially a modern take on the original self-insured policy, and they're even better.

Comparing today's properly structured, maximum-funded IUL policies with traditional life insurance policies (such as Term and Whole Life), modern policies also have superior advantages. With traditional life insurance, for example, folks are looking to get the most insurance for the least amount of cost (or highest death benefit for the lowest premiums). They often ask, "How much do I need to pay to get the death benefit?"

But with The IUL LASER Fund, it's the opposite. You know exactly how much you're going to pay, because you're the one who determines the

Guideline Single Premium (after factoring in the maximum percentage of income and/or net worth allowed by the insurance company). From there, the insurance company bases your death benefit on factors such as age, health, and gender.

Once your IUL policy is properly structured and opened, your job is simply to fill that premium bucket according to the way it was structured. Once maximum-funded, you have self-insured yourself to the maximum amount allowable under TEFRA / DEFRA, and you can reap the rewards of liquidity, safety, predictable rates of return, tax advantages, and tax-free death benefit from there.

REASSURING

And that's that self-assurance of self-insurance. You're more in control not only of the size of your premium bucket, but of your financial legacy. You're using an exceptional financial vehicle to fund your future, and that of your future generations. And that potential for abundance? Reassuring.

Chapter 3 **From Maps to Postage Stamps**

The Fleming brothers arrived in Peterborough in the middle of a heat wave. At first they found the heat hard to bear, but gradually they became acclimatized to their new surroundings, helping about Dr. Hutchison's house, tending the garden, building a new stable, fishing and swimming in the river, and visiting nearby Indian villages.

David Fleming soon found work on the construction of locks and bridges on the Trent River, but Sandford was less fortunate. He bore letters of introduction to such Canadian notables as Casimir Gzowski of the Department of Roads and Harbours, and Bishop Strachan of Toronto, but these men held out little encouragement. Fleming recorded his disappointment in his diary:

Called again at Mr. Gzowski's but he knew of nothing in the province. The great works were nearly finished and the funds were exhausted . . . in fact he thought it a very bad country for professional men and would advise me to return to Scotland again.

A Toronto architect, a Mr. Howard, urged Fleming not to be discouraged, and said that Gzowski wished to protect his monopoly by frightening young engineers out of the country. Happily for Canada, Fleming did not heed Gzowski's advice. Instead, he travelled from Peterborough to Toronto, Hamilton, Guelph, Port Dover and back again, his money running low, showing his sketches to any architect who would look at them in the hope that someone would offer him a job.

Early in 1846, Fleming hit upon the idea of making a detailed survey of Peterborough and publishing copies of the town plan. By June, the survey was complete. Lithography was a new skill in Canada at that time, so Fleming engraved the map on stone himself and did the printing. The maps — the first of their kind in Canada — were a great success. Copies were in such demand that Fleming was encouraged to undertake similar surveys of

Eight weeks from Glasgow to Peterborough seems an impossibly long time by today's measure. The world of the mid-nineteenth century, however, moved at a much slower pace. If Sandford and David could have afforded passage on an ocean steamship, their travelling time would have been greatly reduced. It was the visionary spirit and business sense of a Nova Scotian, Samuel Cunard, which hastened the days of regular steamship passage between the Old World and the New.

The river steamers which plied the St. Lawrence and the Great Lakes were an enormous improvement over the poor road system of the period. Roads were rough and dusty in summer, a sea of mud in spring and fall, and impassable in winter except by sleigh. With the annual freeze-up of Canada's waterways, the transportation of passengers and cargo in winter was reduced to a minimum. Steam railway development in Canada would in due course revolutionize transportation.

When he first arrived in Canada, Fleming stayed in this house in Peterborough, Ontario, the home of his relative Dr. Hutchison.